Acknowledgements

Several friends contributed to the success of the first two editions of *STOCK OPTIONS.*

First and foremost, I am extremely grateful to Mike Griesmer, CPA, formerly a senior tax manager and colleague at *Arthur Andersen LLP.* Mike is currently a tax partner at *McClintock Accountancy Corporation* in Truckee, California. His insightful comments and business acumen helped to make this book unique. A brilliant tax professional, a man of integrity and a loyal friend, Mike Griesmer is the "CPA's CPA."

A number of years have passed since I left the tax department at *Arthur Andersen LLP.* But ties with former colleagues remain strong. Thanks to their comments and critique, I'm pleased to say that some of the best tax professionals in the world made a contribution to this book.

Mr. Norman H. Ruecker, CPA, retired tax partner and former head of *Arthur Andersen's* tax department in San Francisco and one of the city's most highly respected individuals, read and commented on portions of the text. He has truly been a friend.

My thanks to Mike Preston, CPA, friend and former colleague, now head of the tax division at Deloitte Tax LLP in San Francisco. Mike is a first-class guy who has a longstanding reputation for treating people with courtesy and respect.

I would also like to thank Terry Leahy, tax partner at Deloitte LLP in San Francisco, who has consistently been on the leading edge of important tax issues.

Thank you to Lynn Freer from *Spidell's California Taxletter* for the helpful comments she made with respect to previous editions.

In addition, my thanks to Paul Johnson, CPA, formerly a tax consultant at *Coopers & Lybrand.* Paul is one of the world's most loyal friends. My thanks also to Dwayne Dowell, CPA, formerly a tax consultant at *Arthur Andersen LLP.*

Years ago I was fortunate to have enrolled in a finance course taught by Dr. Pieter Vandenberg, Professor of Finance at *San Diego State University.* Dr. Vandenberg's knowledge of the subject, and his ability to convey that knowledge, was exceptional.

I've had the opportunity to share with readers some of what I learned from him.

Other friends made important contributions too, including Alice Barnett, Kate Dumont, Jessie Finn, Nelson Furlano, Linda Geldens, Jaci Groves, Novella and Angelo Menconi, Linda Mitchell, and John Pannozzo.

Robert R. Pastore

For comments, non-technical questions, or special orders

rpastore@usa.net

Robert R. Pastore will respond to your email as soon as possible. If you do not receive a response within 48 hours, please call (415)-934-9515 Monday through Friday from 9am until 5pm Pacific Standard Time.

Continuing Professional Education for CPAs

Professional Education Services, LP, and Spidell Publishing, Inc. are two entities that used the second edition of *STOCK OPTIONS: An Authoritative Guide to Incentive and Nonqualified Stock Options* as the text for a continuing education course – on employee stock options – for certified public accountants.

It is possible that one, or both, of these organizations will develop and offer a new continuing education course on employee stock options, using this revised and expanded edition of *STOCK OPTIONS* as the text.

Jason Richards or Kathy Yates
Professional Education Services, LP
8303 Sierra College Blvd., Suite 146
Roseville, California 95661
1-800-990-2731
1-800-998-5024 (ordering 24 hours/7 days)

Spidell Publishing, Inc.
1158 North Gilbert Street
Anaheim, California 92801-1401
1-714-776-7850

Contents

1

2

RISK AND DIVERSIFICATION

3

NONQUALIFIED STOCK OPTIONS

5

TAX-DEFERRED EXCHANGES

6

TWO TAX-SAVING STRATEGIES

7

ISO Tax Traps   193

8

The Cost of AMT   217

9

ISO-Stock: The December 31 Decision 233

10_____

11_____

12 _____

13 _____

"She" and "He"

This book was written for both female and male optionees. With all due respect to you, the narrative uses the pronoun "he" while examples contain the pronoun "she."

Warning – Disclaimer

This book was written to provide general guidance to a large audience. Yet, every person who reads *STOCK OPTIONS: An Authoritative Guide to Incentive and Nonqualified Stock Options* has unique needs and circumstances – including a unique income tax position. The book is sold with the understanding that the author and publisher are not engaged in rendering legal, accounting, or other professional services. If legal, tax or other expert services are required, a competent professional should be contacted.

STOCK OPTIONS is a supplement to information contained elsewhere, including published articles and other texts. It is not a complete guide to compensatory stock options and other topics contained herein. You are urged to read as much other material as you can on these subjects.

While every effort has been made to make this book error-free, it may contain mistakes, both typographical and in content. In addition, the text is based on tax law, IRS regulations, and other legal cites as of January 31, 2005. The author and PCM Capital Publishing shall not be liable nor responsible to anyone for any loss or damage caused, or alleged to be caused, either indirectly or directly, from the information contained herein.

If you are unwilling to be bound by this disclaimer, you may return the book within 21 days after the date of purchase and your purchase price will be refunded.

1

Introduction

Management realizes that competent **PEOPLE** are crucial to the corporation's success. They often retain such people by granting them options to purchase the company's stock.

Unfortunately, while the *intention* of management and the board of directors is to motivate and reward people through stock options, the *reality* is that much of the potential wealth that *could* come from those options is *wasted*. Why?

The answer is simple. Options are complicated. *If* people maximize the value of their options, it's usually by luck...*blind luck*.

STOCK OPTIONS: An Authoritative Guide to Incentive and Nonqualified Stock Options was written as an educational tool to keep wealth in the hands of optionees who have earned it through hard work and dedication.

This chapter discusses the following sections:

- *Compensatory Stock Options*

- *Relevant Issues for Optionees*

- *Option Repricing*

- *Options with a Reload Feature*

- *What Gives an Option Value?*
- *When to Exercise Options*
- *Fair Market Value of Stock*
- *Collars Limit Exposure to Market Risk*
- *Non-Compete Clauses*

COMPENSATORY STOCK OPTIONS

Corporations often grant stock options to employees and non-employees (optionees) as a form of compensation. Consequently, such grants are commonly referred to as *compensatory* stock options. For purposes of federal income and employment taxation, compensatory stock options are classified as either *incentive stock options* (ISOs) or *nonqualified stock options* (NQSOs).

An option has a *finite* life. If the optionee does *not* exercise the option prior to its expiration, the option *expires* and becomes *worthless*.

INCENTIVE STOCK OPTION

The incentive stock option (ISO), granted only to *employees*, describes an option that has satisfied the qualification requirements under Internal Revenue Code (IRC) Section 422(b). One requirement to qualify for ISO status is that the optionee may exercise the option only during the time he is an employee, or within three months of termination (12 months for an employee who is disabled as defined by the Internal Revenue Code). Optionees should become familiar with the terms of their options because, for example, they may have less than three months after termination to exercise them.

An ISO gives the optionee the right, but not the obligation, to purchase the stock of his employer or its parent or subsidiary corporation, at a fixed price (the *exercise price*), for a period of time not to exceed 10 years from the date the option is granted. The term of the option may not exceed *five* years for an individual that owns stock possessing more than 10 percent of the total combined voting power of all classes of stock of the employer corporation or of its parent or subsidiary corporation.

NONQUALIFIED STOCK OPTION

A nonqualified stock option (NQSO) is a compensatory option that does *not* meet the qualification requirements of an incentive stock option. Nonqualified stock options may be granted to both employees, *and* non-employees (for example, directors and outside consultants).

RELEVANT ISSUES FOR OPTIONEES

Portfolio management, income taxation, and the cash requirements necessary to exercise options are three important issues facing optionees.

PORTFOLIO MANAGEMENT

Unrealized appreciation in compensatory stock options may be large and may comprise a substantial portion of the optionee's total net worth. That net worth could decline substantially if the price of the optioned stock declines. In short, the optionee's portfolio is not well diversified.

Holding a poorly diversified investment portfolio is risky. That risk is compounded when the expected returns from the optionee's investments are highly correlated with the future cash flows that he expects to generate from his labor.

Example: *A significant portion of the optionee's net worth is comprised of employer securities:* Linda is an employee of ABC Corporation (ABC). A large portion of her net worth consists of substantial unrealized appreciation in ABC stock options and other securities of ABC. If the price of ABC stock declines substantially, a large portion of Linda's net worth evaporates. Linda is also dependent upon ABC for her semimonthly paycheck. If Linda *isn't* uncomfortable in this position, she probably *should* be.

Faced with a similar situation, some optionees wisely decide to exercise options, both incentive stock options and nonqualified stock options, and *immediately* sell the stock – triggering the recognition of taxable compensation income. They reinvest the after-tax proceeds from the sale of stock in other assets – stocks, fixed-income securities, real estate, cash equivalents, etc. – as appropriate, given their unique needs and circumstances.

"Recognition of Income"

Phrases such as "the recognition of taxable compensation income", "the optionee recognizes ordinary compensation income", or "the optionee recognizes a capital gain" appear throughout this book.

If the optionee "recognizes" income it means that the income is subject to income tax. Tax law requires the optionee to report such income on his federal income tax return (IRS Form 1040).

INCOME TAXATION

Ordinary Income versus Long-term Capital Gain

In 2003, Congress substantially reduced the maximum income tax rate on long-term capital gain. The *maximum* rate of tax on gain from a sale of stock that was held for more than 12 months is now 15 percent. That 15 percent rate is substantially *less* than the maximum tax rate on ordinary compensation income.

Naturally, then, individuals are anxious – sometimes *too* anxious – to convert what would otherwise be taxed as ordinary income into more-favorably-taxed, long-term capital gain. In fact, a large number of optionees that hold ISOs will be surprised to learn that for them, paying *more* income tax *now* (that is, exercising ISOs and making a same-day sale of stock), rather than *less* income tax *later* (exercising ISOs and holding the stock for 12 months and one day), is a *wealth-maximizing* strategy. It is a wealth-maximizing strategy – especially when the spread between the rate of tax on ordinary income and the rate of tax on long-term capital gain is not large – despite the fact that the optionee pays *more* income tax.

This concept is illustrated in Table 6.8, which reflects the 15 percent maximum tax rate on long-term capital gain as provided under current tax law.

Other Important Tax Issues

The income tax consequences vary for stock options. Transactions that involve incentive stock options are taxed differently from those that involve nonqualified stock options.

Some of the more common tax considerations affecting optionees include:

- Exercising ISOs and selling the stock on the same day versus exercising ISOs and selling the stock 12 months and one day later

- Disqualifying versus non-disqualifying dispositions of stock that had been acquired by exercise of an ISO

- Alternative minimum tax (AMT) issues relating to ISOs and how the AMT can lead an optionee into bankruptcy

- The *basis* of stock acquired by ISO exercise may be different for regular tax purposes than for purposes of AMT

- Tax withholding

- Restrictions imposed by Section 16(b) of the Securities Exchange Act of 1934 and the income tax implications of such restrictions

- Early exercise of vested NQSOs

- Early exercise of *unvested* NQSOs and *unvested* ISOs

- The IRC Section 83(b) election

CASH REQUIREMENTS

By its very terms, an option requires the optionee to pay the exercise price in order to buy the stock. This requirement is an important issue, and a common problem, for optionees who don't have the cash necessary to exercise their options.

To solve that problem, companies with publicly-traded stock may make arrangements with a brokerage firm to the extent the arrangements are not in violation of the Public Company Accounting and Investor Protection Act of 2002 (the "Sarbanes-Oxley Act"), as amended. Such arrangements allow optionees to finance an option exercise with a same-day sale of stock, in a *cashless exercise*.

Under the terms of a cashless exercise, the optionee does *not* pay cash to exercise the option. He exercises the option (in other words, he purchases the stock at the exercise price) and the brokerage firm sells the stock. Both the option exercise and the sale of stock occur on the same day. The optionee receives the excess of the proceeds from the sale of stock over the exercise price, on *settlement date* – without advancing any money to execute the transaction.

Each of these important issues – portfolio management, income taxation, and cash requirements – is discussed extensively in the following chapters. These discussions will ensure that optionees have a more comprehensive understanding of the income tax and cash flow effects of transactions that involve compensatory stock options. With this knowledge, they are far less likely to rely on blind luck when it comes to maximizing the value of their options.

OPTION REPRICING

Companies use stock options to attract, retain and motivate people. Since stock prices rise and *fall*, stock options present another challenge for management.

If the price of the underlying stock falls *below* the option exercise price, the option is said to be "underwater". If the price of the stock falls substantially below the exercise price, the option's fair value may be insignificant or perceived to be insignificant by the people that the corporation wants to retain.

This situation can present a serious problem for the corporation, especially when a substantial portion of employee compensation consists of stock options. To retain key people, the corporation may feel compelled to reduce the option exercise price in what is called *repricing*. Obviously, a reduction in the exercise price makes the option more attractive to the optionee.

Example: The stock price collapses, the grantor corporation cancels existing options that have a high exercise price, and grants new options that have an exercise price equal to the (lower) fair market value of the stock on the grant date of the new options: Three years ago, Company A granted options to key employees. Those options gave them the right to buy Company A stock at $60 per share, the fair market value of the stock on the date of grant. The price of the stock is now $30 per share. The option is *underwater*. Company A's board of directors, concerned that competitors will recruit its employees, votes to cancel the options that have a $60 exercise price, and grant new options that have a $30 exercise price. If the company had *not* repriced the options, optionees could only realize a gain to the extent that the price of Company A stock rises above $60. *After* the repricing, optionees can reap a gain if the price of the stock rises above $30.

PERSPECTIVE ON OPTION REPRICING

In the previous example, Company A reduced the option exercise price from $60 to $30.

To be sure, this is a nice advantage for the optionee. The fair value (discussed later in this chapter) of an option to buy at $30 when the stock is trading at $30 is worth far more than an option to buy the stock at $60. But optionees should be aware that the fair value of an option to buy at $30 – if the stock is trading at $30 – is substantially less than the fair value of an option to buy at $60 if the stock is trading at $60. In short, shareholders got a haircut when the stock price dropped from $60 to $30; but optionees have lost something too – a sharp decline in the *appreciation potential* of their options, a subject discussed, below, in *"What Gives an Option Value?"*

VOLUNTARY STOCK OPTION EXCHANGE

Sometimes companies offer certain employees the option to exchange an existing "old" option for a "new" option to be granted on a date that is more than six months after cancellation date of the "old" option. This offer is called a *voluntary stock option exchange.* Generally, the exercise price of the new option equals the fair market value of the stock on the date the new option is granted, and the new option has terms and conditions that are substantially similar to those of the old option.

Example: The stock price collapses and ABC Corporation announces a voluntary stock option exchange program for employees: ABC's stock price declines from $30 to $10. In July of Year 1, ABC announces that certain employees have the option to cancel stock options previously granted to them, in exchange for stock options to be granted on a date that is more than six months after the cancellation date. The cancellation date is expected to be on or after September 15, Year 1, and the grant date of the new options is expected to be on or after March 16, Year 2 (six months and one day after cancellation date).

Clearly, the offer above appears to be a great one for employees. One consideration, however, is that they do not own any options during the period between cancellation date and grant date of the new options.

If the stock price soars during the period beginning on the date the old option is cancelled and ending on the date the new option is granted, the optionee could end up holding a new option whose strike price is higher than that of the old option he surrendered.

Example: The optionee cancels his "old" stock option in exchange for a "new" stock option, and the stock price soars between cancellation date of the old option and grant date of the new option: On September 15, Year 1, ABC stock is trading at $10 and the exercise price on Lynn's option is $30. She decides to participate in the voluntary stock exchange program and cancels her options to buy ABC stock at $30. The price of ABC stock soars subsequent to the September 15, Year 1 option cancellation date, and on the new grant date (March 16, Year 2) the fair market value of the stock is $40. Therefore, the exercise price of the new option is $40. In short, Lynn exchanged an option to buy ABC stock at $30 for an option to buy at $40.

UNDERWATER OPTIONS AND VOLATILITY

As Chapter 2 illustrates, the Black-Scholes option pricing model allows one to estimate the probability that the fair market value of the underlying stock will decline over a given holding period. That is because, under the Black-Scholes model, the fair value of an option is based, in part, on the probability that the stock price will exceed the option exercise price.

Optionees will discover from Table 2.5 that, contrary to how intuition might guide us, in most cases there is *not* an equal chance that the stock price one year from now will equal the stock price today – if assumptions in the Black-Scholes model are true. This tells us something important – not only with respect to the subject of underwater options (discussed below), but also with respect to the decision to exercise an ISO and hold such ISO-stock for more than 12 months in order to reap favorable income tax treatment on gain.

For example, Table 2.5 shows a 52 percent estimated probability that the fair market value of a stock – that has 30 percent volatility – will be *lower* 12 months from today, if the risk-free annual interest rate is three percent. The estimated probability soars to 70 percent (an increase of 18 percentage points, or 35 percent) that the stock price will be lower 12 months from today, if the volatility of the stock is 110 percent.

In short, the more volatile the underlying stock, the higher the probability that a January 1, Year 1 option grant will be underwater on January 1, Year 2 – other things being equal.

OPTION REPRICING AND IRC SECTION 409A

IRC Section 409A, added to the Internal Revenue Code as part of the *American Jobs Creation Act of 2004*, provides that all amounts deferred under a nonqualified deferred compensation plan for all taxable years are currently includible in gross income to the extent not subject to a substantial risk of forfeiture (defined in IRS Notice 2005-1 Q-10) and not previously included in gross income, unless certain requirements are met. The significance for optionees is that, if Section 409A applies, taxation occurs when the option vests, not when it is exercised. As discussed below, however, Section 409A should affect relatively few optionees – but uncertainties remain with respect to option pricing.

Congress and the IRS (in Notice 2005-1), have made it clear that Section 409A is not intended to change the taxation of compensatory stock options, in cases where the option exercise price is not less than the fair market value of the stock on option grant date (which is the case under most option grants), *and* the option does not include any feature for the deferral of compensation other than the deferral of recognition of income until the later of option exercise or disposition of the option under Regulation 1.83-7.

Most optionees should *not* be affected by Section 409A (but please see Chapter 3 for a discussion of the potential risk to holders of nonqualified options that were granted to them when the underlying stock was not publicly traded), because the option exercise price is generally not set at a discount to the fair market value of the stock on grant date, and the option generally does not include any feature for the deferral of compensation other than the (permitted) deferral of recognition of income mentioned above.

With respect to nonqualified stock options, IRS Notice 2005-1 Q-4 *"What constitutes a deferral of compensation?"* provides "If under the terms of the option, the amount required to purchase the stock *is or could become* [italics added] less than the fair market value of the stock on the date of grant, the grant of the stock option may provide for the deferral of compensation..."

IRC Section 409A is new and questions remain unanswered. The safe course is to *wait for additional guidance* from the IRS. It is premature to conclude that Section 409A would not apply to repricing – even where the option exercise price of the new option is not less than the fair market value of the stock on the grant date of the new option. In fact, as a precaution against the uncertainty surrounding Section 409A, many companies have changed their option plans to read that options *cannot* be repriced...nor reloaded (see below).

OPTIONS WITH A RELOAD FEATURE

An option (the "original" option) that contains a reload feature provides that if the optionee exercises such option and pays the exercise price using stock (the "payment shares") which the optionee already owns, the company will automatically award the optionee a *new* option. The new option is sometimes called a *reload option*, *restoration option*, or *replacement option*.

Generally, if the optionee exercises an option (one containing a reload provision) to buy the company's stock and pays the exercise price with *mature stock* of that company (instead of using cash), the optionee receives one share of stock upon option exercise *and* one *new* option for every share of stock that he uses to pay the exercise price. Sometimes even the new option contains a reload feature so that it too can be "reloaded" on *its* date of exercise.

The exercise price of each *new* option is the fair market value of the stock on the date the corporation grants each new option. The new option *expires* on the *same* date that the "original" option would have expired.

Mature stock is stock that the optionee already owns, including stock acquired on the open market (for example, through a brokerage firm). It also includes stock that he may have purchased through a company plan if the optionee has satisfied certain holding period requirements with respect to such stock.

In Private Letter Ruling 9629028, the IRS ruled that, in lieu of actually transferring shares to the company, the optionee could make a *constructive exchange* of such *payment shares*.

If the payment shares are held by a registered securities broker for the optionee in "street name", the optionee may provide the company with a notarized statement attesting to the number of shares owned that are intended to serve as payment shares. If the stock certificates are held by the optionee, he should provide the company with their certificate numbers.

Upon receipt of such notarized statement or upon confirmation of such share ownership by reference to the company's records, the company treats the payment shares as being constructively exchanged and issues to the optionee a certificate for the *net* number of shares. The net number of shares equals the number of shares subject to the option exercise less the number of payment shares.

Example: Optionee exercises options, and receives a new "reload" option: The outstanding stock of Company A consists of one class of common stock. Julia owns one share of Company A stock that she bought on the open market for $5. The current market price is $20. Julia owns nonqualified stock options to buy two shares of Company A stock at an exercise price of $10 per share. The options expire on January 5, 2007. They contain a reload provision. Julia exercises the options to buy *two* shares of stock and pays the $20 exercise price by transferring to Company A (or merely certifying that she owns one share of Company A stock) the one share of Company A stock that she bought on the open market. She receives two shares of Company A stock *and* a new nonqualified stock option (the reload option). The new option has an exercise price of $20, the fair market value of Company A stock on the date the corporation grants the reload option. The reload option expires on January 5, 2007, the same date that the original option would have expired.

TAX-DEFERRED EXCHANGE

In the example above, Julia transfers one share of Company A stock, which has a fair market value of $20, as payment of the exercise price. Julia's transfer of such stock qualifies as a stock-for-stock *tax-deferred exchange* under IRC Section 1036 "Stock for stock of *same* corporation". Therefore, she does *not* recognize a taxable gain on the date of transfer even though the $20 fair market value of the stock exceeds her $5 original purchase price.

BEFORE AND AFTER OPTION EXERCISE

Before her exercise of the original option, Julia owned and held options to buy *three* shares of Company A stock (she owned one share and held options to buy two shares). *After* exercise of the original option, Julia still owns and holds options to buy *three* shares (she owns two shares and holds an option to buy one share).

If the original option did *not* have a reload provision, Julia would have owned and held options to buy only *two* shares after exercising her two options (she would have owned two shares and held *no* options to buy more shares).

DIFFERENT PROVISIONS

An "original" nonqualified stock option as well as an "original" incentive stock option can have a reload provision.

Reload features differ from one stock option plan to another. Some allow one reload per original option. Others allow multiple reloads.

Sometimes the corporation grants one new option for every share of *stock* that the optionee uses to pay the exercise price. Sometimes the corporation *also* grants one new option for every share of *stock* that the optionee uses to pay withholding taxes on the exercise of a nonqualified stock option.

In other cases, the optionee receives one new option for every *option exercised.*

WHAT GIVES AN OPTION VALUE?

For most optionees, the option exercise price *equals* the fair market value of the stock on the date of option grant.

The *intrinsic value* of the option on the date of grant is *zero* because intrinsic value is the *excess* of the fair market value of the stock over the option exercise price. The *fair value* of the option, however, is *not* zero. In fact, it could be quite high.

Example: *Generally, intrinsic value on grant date equals zero, but the fair value of the option is not zero:* Company A grants a nonqualified stock option to Employee A. On the date of grant, the fair market value of Company A's publicly-traded stock is $10. The option exercise price is $10. On the same day, Company B grants a nonqualified stock option to Employee B. On the date of grant, the fair market value of Company B's publicly-traded stock, and the option exercise price, is $100. Other things being equal (for example, if the *volatility* of both stocks and the *term* of the options are the same), the fair value of Employee B's option is *greater* than the fair value of Employee A's option because B's option offers more *appreciation potential*...even though both options have the *same* (zero) intrinsic value.

To illustrate, if Company A's stock price increases by 100 percent to $20, Employee A may exercise his option (if it has vested), sell the stock, and enjoy a *$10 gain*. If Company B's stock price increases by 100 percent to $200, Employee B may exercise his option (if it has vested), sell the stock, and enjoy a *$100 gain*.

FAIR VALUE OF AN OPTION

The *fair value* of an unexpired *option* is *not* zero. Fair value equals the sum of the option's:

- intrinsic value

  and,

- time value

The fair value of the option is *equal* to its intrinsic value immediately before option *expiration* because at that moment the option's time value equals zero.

Time value is based on many factors including the fair market value of the underlying stock, the option exercise price, the volatility of the underlying stock, dividend payments to shareholders, the time remaining until option expiration date, interest rates, whether or not the option has a reload feature and how many times it can be reloaded, nontransferability of the option, whether it has an anti-dilution provision, whether the optionee receives "dividend equivalent" payments during the period the option remains unexercised, whether the option is "dividend protected" (the exercise price is adjusted downward by the amount of dividends paid to shareholders), and how quickly the option vests.

All of these factors impact the time value of the option. The challenge of computing the option's fair value is a difficult one because it requires so many subjective assumptions.

IMPORTANT FACTORS

Three of the more important factors that impact the fair value of an option are the *volatility* of the stock, the *term* of the option (the amount of time remaining until the option expires), and *dividend* payments to shareholders.

Other things being equal:

- the more volatile the stock, the more valuable the option

- the longer the term, the more valuable the option

- the lower the dividend, the more valuable the option

In addition, a compensatory stock option that has a *reload* feature is more valuable than the same option without a reload feature. Similarly, an option whose exercise price may be reduced (*repriced*) by action of the board of directors is more valuable than the same option without the possibility of ever being repriced. Other things being equal, the option that *vests* (becomes exercisable) more quickly is more valuable. Other things being equal, the option that protects against *dilution* is more valuable, and (as discussed below) a transferable option is more valuable than a nontransferable option.

Volatility of the Stock

It should be reasonably straightforward that, other things being equal, the option with *more* time remaining until expiration date has the *greater* fair value.

It may not be as clear that, other things being equal, the more *volatile* the *stock,* the greater the fair value of an *option* to buy such stock.

The optionee loses *nothing* if the stock price falls below the option exercise price. He has *no downside risk* because if the fair market value of the stock is less than the option exercise price, he simply does not exercise the option.

But he *wins* if the stock price increases. In fact, the option has *unlimited upside potential* because there is no limitation on how high the price of the stock may rise during the term of the option.

Since he can *win* but never *lose* (he only exercises the option if its intrinsic value is greater than zero), it naturally follows that the more volatile the stock, the more valuable the option.

Management and shareholders realize that options motivate employees. They also know that, as mentioned above, optionees can win but never lose; consequently, they may also be motivated to engage in more risky behavior. As the next example illustrates, options can increase shareholder risk.

Example: *Employee stock options may motive employees to engage in more risky behavior:* Angela is an executive at ABC Bank, which makes loans that are secured by real property. ABC grants options to Angela and other members of ABC's management team – and the options have little or no intrinsic value at the current stock price. In an effort to generate more interest income for the bank, management aggressively pursues lending opportunities – even those that its competitors consider too risky. The expectation is that a larger loan portfolio will lead to a higher stock price – and, therefore, an increase in the intrinsic value of their employee stock options. And, if the stock price collapses, employees suffer little or no decline in their net worth because if the stock price does not exceed the option exercise price, optionees simply do not exercise them. The risk to shareholders of ABC Bank from approving loan applications that its competitors reject is that the quality of its loan portfolio deteriorates, a decline in economic activity follows, and the value of the real estate that collateralizes its loans declines substantially, and ultimately results in losses to the bank.

FAIR VALUE WILL NOT BE REALIZED

During the life of the option, its fair value *exceeds* its intrinsic value because of the option's time value. Immediately before option expiration, however, the fair value *equals* the intrinsic value because at that moment the time value equals zero.

Unfortunately, the optionee will generally *not* realize the fair value of the option because compensatory stock options are often accompanied by strict limitations on transferability (although some companies, including Microsoft Corporation, have allowed employees to make a one-time election to transfer underwater options to an investment bank, and capture some of the option's remaining time value; and, stock option plans often permit gifting of nonqualified options to family members).

Since he cannot sell a nontransferable option and realize its fair value, the optionee may realize only the option's *intrinsic value*. That means he sacrifices the option's time value when he exercises such option before its expiration date. Obviously, then, a transferable stock option is more valuable than one that is nontransferable – because it allows for the possibility of capturing some amount of time value upon its sale.

In short, there are two possible events with respect to a nontransferable stock option. Either it is exercised and the holder reaps a gain equal to the option's intrinsic value, or it is not exercised and expires worthless.

WHY IS IT IMPORTANT TO UNDERSTAND FAIR VALUE?

Since the optionee will not realize the fair value of the option, one might ask: *"Why is it important to understand fair value?"* One answer is that optionees have *choices*.

For example, an individual may be considering offers of employment from two or more companies. If the offers contain different stock option packages, the individual must understand what makes an option valuable in order to make an informed decision.

Fair value is important because of the *information* it contains. Other things being equal, the optionee should expect to reap a larger gain from the stock option package that has the higher fair value.

OPTIONS ON PRIVATELY-HELD STOCK

"Outsiders" find it difficult or impossible to know the fair market value of a *stock* that is not actively traded on U.S. securities markets (for example, the New York Stock Exchange or NASDAQ). In fact, it can be difficult for an "insider", armed with a team of investment banking professionals, to compute the fair market value of the stock. The fair value of the *option* is based, in part, on the fair market value of the *stock*.

In short, regardless if one understands what gives an option value, he is more or less *forced* to rely on *subjective* judgments about the company when evaluating its option package.

OPTIONS ON PUBLICLY-TRADED STOCK

U.S. securities markets generally price actively-traded stock at or near "true value". In other words, U.S. securities markets are at least reasonably *efficient* – and some would argue they are highly efficient.

Since the price of an actively-traded *stock* is known, the computation of the fair value of an *option* to buy such stock is more likely to approximate the option's "true value" than if the underlying stock is *not* actively traded. In other words, if the underlying stocks are publicly traded, the fair value of options to buy such stocks is subject to less uncertainty.

EVALUATING AN OPTION PACKAGE

Stock price *volatility* (Example A) and *appreciation potential* (Example B) are important concepts to understand when evaluating an option package.

Example A: Other things being equal, the higher the volatility of the underlying stock, the more valuable an option to buy such stock: Two companies whose stocks trade actively on the New York Stock Exchange offer employment to Jaci. Company A offers

Jaci nonqualified stock options to buy 10,000 shares of stock at $10 per share, the current market price. The options are not transferable. Company B makes an identical offer. Company A's stock option plan is *identical* to Company B's plan. Jaci calls her brokerage firm and learns that Company A's stock has a *beta* of 1.00 while Company B's stock has a beta of 1.50. Beta is a measure of volatility. Generally, the higher the beta, the more volatile the stock. Company B's stock option package has a higher fair value than Company A's because B's stock is more volatile.

Example B: Appreciation potential: Company C, whose stock also trades actively on the New York Stock Exchange, enters the competition to recruit Jaci and offers her nonqualified stock options to buy 10,000 shares of Company C stock at $100 per share, the current market price. The beta of Company C's stock is 1.50, the same as the beta of Company B's stock. Company C's stock option package has more value than B's because Jaci has *appreciation potential* on $1,000,000 of Company C stock (10,000 shares x $100 per share = $1,000,000) versus appreciation potential on only $100,000 of Company B stock (10,000 shares x $10 per share = $100,000).

WHEN TO EXERCISE OPTIONS

The *general rule* is that an optionee should *not* be anxious to exercise compensatory stock options. Generally, he should *not* exercise them years before their expiration date.

The reasoning is simple and logical. First, compensatory stock options are somewhat similar to *interest-free loans* – loans that bear no interest. An interest-free loan has value (to the borrower) and the longer the amount of time remaining until the loan's maturity date, the more valuable it is (to the borrower), other things being equal.

Second, holding options *defers the payment of income taxes* on the taxable income that *would* be triggered by an option exercise.

EXCEPTIONS TO THE GENERAL RULE

There are many exceptions to the general rule that compensatory options should not be exercised well in advance of their expiration date.

Circumstances that may favor earlier exercise include:

- The optionee's need for cash

- The desire to diversify his investment portfolio

- A gradual process of exercising options, and selling the stock, as part of a longer-term strategy to minimize the impact of income taxation

- The fact that he has large capital loss carryovers that may never be utilized, because of the annual limitation on the income tax deductibility of capital losses. Such capital loss carryovers can be used to offset capital gains from the eventual sale of stock previously acquired by exercise of ISOs or NQSOs

- Exercising NQSOs, or exercising ISOs and selling the stock in a disqualifying disposition, to accelerate income into a year in which he has *excess* income tax deductions that will otherwise expire (this strategy effectively results in *tax-free* income)

- Exercising *vested* NQSOs and holding the stock in order to convert appreciation in the stock price after the date of option exercise from ordinary income into capital gain (long-term, or short-term, depending on whether or not he holds the stock for more than 12 months after exercise date)

- Exercising *unvested* NQSOs or *unvested* ISOs *prior to* substantial appreciation in the stock price, and making a timely election under Internal Revenue Code Section 83(b)

- The fair market value of the stock substantially exceeds the option exercise price (therefore, an option to buy such stock may have little time value relative to its intrinsic value)

- The dividend yield on the stock is high (cash dividends are generally not enjoyed by option holders, and they result in a reduction in stock price roughly equal to the amount of the dividend)

FAIR MARKET VALUE OF STOCK

This book contains a number of references to the fair market value of stock. But determining fair market value is sometimes difficult when the stock is not *actively* traded on an exchange or other securities market. Determining the fair market value of publicly-traded stock may also be difficult, for example, – whether or not the stock is actively traded – if the owner holds an amount of stock such that its sale could impact the market price.

If fair market value is in question (for example, the stock is not publicly traded), the shareholder may need to request an appraisal from an experienced and competent stock valuation expert.

PUBLICLY-TRADED STOCK

If the stock is actively traded on an exchange or other securities market, the Internal Revenue Service generally accepts the average of the highest and lowest quoted selling prices on a particular day as that day's fair market value (although, the shareholder may find an expert appraiser who is willing to argue that fair market value is a different amount – and he may or may not be successful in his assertion if challenged by the IRS – depending on the facts and circumstances).

If the stock is publicly traded but not actively traded, there is more opportunity for disagreement as to fair market value. For example, if the shareholder bases fair market value on an average, or volume-weighted average of prices over some "reasonable" period of time, he may or may not face a challenge from the IRS.

NONLAPSE AND LAPSE RESTRICTIONS

IRC Section 83(a) provides that the fair market value of stock transferred in connection with the performance of services shall be determined without regard to any restriction other than a restriction that will never lapse. In other words, a restriction that is not a nonlapse restriction cannot, by itself, serve as the basis for assigning a discount to the fair market value of the stock.

Under Regulation 1.83-3(h), a restriction which, by its terms, will never lapse (that is, a "nonlapse restriction") is a *permanent* limitation on the transferability of property –

(i)   Which will require the transferee of the property to sell, or offer to sell, such property at a price determined under a formula,

and,

(ii)   Which will continue to apply to and be enforced against the transferee or any subsequent holder (other than the transferor).

Regulation 1.83-3(i) states that a *lapse* restriction is a restriction other than a nonlapse restriction.

Regulation 1.83-3(h) states that "a limitation subjecting the property to a permanent right of first refusal in a particular person at a price determined under a formula is a permanent nonlapse restriction." It also provides "an obligation to resell or to offer to sell property transferred in connection with the performance of services to a specific person or persons at fair market value at the time of such sale is not a nonlapse restriction."

That same regulation reads "limitations imposed by registration requirements of State or Federal security laws or similar laws imposed with respect to sales or other dispositions of stock or securities are not nonlapse restrictions." As the judge commented in a Tax Court Memorandum Decision (TC Memo 1979-384), that includes SEC Rule 144 stock, which is restricted stock that has not been registered with the United States Securities and Exchange Commission ("SEC").

Example: *Fair market value of SEC Rule 144 stock:* ABC Corporation stock is publicly traded. Alice receives ABC stock as compensation for the performance of services. But the ABC stock she receives is Rule 144 stock, not ABC stock that is freely traded on an exchange. When Alice determines the fair market value of the Rule 144 stock, she is precluded from taking a discount from the fair market value of freely-traded shares because the restrictions on the Rule 144 stock are, according to Regulation 1.83-3(h), not nonlapse restrictions. This is true despite the fact that there is little or no disagreement that stock with Rule 144 restrictions is less valuable than freely-traded stock; and, it is well established that if Alice would make a private sale of such stock, proceeds from the sale would likely be at a discount from the market price of freely traded shares.

COLLARS LIMIT EXPOSURE TO MARKET RISK

As Chapter 10 *"ISO-Stock Protection Strategies"* explains, the optionee is *not* able to use a collar (that is, buy a put option and sell a call option – on stock he owns) to protect the value of immature ISO-stock, *and* still satisfy the special holding period requirements that would give him preferential tax treatment – because the collar is a straddle that terminates his holding period in the stock.

Yet investors are using collars that are carefully structured to avoid a constructive sale of appreciated stock under IRC Section 1259 (if a constructive sale is triggered, the taxpayer is deemed to have sold appreciated stock that he has *not* sold), and that limit exposure to stock price changes for as long as the collar remains in place – by placing a floor (in the amount of the strike price of the put option) and a ceiling (in the amount of the strike price of the call option) on the investor's position. In fact, it is well documented that many who had established collars early in 2000, including corporate insiders, escaped much of the wrath from the devastating bear market that followed.

HEDGING EMPLOYEE STOCK OPTIONS

Securities and Exchange Commission ("SEC") Rule 16c-4 is in place to prevent a corporate insider from profiting from a decline in the company's stock price. As such, it allows an insider to buy put options on his company's stock, but only to the extent the put position does not cover an amount of shares that exceeds the number of shares he *owns*.

In March 2004, securities firm Credit Suisse First Boston ("CSFB") requested interpretive advice from the SEC as to whether a corporate executive, who is subject to Section 16 of the Securities Exchange Act of 1933, would – under the facts and circumstances presented in its request – be treated as *owning* the shares of stock underlying his compensatory stock option.

Included in such facts and circumstances (many of which are not included here) is that the executive would collar the stock, and at the time the collar is established, the fair market value of the stock substantially exceeds the exercise price of his vested and non-forfeitable employee stock option (that is, the option is substantially "in-the-money"). Further, the collar would consist of "European-style" put and call options (European-style options are exercisable only on expiration date) and the collar would not be an income-producing collar (that is, the executive's proceeds from his sale of the call option would not exceed his cost to purchase the put option). Most importantly, from the perspective of Rule 16c-4, the terms of the transaction would be such that the executive would not benefit in any way from a decline in stock price after collaring the stock. The SEC responded that, based on the facts presented in CSFB's request, the executive would be considered to own the shares underlying his employee stock options.

In short, if structured properly, an insider may enter into collar transactions that limit his exposure to stock price changes, and essentially protect unrealized appreciation on vested and non-forfeitable *employee stock options*.

The SEC response is potentially significant, especially for executives that hold highly-concentrated positions in employer stock, and in options to buy such stock – and whose portfolios are, therefore, not well diversified. That is because, to the extent executives are able to successfully hedge unrealized appreciation in employee stock options, such executives are likely to place a higher value on the option grants they receive. Another consequence may be that, to the extent they are able to protect unrealized appreciation in employee options, these executives will tend to be less anxious to exercise them well in advance of their expiration date.

Copies of the original CSFB request and the SEC response are available from the Office of Chief Counsel Division of Corporation Finance at www.sec.gov.

Example: If terms and conditions of an agreement are structured precisely, an insider is considered to own the shares underlying employee stock options that are substantially in-the-money: Lisa, an employee of ABC Corporation, is an insider who is subject to Section 16 of the Securities and Exchange Act of 1933. She does not own any shares of ABC stock, but she holds employee stock options that give her the right, but not the obligation, to buy 100,000 shares of ABC at an exercise price of $10. The fair market value of the stock is $50. Lisa's options have an intrinsic value of $4 million (100,000 x ($50 - $10) = $4 million). If she enters into a transaction under the exact terms and conditions presented in CSFB's request, she will be treated as owning up to 100,000 shares of ABC stock for purposes of SEC Rule 16c-4. It means that she would not be in violation of Rule 16c-4 if she buys put options that give her the right to sell 100,000 shares of ABC stock at the put option strike price, thus establishing a floor under the value of her employee stock options. Lisa will need the advice of an expert to negotiate her way around the tax law before entering into any hedging transaction, however.

NON-COMPETE CLAUSES

This section addresses one specific question with respect to a non-compete clause included within a stock option agreement. That is: *"Is it possible for a stock option agreement to contain an enforceable non-compete clause that requires the optionee to return all profits from the sale of stock previously acquired by exercise of options if he violates such clause?"*

The answer is "yes" (at least in Texas, Louisiana, and Mississippi, which fall under the jurisdiction of the Fifth Circuit), according to the Fifth Circuit Court of Appeal's 2004 decision in *Olander v. Compass Bank*, 363, F.3d 560 (5th Cir. 2004). To be sure, legal professionals nationwide have their eyes focused on this case, even though the opinion of one circuit court is not binding on other circuit courts.

Under the facts in *Olander v. Compass Bank*, Mr. Olander, an at-will employee of Compass Bank, received compensatory stock options. The stock option agreement contained a clause requiring Olander to return all stock that he held in Compass Bank, and all profits from the sale of stock previously acquired by option exercise – if he violated certain terms (including a non-competition clause) of the agreement, even if a court of law would rule that such terms are not enforceable.

In 2001, Olander resigned from Compass Bank and shortly thereafter began working at Whitney National Bank, a competitor. A suit followed. The U.S. District Court for the Southern District of Texas held, and the Fifth Circuit affirmed such holding, that the non-compete clause was unenforceable. In other words, Compass Bank could not prevent Mr. Olander from working for the competition.

But, the Fifth Circuit also held that the *other* clause – requiring the return of all stock, and all profits from the sale of stock previously acquired by option exercise – *was* enforceable. Consequently, Olander had to return more than $200,000 to Compass Bank. In short, Compass Bank was not successful in preventing Mr. Olander from working at Whitney National Bank, but terms of the stock option agreement made it costly for him to do so.

One consequence of this court decision may be that employers will propose changes to the terms of existing stock option agreements, or draft future stock option agreements that contain language similar to that which proved so valuable to Compass Bank (and so costly to the optionee), or both.

2

Risk and Diversification

Investment professionals often define risk as *uncertainty* and generally measure it by using a statistic called *standard deviation.* They commonly refer to the standard deviation of returns as *volatility.* In short, the higher (lower) the volatility of a stock, the higher (lower) the perceived risk of holding such stock.

As Chapter 1 explains, the greater the volatility of the underlying stock, the greater is the fair value of an option to buy such stock – other things being equal. That means it is important for the optionee to understand volatility. It also means that a generic decision rule cannot be made with respect to the question of whether to hold ISO-stock beyond December 31 of the year of ISO exercise – because the risk of holding ISO-stock of different corporations is not uniform, since different stocks have different levels of volatility (this subject is discussed extensively in Chapter 9 *"ISO-Stock: The December 31 Decision"*).

Table 2.1 illustrates that historical volatility measures the *variability* of actual historical returns relative to the average (mean) of such returns.

The discussion *"Diversification, Correlation and Portfolio Management"* later in this chapter shows that an individual can generally control the level of risk in his investment portfolio by holding several different assets whose expected returns are not highly correlated.

This chapter discusses the following sections:

- *Volatility*

- *Probability of Decline in Stock Price*

- *Diversification, Correlation and Portfolio Management*

VOLATILITY

Annualized volatility is a measure of the *variability* of total return, including dividends. Low volatility indicates that returns are relatively stable over time, while high volatility indicates that returns are subject to significant variation over time.

A point of reference is useful for those trying to grasp the meaning of volatility because volatility is expressed in percent. Without a point of reference, it is difficult to understand the implications of a stock having, for example, a volatility of 50 percent.

As a means for comparison, the annualized volatility (which changes continuously because markets are dynamic) for the Standard & Poors 500 index has often been between 15 and 25 percent.

Many stocks in the Standard & Poors 500 index have volatility in 30 to 65 percent range. Sometimes volatility exceeds 100 percent, an exceedingly high level that alerts the optionee to the likelihood that the price of the stock will be jumping around like a jackrabbit. In short, it means high risk.

UNCERTAINTY REIGNS

The annual compounded return on a diversified portfolio of domestic common stocks was approximately 10 percent during the 20th century. Volatility was approximately twice that amount, however, and it means that returns are subject to much uncertainty.

As one might expect from such volatility, returns were substantially negative in some years and substantially positive in others. In short, uncertainty reigned over returns during the previous century, and optionees should expect that uncertainty will almost certainly reign during the limited term of their options.

This lesson – *volatility exceeding returns* – is highly instructive, especially for optionees. That is because an optionee holds options to buy *one* underlying stock – not options to buy a (less volatile) diversified portfolio of many different stocks. Consequently, the future value of that one stock is almost always far more uncertain than the future value of a diversified portfolio.

In short, those holding options, the intrinsic value of which is substantial and comprising a large part of their net worth, will generally find it wise to exercise at least some of them and immediately sell the stock – unless they have the ability to bear substantial risk.

HISTORIC AND FUTURE VOLATILITY

Historical volatility is often used as the basis for projecting future volatility. One must exercise caution, however, when using historical volatility to formulate expectations about future volatility because financial markets are dynamic.

For example, it is risky to assume that if the volatility of ABC Corporation stock has been measured at 80 percent over the most recent 5-year period that it will continue at a level near 80 percent over the 5-year period that starts today.

In short, for a variety of reasons, volatility tends to change over time. Reasons include changes in the level of specific risk associated with the company, or with changes in the company's capital structure (i.e., the amount of debt versus equity financing).

Other reasons have more to do with changes in the macroeconomic climate (that is, general economic activity), or political risks (for example, operations in countries that have unstable governments), or unexpected results stemming from litigation, or a hostile takeover attempt. There are many uncertainties facing companies and these are but a few that can explain why future volatility may be higher or lower than historical volatility.

HISTORICAL VOLATILITY

It is important for investors to understand the meaning of volatility because, while they do not have the ability to control the returns that they will ultimately earn, *investors have the ability to set their portfolios to a risk level* that is consistent with their particular needs and circumstances. What happens after that is in the hands of the markets, over which the investor has no control.

Perhaps the best way to appreciate the meaning of volatility is to understand how one computes it. In fact, computing volatility is quite simple using a computer spreadsheet – as one can see from Table 2.1, which shows how to compute volatility for a stock that does not pay a dividend.

Table 2.1, column A refers to *"Period Number"*. For example, if one is computing the historical volatility of ABC Corporation stock using *weekly* data, period number 0 would be the starting point and period number 1 would be a date that is one week later. Likewise, if he is using *monthly* data, period number 1 would be a date that is one month later than period 0.

Table 2.1, column B presents historical stock prices. The stock price was $101 in period 2, $102 in period 3, and $110 in period 30.

Table 2.1, column C is simply the stock price in period n divided by the stock price in period $n-1$ (i.e., $n-1$ refers to the previous period). For example, the stock price in period 1 is $101 and the stock price in period 0 was $100. The ratio is 1.010000 ($101 divided by $100 = 1.010000).

Table 2.1, column D is the natural logarithm ("natural log") of the value in column C. For example, the natural log of 1.010000 is .009950. Since e = 2.7182818, e raised to the power .009950 equals 1.010000, which is the amount in column C.

Note two values at the bottom of the table:

- *Periodic volatility*

- *Annualized volatility*

HISTORICAL PERIODIC VOLATILITY

Historical *periodic volatility* is the standard deviation of the continuously compounded rates of return for the sample data. Each of the 30 continuously compounded rates of return in this example is reported in Table 2.1, column D.

The periodic volatility (that is, the standard deviation of the 30 rates of return in column D) is .036835 (3.6835 percent). In order to facilitate meaningful comparisons, periodic volatility is converted into annualized volatility as shown below.

Note that if the stock prices in Table 2.1, column A are annual prices (that is, period 1 is the end of Year 1 and period 2 is the end of Year 2, etc.) then periodic volatility equals annualized volatility because, as shown in the next section, the square root of one is one.

HISTORICAL ANNUALIZED VOLATILITY

As explained below, if one multiplies periodic volatility by the "applicable square root" he arrives at *annualized volatility*. The applicable square root is the square root of:

- 258 (or something close to that number) if the stock prices in the table are daily prices
- 52 if the stock prices in the table are weekly prices
- 12 if the stock prices in the table are monthly prices
- 4 if the stock prices in the table are quarterly prices
- 1 if the stock prices in the table are annual prices

VOLATILITY IF STOCK PRICES ARE *DAILY* PRICES

In Table 2.1, annualized volatility equals periodic volatility in the amount of .036835 multiplied by the square root of 258 if the stock prices in the table are *daily* prices (that is, the period under study covers a total of 30 trading days) – because there are approximately 258 trading days in a year. The annualized volatility is therefore .591665 (59.1665 percent) if the stock prices are daily prices (that

Table 2.1
How to Compute Volatility for a Non-dividend-paying Stock

(A) Period Number "n"	(B) Stock Price (SP)	(C) SPn divided by SPn-1 see Note 1	(D) Natural Log of Column C
0	100		
1	101	1.010000	0.009950
2	102	1.009901	0.009852
3	103	1.009804	0.009756
4	104	1.009709	0.009662
5	102	0.980769	-0.019418
6	100	0.980392	-0.019803
7	99	0.990000	-0.010050
8	98	0.989899	-0.010152
9	97	0.989796	-0.010257
10	98	1.010309	0.010257
11	103	1.051020	0.049762
12	101	0.980583	-0.019608
13	92	0.910891	-0.093332
14	95	1.032609	0.032088
15	93	0.978947	-0.021277
16	88	0.946237	-0.055263
17	94	1.068182	0.065958
18	98	1.042553	0.041673
19	103	1.051020	0.049762
20	101	0.980583	-0.019608
21	99	0.980198	-0.020001
22	106	1.070707	0.068319
23	108	1.018868	0.018692
24	111	1.027778	0.027399
25	104	0.936937	-0.065139
26	106	1.019231	0.019048
27	106	1.000000	0.000000
28	105	0.990566	-0.009479
29	105	1.000000	0.000000
30	110	1.047619	0.046520

If the stock prices listed above are daily prices, then:

Periodic volatility	=	0.03683548	=	3.68% standard deviation of amounts in column D (see Note 2)
Annualized volatility	=	0.591665	=	59.17% periodic volatility x square root of the number of trading days in a year (approximately 258)

If the stock prices listed above are weekly prices, then:

Periodic volatility	=	0.03683548	=	3.68% standard deviation of amounts in column D (see Note 2)
Annualized volatility	=	0.265624	=	26.56% periodic volatility x square root of 52

If the stock prices listed above are monthly prices, then:

Periodic volatility	=	0.03683548	=	3.68% standard deviation of amounts in column D (see Note 2)
Annualized volatility	=	0.127602	=	12.76% periodic volatility x square root of 12

Note 1: Column C = stock price for period "n" divided by stock price for the previous period "n - 1"
    Example: stock price for period 5 = $102; stock price for period 4 = $104; column C = 102/104 = .980769

Note 2: This standard deviation is the standard deviation of a sample (using Lotus 1-2-3, the formula is @stds) is, the stock price at the end of trading on Monday is $101 and the stock price at the end of trading on Tuesday is $102, etc.).

VOLATILITY IF STOCK PRICES ARE *WEEKLY* PRICES

In Table 2.1, annualized volatility equals periodic volatility in the amount of .036835 multiplied by the square root of 52 if the stock prices in the table are *weekly* prices (that is, the period under study covers a total of 30 weeks). The annualized volatility is therefore .265624 (26.5624 percent) if the stock prices in the table are weekly prices (that is, the stock price at the end of week 1 is $101 and the stock price at the end of week 2 is $102, etc.).

VOLATILITY IF STOCK PRICES ARE *MONTHLY* PRICES

In Table 2.1, annualized volatility equals periodic volatility in the amount of .036835 multiplied by the square root of 12 if the stock prices in the table are *monthly* prices (that is, the period under study covers a total of 30 months). The annualized volatility is therefore .127602 (12.7602 percent) if the stock prices are monthly prices (that is, the stock price at the end of month 1 is $101 and the stock price at the end of month 2 is $102, etc.).

VOLATILITY OF AN OPTION'S INTRINSIC VALUE

Table 2.1 shows the historical volatility of ABC stock over 30 time periods of equal length. To illustrate the magnified volatility of the intrinsic value of an *option* relative to the volatility of the underlying *stock*, Table 2.2 shows the historical volatility of the intrinsic value of an option to buy such stock at an exercise price of $85 per share (please note that Table 2.2 delivers a correct answer providing that all of the amounts in column D are positive; that is because the amounts in column D are the denominator for the computation in column E and one cannot divide the numerator by zero).

The following list summarizes the substantially higher annualized volatility of that option's intrinsic value as compared to the volatility of the underlying stock:

- If the 30 stock prices in the table are daily prices, volatility of the intrinsic value = 583 percent (versus 59 percent for ABC stock)

- If the 30 stock prices in the table are weekly prices, volatility of the intrinsic value = 262 percent (versus 27 percent for ABC stock)

- If the 30 stock prices in the table are monthly prices, volatility of the intrinsic value = 126 percent (versus 13 percent for ABC stock)

In short, the volatility of the intrinsic value of a stock option exceeds the volatility of the underlying stock – generally by a wide margin. In the above example, volatility of the option's intrinsic value was approximately 10 times the volatility of the underlying stock.

It is important to understand that an option is a derivative that has leverage, and the extent of such leverage varies depending upon the option exercise price – other things being equal. To illustrate how leverage changes with changes in the option exercise price, consider that the option exercise price in Table 2.2 was $85. If the option exercise price had been $50, instead of $85, the percentage changes in such option's intrinsic value would have been less pronounced (that is, the option's intrinsic value would have been less volatile). If the option exercise price had been greater than $85, volatility would have been more pronounced.

IMPLIED VOLATILITY

Historical volatility can be a useful reference point for investors addressing risk. Discussions about volatility, however, often refer to a more relevant measure for optionees – *implied volatility.*

As explained below, implied volatility of the underlying stock is that current level of volatility, which is determined in a competitive

Table 2.2
Volatility of an Option that has an $85 Exercise Price

(A) Period Number "n"	(B) Stock Price (SP)	(C) Option Exercise Price	(D) Option Intrinsic Value IV	(E) IVn divided by IVn-1	(F) Natural Log of Column E
0	100	85	15		
1	101	85	16	1.066667	0.064539
2	102	85	17	1.062500	0.060625
3	103	85	18	1.058824	0.057158
4	104	85	19	1.055556	0.054067
5	102	85	17	0.894737	-0.111226
6	100	85	15	0.882353	-0.125163
7	99	85	14	0.933333	-0.068993
8	98	85	13	0.928571	-0.074108
9	97	85	12	0.923077	-0.080043
10	98	85	13	1.083333	0.080043
11	103	85	18	1.384615	0.325422
12	101	85	16	0.888889	-0.117783
13	92	85	7	0.437500	-0.826679
14	95	85	10	1.428571	0.356675
15	93	85	8	0.800000	-0.223144
16	88	85	3	0.375000	-0.980829
17	94	85	9	3.000000	1.098612
18	98	85	13	1.444444	0.367725
19	103	85	18	1.384615	0.325422
20	101	85	16	0.888889	-0.117783
21	99	85	14	0.875000	-0.133531
22	106	85	21	1.500000	0.405465
23	108	85	23	1.095238	0.090972
24	111	85	26	1.130435	0.122602
25	104	85	19	0.730769	-0.313658
26	106	85	21	1.105263	0.100083
27	106	85	21	1.000000	0.000000
28	105	85	20	0.952381	-0.048790
29	105	85	20	1.000000	0.000000
30	110	85	25	1.250000	0.223144

If the stock prices listed above are daily prices, then:

Periodic volatility of option	=	0.363256142	=	36.33% standard deviation of amounts in column D (see Note 2)
Annualized volatility of option	=	5.834758	=	583.48% periodic volatility x square root of the number of trading days in a year (approximately 258)

If the stock prices listed above are weekly prices, then:

Periodic volatility of option	=	0.363256142	=	36.33% standard deviation of amounts in column D (see Note 2)
Annualized volatility of option	=	2.619477	=	261.95% periodic volatility x square root of 52

If the stock prices listed above are monthly prices, then:

Periodic volatility of option	=	0.363256142	=	36.33% standard deviation of amounts in column D (see Note 2)
Annualized volatility of option	=	1.258356	=	125.84% periodic volatility x square root of 12

Note 1: Column E = the option's intrinsic value for period "n" divided by the option's intrinsic value for the previous period "n - 1"
    Example: intrinsic value for period 5 = 17; intrinsic value for period 4 = 19; column E = 17/19 = .894737

Note 2: This standard deviation is the standard deviation of a sample (using Lotus 1-2-3 the formula is @stds) and free market (for example, in trading on the Chicago Board Options Exchange), that justifies the current market price (the "option premium") of an actively-traded option to buy such stock.

IMPLIED VOLATILITY IS FORWARD-LOOKING

Implied volatility, in contrast with historical volatility, is *current and forward-looking*. It reflects current stock market conditions and publicly-available information (and sometimes even material nonpublic information) with respect to the underlying stock.

Consequently, implied volatility is a more reliable indicator of future volatility than is historical volatility. Implied volatility is not available, however, for all stocks because publicly-traded options do not exist for all stocks.

Example: Implied volatility is less than historical volatility: Options to buy the common stock of Company A are actively-traded on the Chicago Board Options Exchange ("CBOE"). According to the Black-Scholes option pricing model, the option premium (that is, the option price) for a December $100 call option on Company A stock should be $6, based upon historical volatility in the amount of E percent. But, the option premium on Company A stock is not $6 per share. It is only $4. This price discrepancy does not necessarily mean that the Black-Scholes model contains an error (although every option pricing model employs its own assumptions that result in pricing that is not perfectly uniform), or that the CBOE is an inefficient market. Instead, it more likely means that implied volatility for Company A stock is currently less than historical volatility in the amount of E percent. More specifically, market participants are willing to pay for *expected* future volatility – and are not willing to pay for historical volatility.

Example: Implied volatility exceeds historical volatility: The facts are the same as in the previous example except that the option premium is $8, not the $6 that Black-Scholes indicates it should be based on historical volatility in the amount of E percent. In short, since market participants are willing to pay more than the $6 option premium indicated by Black-Scholes, we know that the implied volatility of Company A stock exceeds historical volatility – other things being equal.

IMPLIED VOLATILITY VARIES

Optionees need to be aware that, for reasons beyond the scope of this discussion, implied volatility, as measured by the Black-Scholes model, often varies for publicly-traded options on the *same* underlying stock – depending on the amount of time remaining until option expiration date.

The option's strike price also tends to impact implied volatility under the Black-Scholes model. And published research demonstrates that an *at*-the-money option tends to be a more reliable indicator of future stock price volatility than an option that is not at-the-money.

Example: Option expiration date may impact implied volatility: ABC Corporation stock is trading at $100. An actively-traded December $100 call option is trading at a price that, using the Black-Scholes model, implies future volatility of 50 percent. At the same time, an actively-traded March $100 call option is trading at a price that implies future volatility of 46 percent.

Example: An at-the-money, publicly-traded call option tends to be a better indicator of future stock price volatility: In the previous example, ABC stock is trading at $100 and implied volatility has been measured for an ABC option with a $100 strike price (that is, the ABC option is "at-the-money"). Other things being equal, the implied volatility of that option is likely to be a better indicator of future stock price volatility than an option that is either in-the-money or out-of-the-money.

THE "OPTION CALCULATOR" AT CBOE.COM

The Chicago Board Options Exchange, which generally discloses the option pricing model it uses (different models generally employ different assumptions, and therefore may lead to different results), offers free use of its *"Option Calculator"* at *cboe.com* for those who wish to compute estimates of both option values and implied volatility.

For example, if he wishes to compute implied volatility, the optionee simply enters the following four inputs:

- Current price (premium) of the publicly-traded option

- Current stock price

- Option exercise (strike) price

- Time remaining until option expiration date

The *Option Calculator* responds with the implied volatility of the underlying stock. That level of volatility is the amount of volatility that option buyers are currently willing to pay for when they buy such option in the public markets.

The *Option Calculator* is one source of implied volatility. Some brokerage firms will also provide estimates of implied volatility if a client would request such information.

PROBABILITY OF DECLINE IN STOCK PRICE

Some define risk as the probability of a decline in the stock price, or the probability of a "more than X percent" decline in the stock price. Such measures are not universally adopted as a formal measure of risk, however. One reason is that it does not indicate how large the decline could be. Despite this flaw, having an indication of the probability that the stock will decline by more than X percent offers perspective regarding risk.

Table 2.3 shows the *estimated* probability (for a non-dividend-paying stock) that the price of the stock will decline by more than 10 percent over various holding periods and under the assumption of various stock price volatilities. As explained below, the probabilities in these tables were derived from the Black-Scholes option pricing model.

Table 2.3
Nondividend-paying Stock
Estimated Probability That Stock Price Will Decline More Than 10 Percent
Over Various Holding Periods When the Risk-free Annual Interest Rate is 3 Percent

Holding Period =	1 month	3 months	6 months	9 months	12 months
Volatility					
20%	4%	14%	22%	26%	28%
30%	12%	25%	32%	36%	38%
50%	25%	37%	44%	47%	49%
70%	33%	44%	50%	54%	56%
90%	39%	49%	55%	59%	62%
110%	43%	53%	59%	63%	67%

Table 2.4
Estimated Probability That Stock Price Will Decline More Than 5 Percent
Over Various Holding Periods When the Risk-free Annual Interest Rate is 3 Percent

Holding Period =	1 month	3 months	6 months	9 months	12 months
Volatility					
20%	18%	30%	35%	37%	38%
30%	28%	38%	42%	44%	45%
50%	38%	46%	50%	52%	54%
70%	43%	50%	54%	57%	59%
90%	47%	54%	59%	62%	64%
110%	50%	57%	62%	66%	68%

Table 2.5
Estimated Probability That Stock Price Will Decline
Over Various Holding Periods When the Risk-free Annual Interest Rate is 3 Percent

Holding Period =	1 month	3 months	6 months	9 months	12 months
Volatility					
20%	49%	49%	50%	48%	48%
30%	50%	51%	51%	52%	52%
50%	52%	54%	55%	57%	58%
70%	53%	56%	59%	60%	62%
90%	55%	58%	62%	64%	66%
110%	56%	60%	64%	67%	70%

As explained in the accompanying text, these tables are derived from the Black-Scholes model, which contains certain assumptions that likely are not valid. Consequently, the probabilities shown are, by extension, merely "rough" estimates.

Table 2.4 shows the estimated probability that the stock price will decline by more than 5 percent. Table 2.5 shows the estimated probability that the stock price will decline from its current price.

CAUTION: These tables do not show precise probabilities. They are "rough" estimates that merely offer perspective. That is, for example, Table 2.5 shows that there is not a 50-50 chance that a stock price will increase or decrease; instead, it shows that the probability of decline is greater (often substantially greater) than 50 percent for non-dividend paying stocks with extremely high volatility.

All three tables assume an annualized risk-free continuously-compounded interest rate of 3 percent. Since the estimated probabilities are only mildly sensitive to changes in interest rates, these tables are relevant over a wide spectrum of interest rates. Finally, the probabilities are rough approximations – and should be interpreted accordingly.

Note: The estimated probabilities in Tables 2.3, 2.4 and 2.5 are derived from the Black-Scholes model, which contains a number of assumptions, some of which are likely not valid. Consequently, by extension, the probabilities presented are not totally valid either.

Example: *Estimated probability that the price of ABC Corporation stock will decline by more than 10 percent:* Grace exercised an incentive stock option to buy ABC Corporation ("ABC") stock on February 1, Year 1. She continues to hold such ISO-stock. It is now December 31, Year 1 and Grace is trying to decide whether to sell the stock in Year 1, in order to avoid the recognition of taxable income for purposes of AMT. She wants to know the probability that ABC stock will decline by more than 10 percent during the remaining one-month period (December 31, Year 1 until February 2, Year 2) that she must continue to hold the ISO-stock in order to satisfy the special holding period requirement for a qualifying disposition. ABC stock does not pay a dividend.

Options on ABC are traded on the CBOE. Grace consults the *Option Calculator* at *cboe.com* to find the implied volatility on ABC stock. She checks the price of an ABC option that will expire on or near February 2, Year 2.

She enters the following information into the *Option Calculator*:

- Current market price of the option (the option "premium")
- Option exercise (strike) price
- Current price of ABC stock
- Time remaining until the publicly-traded option expires

The *Option Calculator* responds with an implied volatility of 70 percent. Grace consults Table 2.3 – *fully understanding its limitations described above* – and finds that the estimated probability (as derived from the Black-Scholes model) of a stock declining more than 10 percent over a one-month period is approximately 33 percent if the volatility of such stock is 70 percent. Grace uses this 33 percent "rough" estimate as one piece of information when making her decision to hold or not hold ABC stock beyond December 31, Year 1 (please see Chapter 9 "*ISO-Stock:The December 31 Decision*").

PROBABILITY OF DECLINE AND VOLATILITY

Optionees should also notice in Table 2.3 the important relationship between volatility and the estimated probability of decline in stock price. For example, as mentioned above, the estimated probability of a more than 10 percent decline in stock price is 33 percent, if the volatility is 70 percent; that 33 percent is almost three times the 12 percent estimated probability for a stock that has a volatility of 30 percent.

BLACK-SCHOLES OPTION-PRICING MODEL

The estimated probabilities (for a non-dividend-paying stock) in Tables 2.3, 2.4, and 2.5 are derived from the Black-Scholes model shown below. That is, instead of using the model to solve for the fair value of an option, the model can be used to estimate the probability that the stock price will equal or exceed some predetermined level. That is possible because the factor Xe^{-rT} in the model is simply the present value of the option exercise price and $N(d_2)$ is the probability that the stock price will be greater than or equal to the option exercise price on the date of option expiration.

Under Black-Scholes, the fair value, C_O, of a *call* option on a non-dividend-paying stock (a call option is an option to *buy* stock) is estimated as:

$$C_O = S_O N(d_1) - Xe^{-rT}N(d_2)$$

Where,

$$d_1 = \frac{\ln(S_0/X) + (r + \sigma^2/2)T}{\sigma T^{1/2}}$$

$d_2 \quad = d_1 - \sigma T^{1/2}$

$C_O \quad$ = Option value

$S_O \quad$ = Current stock price

$X \quad$ = Option exercise price

$e \quad$ = 2.71828

$\sigma \quad$ = Standard deviation (volatility) of returns on the stock

$R \quad$ = The annualized continuously-compounded risk-free interest rate

$T \quad$ = Time remaining until option expiration date

$N(d_1) \quad$ = Probability that a random selection from a standard normal distribution will be less than d_1

$N(d_2) \quad$ = Probability that a random selection from a standard normal distribution will be less than d_2

BLACK-SCHOLES TENDS TO OVERSTATE FAIR VALUE

It is well documented that the Black-Scholes model tends to *overstate* the fair value of compensatory stock options. Consequently, an opportunity sometimes arises for optionees who are willing to exchange such options for shares of the underlying stock.

Example: Optionee exchanges overvalued, underwater options for shares of publicly-traded common stock: ABC Corporation previously granted Carrie nonqualified stock options to buy 300,000 shares of ABC stock. The options are currently underwater. Using the Black-Scholes model to compute the fair value of such options, Carrie and ABC Corporation agree that the total fair value is $1 million. ABC stock is publicly traded, and the current price is $10. ABC transfers 100,000 shares of its stock, valued at $1 million, in exchange for Carrie's options. At the time of the exchange, the arrangement is clearly in Carrie's favor because she gives up options that are overvalued by the Black-Scholes model, in exchange for stock whose value is determined in a U.S. securities market.

In the previous example, the arrangement is clearly in Carrie's favor *at the time of exchange* – on a fair value basis. The future is unknown, however, and the price of ABC stock could soar. Carrie now holds 100,000 shares of stock, instead of options to buy 300,000 shares. It means that the exchange reduces her potential for gain.

DIVERSIFICATION, CORRELATION AND PORTFOLIO MANAGEMENT

Every company has *firm-specific* risks (sometimes referred to as *unique risk, unsystematic risk* or *diversifiable risk*).

For example, a company may find it difficult to attract and retain competent management. It may find itself victim to a misappropriation of funds. Or – like Union Carbide Corporation's unfortunate experience with deadly gas in Bhopal, India or

Odwalla, Inc.'s experience with the E.coli bacteria – the firm could suffer disruptive effects and costly consequences.

From a portfolio management perspective, however, the potential for an adverse impact on portfolio value from firm-specific risk is reduced by holding the common stock of several companies. This is true, for example, because Union Carbide's firm-specific risks are *independent* from Odwalla's. As long as firm-specific risks are *independent* from one another, holding the common stock of several companies reduces portfolio risk.

MARKET RISK OR SYSTEMATIC RISK

The previous section discusses the fact that independent risks are diversifiable. But, not all risks are independent from one another and, therefore, such risks are not diversifiable. Risks that are common to all firms (for example, the risk of deterioration in general economic conditions) cannot be eliminated through diversification.

Risk that cannot be diversified away is called *market risk, systematic risk* or *non-diversifiable risk* and investors should *expect* to be rewarded for assuming such risk in the form of higher returns. But, there is no guarantee. In fact, it is no secret that actual returns can be negative regardless of how well diversified the portfolio.

CORRELATION AND PORTFOLIO RISK

Scholars and professional investment managers discovered, and proved mathematically, that the *number* of securities held by the portfolio isn't necessarily as important as how the investment returns on the securities *interact* with one another.

Diversification increases when the portfolio holds assets whose expected returns exhibit *low* or *negative* covariance with one another (in other words, when the expected returns on individual assets within the portfolio have a low or negative correlation coefficient).

Low correlation means that the expected returns on the two asset classes will not move in tandem. Negative correlation means that the expected return on each will have a different *sign* – for example, it is expected that if Asset Class A earns a *positive* rate of return, Asset Class B will generate a *negative* rate of return, and vice-versa.

Since future returns are unpredictable, however, low or negative *historical* correlations do not guarantee low or negative *future* correlations. It means that while we are able to construct portfolios that we *expect* will provide shelter in a storm, there are no guarantees that assets will provide *actual* returns that have low correlation. In short, there is at least one certainty with respect to future returns on stocks; uncertainty has not been repealed.

To summarize, if the expected returns on two asset classes are less than perfectly correlated, holding both (as opposed to holding only one) tends to reduce portfolio risk. Investors must understand, however, that the level of correlation depends on the time period measured and therefore is not a constant. Further, investors must be alert to the fact that even a not-so-clever statistician is able to present accurate data that shows high correlation between the production of pigs and the production of pig iron.

USING CORRELATION TO MANAGE PORTFOLIO RISK

Combining assets with low or negative correlation tends to smooth investment returns. Holding a portfolio of securities whose expected returns have low or negative correlation with one another tends to reduce future volatility of such portfolio.

Table 2.6 lists the holdings of two hypothetical portfolios, A and B. Each portfolio holds 10 percent of its assets in the common stock of each of ten publicly-traded companies.

Portfolio A differs from Portfolio B in only one respect. Portfolio A holds 10 percent of its assets in Procter & Gamble Corporation (P&G) common stock while Portfolio B holds 10 percent of its assets in Newmont Mining Company (Newmont Mining) common stock. Which portfolio should be perceived as more risky? The answer: Portfolio A. Why?

Table 2.6

Combining Assets that have Low or Negative Correlation Tends to Reduce Portfolio Risk

PORTFOLIO A	PORTFOLIO B
Alcoa	Alcoa
Caterpillar	Caterpillar
Citigroup	Citigroup
DuPont	DuPont
General Electric	General Electric
General Motors	General Motors
Home Depot	Home Depot
Johnson & Johnson	Johnson & Johnson
Wal-Mart	Wal-Mart
Procter & Gamble	*Newmont Mining*

Procter & Gamble's business is expected to prosper during periods of economic expansion. Other things being equal and absent unusual events, the other companies comprising Portfolio A are also expected to benefit from favorable economic conditions and suffer from unfavorable economic developments. Therefore, investors expect that returns from holding P&G's common stock will be positively correlated with returns on the other nine common stock holdings in Portfolio A.

But, something is *different* about the expectations at Newmont Mining. Newmont Mining derives most of its revenues and cash flow from gold mining operations. The expected returns on Newmont Mining common stock have a low or negative correlation with the expected returns from each of the other nine common stock investments held by Portfolio B. In contrast to P&G, Newmont Mining is expected to benefit from *un*favorable and *un*certain economic environments.

Unfavorable and uncertain economic environments often spark investor interest in gold and shares of companies that own substantial amounts of what the gold mining industry characterizes as "proven and probable" gold ore reserves. *Clearly, because of the low or negative correlation of expected returns resulting from the addition of Newmont Mining common stock to the portfolio (as opposed to the addition of P&G whose expected returns are positively correlated with the rest of the portfolio), Portfolio B is perceived to be less risky than Portfolio A.*

Example: Lisa holds all of her investment portfolio in stock of 50 companies. She owns stock in 50 *domestic* companies that operate in several different industries. Her portfolio is not well diversified because the expected return on each of the domestic stocks is highly correlated.

Example: Catherine also holds all of her investment portfolio in stock of 50 companies. She owns stock in 45 *domestic* companies, and 5 *foreign* companies. Catherine's portfolio is more diversified than Lisa's because expected returns on stock of the foreign companies are not highly correlated with those of the domestic companies.

Example: Like Lisa and Catherine in the examples above, 100 percent of Barbara's portfolio is invested in the stock of 50 companies. She owns stock in 40 *domestic* companies, 5 *foreign* companies, and 5 companies (not just one, because gold mining companies have unique risks and diversification reduces those risks) that produce substantial amounts of *gold* and have substantial proven and probable gold ore reserves. Barbara's portfolio is more well diversified that both Lisa's and Catherine's because Barbara owns gold mining shares whose expected returns have no, low, or possibly even negative correlation with the returns on the 40 domestic stocks and 5 foreign stocks.

Example: Tina's portfolio is even more diversified than the previous three investors because she holds *domestic, foreign,* and *gold* stocks – and *fixed-income* securities (for example, bonds).

HOW MANY STOCKS ARE REQUIRED?

The law of *diminishing* returns applies to portfolio diversification. The investor achieves substantial diversification benefits by increasing his stock portfolio from one stock to two stocks. Adding a third stock improves diversification further, but generally the third stock does not improve diversification as much as the second stock does.

By holding the stocks of 10 companies that operate in different industries whose projected operating cash flows are not highly correlated, the investor eliminates a *substantial* portion of firm-specific risk. To eliminate *most* firm-specific risk, however, the portfolio should hold dozens of different stocks in companies that operate in several different industries, including the stocks of foreign companies. Preferably, those foreign companies should not be large multinationals because the returns on stocks of large multinationals are likely to be more highly correlated with those of the stock of U.S. companies.

Example: For diversification purposes, shares of multinational corporations are not the first choice: German Enterprise, a fictitious company operates solely in Germany and its cash flows from operations stem almost exclusively from Germany and countries that are members of the European Economic Community. German Multinational, another fictitious company, operates worldwide and derives a substantial portion of its operating cash flows from activities in the United States. Common stock of the former company is likely to offer more diversification benefits – for a U.S. resident – than the latter.

MANAGING PORTFOLIO RISK OF AN OPTIONEE

The needs and circumstances of every optionee are unique, and therefore optionees have a different risk tolerance. Less aggressive optionees that have assets in retirement plans (for example, a 401k plan or individual retirement account ("IRA")) or in taxable accounts generally should consider altering the risk level in such accounts if they hold employee stock options.

Example: Optionee holds assets whose expected returns will have low correlation with the expected return on her employer stock: Lynn is an employee of ABC Corporation, an established software developer in Silicon Valley, California. She owns employee stock options that have significant intrinsic value. She also owns a home in Silicon Valley. Lynn chooses to hold assets, in her employer's 401(k) plan, the expected returns of which have a low correlation with the expected returns from ABC Corporation stock. Such investments include, for example, shares of stock in various companies that produce gold and have extensive proven and probable gold ore reserves. She also owns stock in various domestic and foreign companies that operate in different industries. Holdings also include fixed-income securities. She holds no stock in companies that develop software, and limited or no stock holdings in companies whose fortunes are highly dependent upon a vibrant economy in Silicon Valley.

OPTIONS ARE AN INFLATION HEDGE

Aside from theft, fraud, and confiscation, nothing is more potentially devastating to holders of financial assets than high levels of *unexpected* price inflation.

Studies cite a long list of reasons why unexpected price inflation can be costly and disruptive. But, price inflation offers the optionee a potential advantage over other investors when his option exercise price is a *fixed* dollar amount.

Example: *Fixed-price option offers an "imperfect" hedge against inflation:* Veronica holds a vested employee stock option to buy ABC Corporation stock at $10 per share at any time until December 31, Year 10. The option offers Veronica a somewhat "imperfect" hedge against high rates of unexpected price inflation, for as long as her employment continues but not longer than option expiration date, because her option exercise price is fixed at $10. Her inflation hedge is potentially valuable, yet not necessarily so because there is some probability that the price of ABC stock will never exceed the $10 exercise price, regardless of how high the future rate of inflation.

3

Nonqualified Stock Options

This chapter explains the *federal* income tax consequences with respect to transactions that involve nonqualified stock options. Although *state* income tax law often works in tandem with federal law, often is different from always.

All discussions with respect to the taxation of nonqualified stock options assume that the fair market value of the underlying stock on the option grant date is not less than the option exercise price, and the option does not include a deferral feature other than the feature that the option holder has the right to exercise the option in the future.

This book covers most option grants, therefore, because the option exercise price is generally *equal* to the stock's fair market value on grant date, and the only deferral feature is that the optionee has the right to exercise the option in the future.

The optionee generally does *not* recognize taxable income on the date that a corporation *grants* him a nonqualified stock option. Instead, he generally recognizes ordinary compensation income on the date that he *exercises* the option.

Ordinary compensation income is subject to federal income tax withholding, social security tax withholding, and Medicare tax withholding – *whether or not the optionee sells the stock.* These withholding taxes can be an unpleasant surprise to unsuspecting optionees – especially those who are under the (false) impression that withholding taxes are not required until the stock is sold.

While he *generally* recognizes ordinary compensation income on the date of option *exercise,* the recognition of ordinary compensation income is *delayed* (see the section *"Income Recognition is Sometimes Deferred"* later in this chapter) if, on the date of option exercise, the stock acquired by such exercise is *both* (A) subject to a substantial risk of forfeiture, *and* (B) not transferable.

If *both* (A) *and* (B) apply to the stock on the date of option exercise, the optionee recognizes ordinary compensation income on the first day that the stock acquired is *either* not subject to a substantial risk of forfeiture *or* transferable. This tax treatment applies *unless* the optionee makes a timely election, under Internal Revenue Code (IRC) Section 83(b), to recognize ordinary compensation income on the date of option exercise. When and how to file the potentially *tax-saving* IRC Section 83(b) election is an important part of this chapter.

This chapter discusses the following sections:

- *Important Dates*

- *IRC Section 83(b) Election*

- *Options with a Reload Feature*

- *Withholding and Employment Taxes*

- *Transfers of Interests Incident to Divorce*

- *Gifts of Options*

IMPORTANT DATES

GRANT DATE

In most cases, the optionee does *not* recognize taxable income on the date the company grants him an option. This income tax treatment sometimes applies because the terms of the option have been cleverly drafted to escape income taxation on the grant date.

More likely, however, the optionee does not recognize income on the date of grant because the option does not have a *readily ascertainable fair market value* (for example, the option is not publicly traded) on the date of option grant. The option does not have a readily ascertainable fair market value even though, for example, *standardized* option contracts on the company's stock may be publicly traded on the Chicago Board Options Exchange.

If the option does *not* have a readily ascertainable fair market value, Section 83 of the Internal Revenue Code and U.S. Treasury Regulation 1.83-7 provide that the optionee does *not* recognize taxable income on the date of grant.

FAIR MARKET VALUE AND IRC SECTION 409A

As mentioned above, all discussions in this book with respect to the taxation of nonqualified stock options assume that the option exercise price is not less than the fair market value of the stock on grant date. That is because IRC Section 409A *"Inclusion in gross income of deferred compensation under non-qualified deferred compensation plans"*, which was added by the *American Jobs Creation Act of 2004*, provides different tax rules if the option exercise price is less than fair market value of the stock on grant date. IRS Notice 2005-1, Q-3 states that "The application of Section 409A is not limited to arrangements between an employer and an employee", and for example, may apply to an option grant to an independent contractor.

If the option exercise price is less than the fair market value of the stock on grant date, a taxable event under IRC Section 409A generally occurs on the date the option vests (instead of the date that the option is exercised). In short, the option is considered to be nonqualified deferred compensation.

In contrast, the Conference Report reads: "For purposes of this provision, it is not intended that the term "nonqualified deferred compensation plan" include an arrangement taxable under Section 83 providing for the grant of an option on employer stock with an exercise price that is not less than the fair market value of the underlying stock on the date of grant if such arrangement does not include a deferral feature other than the feature that the option holder has the right to exercise the option in the future." In short, the intent of Congress was not to extend the reach of Section 409A to compensatory options, if the option exercise price is not less than the fair market value of the stock on grant date.

As the next example illustrates, Section 409A is particularly challenging for companies (and that challenge could ultimately have an adverse impact on employees of those companies) that grant nonqualified stock options when the underlying stock is not publicly traded. That is because two parties will rarely agree on the fair market value of such stock; and a future challenge of fair market value by the Internal Revenue Service could prove costly for employees and employers.

If forthcoming guidance from the U.S. Treasury or IRS does not provide privately-held companies with an exemption from Section 409A (with respect to discounted options), there is a chance that courts will be busy addressing cases that involve the valuation of stock on option grant date. Apparently, the IRS has acknowledged this possibility because, in IRS Notice 2005-1 it wrote, with respect to nonqualified stock options, "...the Treasury Department and the Service also request comments on appropriate techniques for valuation of stock subject to options or stock appreciation rights where the value of such stock is not established by and in an established securities market, in order to ensure that such valuation reflects the actual fair market value of the stock."

Example: *Option exercise price is less than what the fair market value was on grant date, and therefore, taxation occurs when the option vests:* ABC Corporation stock is not publicly traded. On January 2, Year 1, Cynthia is granted nonqualified stock options, which vest over 5 years. The option exercise price is 10 cents. A couple of years later, the IRS asserts that the fair market value of the stock was $1 on the option grant date, not 10 cents, and that Cynthia should have reported (and did not) compensation income on IRS Form 1040 for the taxable year in which the options vested. Cynthia (and ABC Corporation, which did not properly report – on IRS Forms 941 and Form W-2 – that compensation income was paid to her) finds herself subject to additional tax, interest, and penalties.

EXERCISE DATE

IRC Section 83 provides that when an individual performs services for another party and property is transferred to him for such services, the individual recognizes ordinary compensation income "at the first time the rights...in such property are *transferable* or are not subject to a *substantial risk of forfeiture.*" Stated differently, he recognizes ordinary compensation income on *vesting date.*

In other words, the optionee recognizes ordinary compensation income on the date of option *exercise* if, on the date of option exercise, his rights in the stock that he acquires upon option exercise are *either* transferable *or* not subject to a substantial risk of forfeiture.

The recognition of ordinary compensation income is *delayed* if, on the date of option exercise, the stock acquired upon such exercise is *both*:

(A) subject to a substantial risk of forfeiture

and

(B) not transferable

Stated differently, if the stock is subject to a substantial risk of forfeiture, *and* is not transferable, it is not vested.

OPTION EXERCISE TRIGGERS TAXABLE INCOME

Generally, the *exercise* of a nonqualified stock option triggers the recognition of ordinary compensation income because the stock received upon option exercise *is* either transferable or not subject to a substantial risk of forfeiture on the date of option exercise.

If the optionee *does* recognize ordinary compensation income on the exercise date, the *amount* of income that he recognizes equals the excess of the fair market value of the stock on the date of option exercise over the exercise price. The exercise price is the "amount paid" for the stock, as described in IRC Section 83(a)(2) and Regulation 1.83-1(a)(1)(ii).

Example: Exercise of a nonqualified stock option triggers compensation income: On July 15, Sharee exercises a vested nonqualified stock option to buy Company A stock. The stock is transferable on the date of option exercise. Sharee's exercise price is $10. The fair market value of the stock on the date of option exercise is $15. Sharee recognizes ordinary compensation income on July 15. The *amount* of income that she recognizes equals $5, the excess of the fair market value of the stock on the date of option exercise over the option exercise price.

HOLDING PERIOD OF STOCK ACQUIRED

The optionee's exercise of a vested nonqualified stock option starts the holding period on the stock acquired by such exercise.

Example: Option exercise starts the holding period on the stock acquired: Sharee exercises a vested nonqualified stock option on July 15, Year 1. If she sells the stock on or after July 16, Year 2, a date that is more than 12 months after option exercise, any capital gain or loss is treated as *long-term* capital gain or loss.

The holding period is important because it determines whether any capital gain or loss from the eventual sale of stock is treated as *short-term* or *long-term* capital gain or loss. Under current law, if the holding period is more than 12 months, any capital gain or loss is treated as long-term capital gain or loss. If the holding period is *not* more than 12 months, any capital gain or loss is treated as short-term capital gain or loss.

BASIS OF STOCK ACQUIRED

If he *does* recognize income on the date of option exercise, the optionee's *basis* in the stock he acquires is generally the fair market value of the stock on the date of option *exercise*. That is because Regulation 1.61-2(d)(2)(i) provides that basis equals the amount paid for the stock, plus the amount that the optionee includes in gross income.

Basis becomes an important issue when the stock is *sold*. Capital gain or loss on the eventual sale of stock equals the difference between the *proceeds* from the sale and the *basis* in the stock.

Example: Basis equals the fair market value of the stock on the date of option exercise: In the previous example, the fair market value of the stock on the date of option exercise is $15. Therefore, Sharee's basis in the stock is $15. If she later sells the stock for $20, she realizes a $5 capital gain.

This book often refers to the basis of stock acquired by exercise of a nonqualified stock option as being fair market value of the stock on the date of option exercise, because that is almost always the case. That is almost always the case because basis equals the amount paid to buy the stock (the exercise price), plus the amount of taxable income recognized by the optionee.

As explained below, the basis of stock acquired by nonresident alien individuals is not always fair market value on date of option exercise.

Nonresident Alien Individuals

The *American Jobs Creation Act of 2004* added IRC Section 83(c)(4), which changes the rules for determining basis in property received in connection with the performance of services in the case of an individual who was a nonresident alien (that is, he was not a citizen of the U.S. *and* not a resident of the U.S.) at the time of the performance of services – if the property received is treated as income from sources outside the United States.

The Committee Reports Conference Agreement provides: "In that case the individual's basis in the property does not include any amount that was not subject to income tax (and would have been subject to income tax if paid as cash compensation when the services were performed) under the laws of the United States or any foreign country."

IRC Section 83(c)(4) states that "For purposes of determining an individual's basis in property transferred in connection with the performance of services, rules similar to the rules of section 72(w) shall apply."

Forgiveness of Indebtedness Treated as "Amount Paid"

As mentioned above, the taxpayer recognizes ordinary compensation income on the date of option exercise to the extent that the fair market value of the stock on date of option exercise exceeds the amount paid for such stock. Regulation 1.83-4(c) states "If indebtedness that has been treated as an amount paid under Regulation 1.83-1(a)(1)(ii) is subsequently cancelled, forgiven or satisfied for an amount less than the amount of such indebtedness, the amount that is not, in fact, paid shall be includible in the gross income of the service provider in the taxable year in which such cancellation, forgiveness or satisfaction occurs."

In Revenue Ruling 2004-37, the employee received a stock option grant in Year 1 and the option did not have a readily ascertainable fair market value on the date of grant. Therefore, the option grant was not a taxable event. In Year 2, the optionee exercised the nontransferable, nonqualified stock option, and his employer transferred to him employer stock that had a fair market value of $100,000 on the date of option exercise. The optionee issued a $75,000 interest-bearing recourse note at a market interest rate (only interest expense was payable by the optionee during the time the note was outstanding), which was secured by the stock he received, to his employer in satisfaction of the option exercise price. The stock was vested on the date of option exercise. Under IRC Section 83, the optionee recognized $25,000 of compensation income in Year 2, computed as the $100,000 fair market value of the stock received over the $75,000 amount paid. The stock price subsequently declined and had a fair market value of only $50,000 on January 1, Year 4. In Year 4, the employer and employee agreed to reduce the stated principal amount of the note from $75,000 to $50,000. The IRS ruled that the $25,000 reduction in the stated principal amount of the note triggered $25,000 of compensation income in Year 4, and that such income was subject to social security tax withholding, Medicare tax withholding, and income tax withholding.

The conclusion in Revenue Ruling 2004-37 does not mean that every alteration in the terms of a note used to pay the option exercise price triggers compensation income. The IRS did, however, mention that – under the facts above – if the employer and employee were, for example, to reduce the interest rate on the note or change the note from recourse to nonrecourse, that modification would result in compensation income.

INCOME RECOGNITION IS SOMETIMES DEFERRED

Recall that the recognition of ordinary compensation income is *delayed* if, on the date of option exercise, the stock acquired upon such exercise is *both*:

(A) subject to a substantial risk of forfeiture

   and

(B) not transferable

If *both* (A) *and* (B) apply to the stock on the date of option exercise, the optionee recognizes ordinary compensation income on the first day that his rights in the stock acquired by such exercise are *either* not subject to a substantial risk of forfeiture, *or* transferable (that is, he recognizes ordinary compensation income on the date the stock vests).

SUBSTANTIAL RISK OF FORFEITURE

The meaning of *"substantial risk of forfeiture"* is described in U.S. Treasury Regulation 1.83-3(c), which states that "whether a risk of forfeiture is substantial or not depends on the facts and circumstances." As one might imagine, it is not always clear whether a risk of forfeiture is substantial.

In general, a substantial risk of forfeiture exists where rights in the property transferred are conditioned, directly or indirectly, upon the future performance of substantial services (or refraining from performance), or the occurrence of a condition related to the purpose of the transfer, and the possibility of forfeiture is substantial if such condition is not satisfied.

A substantial risk of forfeiture exists, for example, when terms of the transfer give the employer the right to repurchase the stock from the optionee at the same price that the stock was sold to the optionee if he terminates employment *before* the stock is *vested*. On the other hand, property is not transferred subject to a substantial risk of forfeiture to the extent that the employer is required to pay the fair market value of a portion of such property to the employee upon the return of such property.

Regulation 1.83-3(c)(1) provides that "The risk that the value of the property will decline during a certain period of time does not constitute a substantial risk of forfeiture." Regulation 1.83-3(c)(2) provides that "...requirements that the property be returned to the employer if the employee is discharged for cause or for committing a crime will not be considered to result in a substantial risk of forfeiture".

Regulation 1.83-3(c)(1) also states that "a nonlapse restriction, standing by itself, will not result in a substantial risk of forfeiture." Please see Chapter 1 *"Introduction"* for a discussion of lapse and nonlapse restrictions.

Enforcement of the Forfeiture Condition

As mentioned above, the possibility of forfeiture must be substantial if such condition is not satisfied – in order to have a substantial risk of forfeiture. That is, there must be a reasonable expectation that the forfeiture condition will be enforced by the corporation. Regulation 1.83-3(c)(3) reads: "For example, if an employee would be considered as having received rights in property subject to a substantial risk of forfeiture, but for the fact that the employee owns 20 percent of the single class of stock in the transferor corporation, and if the remaining 80 percent of the class of stock is owned by an unrelated individual (or such an individual's family) so that the possibility of the corporation enforcing a restriction on such rights is substantial, then such rights are subject to a substantial risk of forfeiture. On the other hand, if

4 percent of the voting power of all the stock of a corporation is owned by the president of such corporation and the remaining stock is so diversely held by the public that the president, in effect, controls the corporation, then the possibility of the corporation enforcing a restriction on rights in property transferred to the president is not substantial, and such rights are not subject to a substantial risk of forfeiture."

TRANSFERABILITY OF PROPERTY

Whether stock is *transferable* or *nontransferable* is not always clear because such terms are specially defined. Even the United States Tax Court and the U.S. Court of Appeals have disagreed as to whether a particular share of stock was transferable or nontransferable. Optionees need to be aware that stock, which *appears* to be *transferable,* may in fact be *nontransferable* – and vice versa.

"Transferability of property" is defined in U.S. Treasury Regulation 1.83-3(d). It states that "...property is transferable if the person performing the services or receiving the property can sell, assign, or pledge (as collateral for a loan, or as security for the performance of an obligation, or for any other purpose) his interest in the property to any person other than the transferor of such property and if the transferee is not required to give up the property or its value in the event the substantial risk of forfeiture materializes."

LOCK-UP PERIODS

Investment banking firms generally require a "lock-up" period if they underwrite an initial public offering ("IPO") of stock. Under a lock-up agreement, which begins on the date of IPO and often lasts about six months, certain shareholders agree not to sell, otherwise dispose of, or hedge any common shares, options, warrants, or convertible securities of the issuing corporation.

In Private Letter Ruling 200338010 the IRS stated that a lock-up does not constitute a substantial risk of forfeiture.

BLACKOUT PERIODS

Employers generally impose "blackout" periods, during which employees are prohibited from buying or selling the company's stock. Employees are well aware that the price of the stock could decline during the blackout period. But, a blackout period does not present any risk to the employee that he will forfeit his stock. The stock is not subject to a substantial risk of forfeiture.

SEC RULE 144 STOCK

SEC Rule 144 of the Securities Act of 1933 exists so that companies can issue restricted stock without having to register such stock with the United States Securities and Exchange Commission. Restrictions that accompany SEC Rule 144 stock do not make such stock subject to a substantial risk of forfeiture, however. In addition, Rule 144 stock is transferable, as evidenced by the fact that the restrictions accompanying the stock do not prohibit the sale of such stock in a private transaction.

SPECIAL RULE WHEN SECTION 16(b) APPLIES

A *special rule* under IRC Section 83 provides "So long as the sale of property at a profit could subject a person to suit under section 16(b) of the Securities Exchange Act of 1934, such person's rights in such property are –

(A) subject to a substantial risk of forfeiture

and

(B) not transferable."

In other words, if the optionee could be subject to suit under Section 16(b) of the Securities Exchange Act of 1934 if he were to sell the stock on the date of option exercise, the special rule under IRC Section 83 provides that the stock is treated as being *both* nontransferable *and* subject to a substantial risk of forfeiture on the date of option exercise.

Since *both* conditions (A) *and* (B) apply to the stock on the date of option exercise, the optionee does *not* recognize ordinary compensation income on the date of option exercise. In other words, the exercise of the option does *not* trigger an income tax liability for the optionee *on the date of option exercise*.

IS SECTION 16(b) STILL RELEVANT?

Section 16(b) of the Securities Exchange Act of 1934 provides that "For the purpose of preventing the unfair use of information..." corporate "insiders" (shareholders who own more than 10 percent of stock registered pursuant to the Securities Exchange Act of 1934, officers, or directors) are subject to "restrictions" on purchases and sales of securities under what are commonly known as the six-month "short-swing" rules. If the insider violates the short-swing rules, he may be subject to suit and forced to return his profits to the corporation.

In 1991, amendments were made to the Securities Exchange Act of 1934, and in 1996 the Securities and Exchange Commission (SEC) released new rules under Section 16(b). Those amendments and revised SEC rules have made Section 16(b) less restrictive. Yet, insiders need to be aware that short-swing rules under Section 16(b) still exist.

After 1991, the six-month holding period under Section 16(b) starts when an option is *granted*. Therefore, as discussed in IRS Private Letter Ruling 200338010 "...after 1991, section 16(b) interacts with section 83 of the Code as follows: if, for example, shares acquired through the exercise of a nonstatutory option in a transfer taxable under the rules of section 83, such shares will *not* be subject to section 16(b) liability unless they are acquired during the six-month period beginning with the date of grant of the option." In short, shares acquired by option exercise will not be subject to section 16(b) liability unless the optionee exercises the option during that six-month period.

In the majority of cases, optionees do not exercise an option within six months after grant date. Some do, however.

SECTION 16(b) "RESTRICTIONS" DO NOT PROHIBIT SALES

Section 16(b) of the Securities Exchange Act of 1934 does *not* prohibit the shareholder from selling the stock. Section 16(b) provides that if the short-swing rules are violated, the shareholder may be subject to suit and forced to return his profits to the corporation.

SPECIAL RULE: WHEN IS INCOME RECOGNIZED?

U.S. Treasury Regulation 1.83-3(j) provides that the stock is "...treated as subject to a substantial risk of forfeiture and as not transferable until the earlier of (i) the expiration of such six-month period, or (ii) the first day on which the sale of such property at a profit will not subject the person to suit under section 16(b) of the Securities Exchange Act of 1934."

In other words, the optionee recognizes ordinary compensation income when the Section 16(b) restriction *ends*. He recognizes ordinary compensation income on the *earlier* of (i) the expiration of such six-month period, or (ii) the first day on which the sale of such property at a profit will not subject the person to suit under Section 16(b) of the Securities Exchange Act of 1934.

Example: Section 16(b) restrictions apply to the stock because the option is exercised within six months after grant date: Lauren exercises a nonqualified stock option within six months after grant date. The stock acquired is subject to Section 16(b) restrictions that continue through June 29. She recognizes ordinary compensation income on June 30, the first day on which she may sell the stock without violating Section 16(b) of the Securities Exchange Act of 1934.

SPECIAL RULE: HOW MUCH INCOME IS RECOGNIZED?

The amount of ordinary compensation income that the optionee recognizes equals the excess of the fair market value of the stock on the first day that he may sell the stock without violating Section 16(b) over the option exercise price.

Example: *The amount of compensation income the optionee will recognize is unknown at the time of option exercise:* Lauren exercises a nonqualified stock option to buy Company A stock on July 15, the day the option is granted. Section 16(b) restrictions apply from July 15 and continue for six months. Her exercise price is $10. The fair market value of the stock on the first day that she may sell it without violating Section 16(b) is $60. On that day, Lauren recognizes $50 of ordinary compensation income, the excess of the $60 fair market value of the stock on the first day that she may sell it over her $10 exercise price.

SPECIAL RULE: HOLDING PERIOD OF STOCK ACQUIRED

The optionee's holding period *begins* on the first day that the optionee may sell the stock without violating Section 16(b) of the Securities Exchange Act of 1934.

The legal authority for this is found in U.S. Treasury regulations. U.S. Treasury Regulation 1.83-4(a) provides that the holding period *begins* on the date the stock is "substantially vested". U.S. Treasury Regulation 1.83-3(b) provides that property is substantially vested when it is *either* transferable *or* not subject to a substantial risk of forfeiture.

Example: Holding period does not begin on the date of option exercise: Lauren, a member of Company A's board of directors, exercises a nonqualified stock option to buy Company A stock. At the time of option exercise, Lauren is subject to Section 16(b) restrictions on the stock she acquires by such exercise. The Section 16(b) restrictions continue through June 29, Year 1. Lauren's holding period *begins* on June 30, Year 1, the first day that she may sell the stock without violating Section 16(b) of the Securities Exchange Act of 1934. If she sells the stock on or after June 30, Year 2, any capital gain or loss on such sale is treated as *long-term* capital gain or loss.

SPECIAL RULE: BASIS OF STOCK ACQUIRED

If the recognition of ordinary compensation income is *delayed* until *after* the date of option exercise, the optionee's *basis* in the stock is the fair market value of the stock on the first day that he may sell it without violating Section 16(b) of the Securities Exchange Act of 1934.

Example: Basis of stock acquired: The fair market value of the stock on the first day that Lauren may sell it without violating Section 16(b) is $60. Her basis in the stock is $60. If she later sells the stock for $70, she realizes a $10 capital gain.

SALE DATE

On the date of *sale*, the optionee recognizes a *capital gain or loss* in the amount of the difference between the proceeds from the sale and his *basis* in the stock.

SHORT-TERM VERSUS LONG-TERM CAPITAL GAIN OR LOSS

Under current law, gain or loss on the sale of stock is treated as *short-term* capital gain or loss if the holding period is less than or equal to 12 months. If the holding period is *longer* than 12 months, any capital gain or loss is treated as *long-term* capital gain or loss.

IRC SECTION 83(b) ELECTION

As discussed earlier, the recognition of ordinary compensation income is *delayed* if, on the date he exercises a nonqualified stock option, the stock acquired by such exercise is *both* subject to a substantial risk of forfeiture *and* not transferable. In short, the recognition of ordinary compensation income is delayed until the date the stock vests.

When this tax treatment applies, optionees may find it wise to *accelerate* the recognition of income to the date of option *exercise*. They do this by filing an *election* under Internal Revenue Code Section 83(b).

Please see Chapter 11 *"Stock Grants"* for more information on the Section 83(b) election.

Example: *The optionee accelerates the recognition of compensation income to option exercise date, by making a Section 83(b) election:* On July 15, Year 1, Lauren exercises a nonqualified stock option, which was granted to her less than six months earlier, to buy Company A stock. Her exercise price is $10. The fair market value of the stock on the date of option exercise is $15. On July 15, Year 1, Lauren is subject to Section 16(b) restrictions on the stock she acquires by option exercise. Lauren files a timely IRC Section 83(b) election because she projects that the fair market value of the stock will increase to $100 on the first day that she may sell it. Because of the Section 83(b) election, she recognizes $5 of ordinary compensation income on July 15, the date of option exercise. The $5 of income equals the excess of the fair market value of the stock on the date of option exercise over the exercise price.

HOLDING PERIOD OF STOCK ACQUIRED

U.S. Treasury Regulation 1.83-4(a) provides "...if the person who has performed the services in connection with which property is transferred has made an election under section 83(b), the holding period of such property shall begin just after the date such property is transferred."

In other words, if the optionee exercises an unvested nonqualified stock option and makes an IRC Section 83(b) election, he accelerates to exercise date the start of the holding period of the stock acquired. If he would not make a Section 83(b) election, Regulation 1.83-3(b) provides that the holding period would not begin until the stock is "substantially vested."

Example: *Optionee accelerates the beginning of the holding period by making a Section 83(b) election:* Lauren exercises a nonqualified stock option on July 15, Year 1 and makes a timely IRC Section 83(b) election. If she sells the stock on or after July 16, Year 2, any capital gain or loss is treated as long-term capital gain or loss.

Table 3.1
Comparison of Income Tax Treatment on Exercise of Nonqualified Stock Option

Example:

Exercise price	$ 10
Fair market value (FMV) of stock on grant date	10
Fair market value (FMV) of stock on exercise date	15
Fair market value (FMV) of stock on vesting date	100
Proceeds from eventual sale of stock	100

(1) The options do not have a readily ascertainable fair market value on grant date. Therefore, no tax consequences on grant date.

	Three Different Scenarios	Option Grant Date	Option Exercise Date	Stock Vesting Date	Holding Period Begins	Basis of Stock Acquired by Option Exercise	Capital Gain (loss) on Sale of Stock @ $100
A	The stock acquired by the exercise of the option is *vested on the date of option exercise*	No tax consequences (1)	$5 compensation income = $15 FMV on exercise date minus $10 exercise price	No tax consequences	Exercise date	$15 = $10 exercise price + $5 compensation income = FMV of the stock on date of option exercise	$85 = $100 minus $15 basis. Long-term capital gain or loss if holding period is more than 1 year
B	The stock acquired by the exercise of the option is *not vested on the date of option exercise*	No tax consequences (1)	No tax consequences	$90 compensation income =$100 FMV on vesting date minus $10 exercise price	Vesting date	$100 = $10 exercise price + $90 compensation income = FMV of stock on the date the stock vests	$0 = $100 minus $100 basis. Long-term capital gain or loss if holding period is more than 1 year
C	The stock acquired by the exercise of the option is *not vested on the date of option exercise* but optionee makes 83b election	No tax consequences (1)	$5 compensation income = $15 FMV on exercise date minus $10 exercise price	No tax consequences	Exercise date	$15 = $10 exercise price + $5 compensation income = FMV of stock on the date of option exercise	$85 = $100 minus $15 basis. Long-term capital gain or loss if holding period is more than 1 year

BASIS OF STOCK ACQUIRED

If the optionee files a timely IRC Section 83(b) election, U.S. Treasury Regulation 1.83-2(a) provides that his basis in the stock acquired "...shall be the amount paid for the property increased by the amount included in gross income under section 83(b)." Generally, then, basis equals fair market value on date of exercise.

Example: Basis equals amount paid plus the amount of compensation income recognized: Lauren exercises a nonqualified stock option and files a timely IRC Section 83(b) election. The amount paid (the exercise price) plus the amount of compensation recognized (the excess of fair market value over the exercise price) is $15. Her basis in the stock acquired is $15. If she later sells the stock for $20, she realizes a $5 capital gain.

SUMMARY

When the optionee exercises a *nonqualified stock option,* followed by a timely IRC Section 83(b) election:

- He recognizes *ordinary compensation income* on the date of option exercise, in the amount of the excess of the fair market value of the stock on the date of option exercise over the exercise price.

- He does *not* recognize any income when the restriction ends. He reports a capital gain or loss when he *sells* the stock.

- His *basis* in the stock acquired is the exercise price plus the amount of compensation income recognized.

- The *holding period* begins when the option is exercised.

WHY MAKE A SECTION 83(b) ELECTION?

The IRC Section 83(b) election is a *tax-saving* strategy when the fair market value of the stock acquired by option exercise increases substantially during the period following the date of option exercise and the optionee sells the highly-appreciated stock after satisfying the holding period requirement for long-term capital gain (if his holding period is more than 12 months, gain is treated as *long-term capital gain*; if the holding period is *not* more than 12 months, gain is treated as *short-term capital gain*).

Under such a scenario, the *total* amount of income subject to tax is the *same* as if the optionee would *not* have made an IRC Section 83(b). The *advantage* of the Section 83(b) election, however, is that *more* of the income subject to tax is comprised of favorably-taxed long-term capital gain and *less* is comprised of ordinary compensation income.

OTHER POTENTIAL ADVANTAGES

As stated above, if the holding period is *not* more than 12 months, any gain is treated as *short-term* capital gain. Even *short-term* capital gain is potentially more advantageous than the recognition of ordinary compensation income because the optionee may have capital *losses* in his investment portfolio. Those capital losses can offset short-term capital gain from the sale of his optioned stock.

In addition, tax withholding is required on ordinary income compensation. If the IRC Section 83(b) election acts to reduce the amount of ordinary compensation income, it also acts to reduce the amount of tax withholding.

Example: The Section 83(b) election results in less compensation income, because the stock price on vesting date exceeds the stock price on option exercise date: Lauren exercises a nonqualified stock option and makes a timely Section 83(b) election. On the date of option exercise, she recognizes $5 of ordinary compensation income, the excess of the stock's $15 fair market value on the date of option exercise over her $10 exercise price. The $5 of income is subject to withholding. On the first day that her rights in the stock were *either* not subject to a substantial risk of forfeiture *or* transferable (that is, on vesting date), the fair market value of the stock was $100. If she had *not* made the Section 83(b) election, she would have recognized $90 of ordinary compensation income (on vesting date) that would have been subject to withholding.

CONVERTING ORDINARY INCOME INTO CAPITAL GAIN

Recall that the recognition of ordinary compensation income is sometimes *delayed* because of a Section 16(b) restriction and that the optionee recognizes ordinary compensation income when such restriction *ends*. The *amount* of ordinary compensation income that the optionee recognizes equals the fair market value of the stock on the first day that the optionee may sell the stock without violating Section 16(b) over the option exercise price.

In the earlier example, Lauren projects that the fair market value of the stock will increase to $100 on the first day that she may sell it. Therefore, she makes a timely IRC Section 83(b) election and recognizes ordinary compensation income on the date of option exercise.

The amount of income she recognizes on the July 15, Year 1 date of option exercise equals $5, the excess of the $15 fair market value of the stock on the date of option exercise over her $10 exercise price. She sells the stock for $100 in August of Year 2 and recognizes an $85 long-term capital gain, the excess of the $100 proceeds over her $15 basis.

If she did *not* make the IRC Section 83(b) election and the fair market value of the stock *is* $100 on the first day that she may sell it, Lauren would have realized $90 of ordinary compensation income on the first day that she could sell the stock. The $90 of ordinary compensation income is computed as the excess of the $100 fair market value of the stock on the first day that she could sell it over her $10 option exercise price. She would have recognized *zero* capital gain in August of Year 2, the excess of the $100 proceeds from the sale over her $100 basis.

CONTROL OVER THE TIMING OF INCOME

In the above example, Lauren reduced her income tax liability. The IRC Section 83(b) election resulted in the recognition of *less* ordinary compensation income and *more* long-term capital gain.

The IRC Section 83(b) election also gives Lauren *control* over the *timing* of income recognition. That is because any taxable capital gain or loss on such stock is not triggered until the date she sells it. This could be a significant advantage if she is able to time the sale of stock to take advantage of any unique circumstances that might apply to her tax situation, or if there is a change in the tax law, or both.

EXERCISING UNVESTED OPTIONS

Generally, optionees may exercise options on or after the *vesting date*. The vesting date is the date on which the optionee has finally earned the right to exercise the option. In most cases, the option becomes immediately exercisable on the vesting date.

Some optionees, however, have the opportunity to exercise options (*both* nonqualified *and* incentive stock options) *before* they vest in what is sometimes called an *early exercise option*.

As discussed previously, Congress made it clear that IRC Section 409A is not intended to apply to a nonqualified stock option in cases where the option exercise price is not less than the fair market value of the underlying stock on the date of grant – if such arrangement does not include a deferral feature other than the feature that the option holder has the right to exercise the option in the future." In IRS Notice 2005-1, Q-4 the IRS wrote "…the right to receive substantially nonvested stock (as defined in Regulation 1.83-3(b)) upon the exercise of a stock option does not constitute a feature for the deferral of compensation." That statement should apply here, because when an optionee exercises an unvested option he is exercising a right to receive stock that is not vested on exercise date.

This chapter addresses the income tax treatment of transactions that involve the exercise of unvested *nonqualified stock options*. Chapter 4 addresses the income tax treatment of transactions that involve the exercise of unvested *incentive stock options*.

WHY EXERCISE PRIOR TO VESTING?

The early exercise option is effectively an IRC Section 83(b) *tax strategy* when the stock acquired by the exercise of such option is *both* subject to a substantial risk of forfeiture *and* not transferable on the date of option exercise.

The optionee exercises *unvested nonqualified stock options* **and** makes a timely Section 83(b) election to recognize ordinary compensation income on the date of option exercise. In most situations, it is difficult to imagine that it would be wise to take advantage of an early exercise opportunity and *not* make a timely Section 83(b) election.

The *objective* of this tax strategy is to exercise unvested options *before* substantial appreciation occurs in the fair market value of the stock. If events materialize as expected and the fair market value of the stock increases, the strategy results in the recognition of *less* ordinary compensation income and *more* capital gain (short or long-term depending on the holding period).

RISK

The *risk* of early exercise is that the optionee exercises the option and the fair market value of the stock does *not* increase substantially, or decreases. Meanwhile, the optionee's money, in the amount of the exercise price, is tied up in the stock *and* he has paid withholding taxes on the recognition of ordinary compensation income.

REPURCHASE OPTION

If he *does* make an early exercise and later ceases to be an employee, or director of or a consultant to the corporation, terms of the early exercise option generally give the corporation the right to *repurchase*, at the optionee's *original* purchase price, any or all shares that have *not* vested as of the termination date. Generally, the early exercise option also provides that shares acquired by the optionee, which are subject to repurchase by the corporation, are *not transferable*.

The corporation's right to repurchase unvested shares is sometimes called an *unvested share repurchase option*.

Example: The optionee's employment terminates and the employer exercises its right to repurchase shares of stock that have not vested: Lauren, an employee of Company A, makes an early exercise of 100 *unvested* nonqualified stock options at an exercise price of $1 per share. The early exercise agreement provides that Company A may repurchase, for $1 per share, any or all shares that have *not* vested as of the date Lauren's employment terminates. Sometime later, Lauren's employment does terminate and on the date of termination 60 shares are unvested. Company A exercises its unvested share repurchase option and pays Lauren a total of $60 for the 60 unvested shares.

EXERCISE OF REPURCHASE OPTION

Terms of the unvested share repurchase option generally provide that the corporation, or another person selected by the corporation, has the right to *exercise* such option within a fixed period of time after termination by serving written notice to the optionee. Generally, if the corporation does *not* exercise the unvested share repurchase option within the stated period of time following termination, and the time for exercise of such option has not been extended by the corporation and the optionee, the unvested share repurchase option *terminates*.

ESCROW

Generally, terms of the unvested share repurchase option require the optionee to deposit unvested stock certificates or certificates evidencing such unvested shares into an *escrow* account. Shares are released from escrow as they vest.

GENERALLY, INCOME RECOGNITION IS DEFERRED

Recall that the recognition of ordinary compensation income is *delayed* if, on the date of option exercise, the stock that the optionee acquires as a result of such exercise is *both*:

(A) subject to a substantial risk of forfeiture

   and

(B) not transferable

Also recall that a *substantial risk of forfeiture* exists on the date of option exercise when terms of the transfer give the corporation the right to repurchase the stock at the same price that the stock was sold to the optionee if the optionee ceases to perform services for the corporation before the date the stock is *vested*.

Since shares that are subject to a repurchase option are generally *not transferable* on the date the optionee makes an early exercise, *and* since terms of the early exercise option generally give the corporation the right to repurchase the stock at the same price that the stock was sold to the optionee if the optionee terminates employment before the date the stock is vested, the recognition of ordinary compensation income is generally *delayed* until *after* the date of option exercise.

This tax treatment arises because *both* (A) *and* (B) apply to the stock on the date of option exercise. The optionee files a timely IRC Section 83(b) election if he wishes to accelerate the recognition of ordinary compensation income to the date of option exercise.

Example: The stock is not vested on the date of option exercise and the optionee does not recognize compensation income on the date of option exercise: Lauren exercises an unvested NQSO. At the time of option exercise, *both* (A) *and* (B) apply to the stock acquired by such exercise (that is, the stock is not vested on the date of exercise). Lauren does *not* recognize ordinary compensation income on the date of option exercise.

Example: The stock is not vested on the date of option exercise but the optionee recognizes compensation income on the date of option exercise because she makes a Section 83(b) election: Lauren exercises an unvested NQSO. At the time of option exercise, *both* (A) *and* (B) apply to the stock acquired by such exercise (that is, the stock is not vested on the date of exercise). Lauren files a timely IRC Section 83(b) election, which triggers the recognition of ordinary compensation income on the date of option exercise.

TAXATION OF FORFEITED STOCK

U.S. Treasury Regulation 1.83-2(a) provides "If property for which a section 83(b) election is in effect is forfeited while substantially unvested, such forfeiture shall be treated as a sale or exchange upon which there is realized a loss equal to the excess (if any) of –

(1) The amount paid (if any) for such property, over,

(2) The amount realized (if any) upon such forfeiture."

In other words, if the optionee exercises a nonqualified stock option, files an IRC Section 83(b) election, and subsequently *forfeits* the stock (for example, his employment terminates and the corporation exercises its unvested share repurchase option to buy the stock he previously acquired by option exercise), the forfeiture is treated as a *sale* or *exchange*.

Regulation 1.83-2(a) provides that the optionee's *basis* in such forfeited stock, for purposes of computing gain or loss on such sale or exchange, is his option *exercise price* (the amount he paid for the stock). His basis is *not* the fair market value of the stock on the date of option exercise, as it *would* be if he did *not* forfeit the stock and eventually *sold* it.

The optionee's basis equals the option exercise price *despite* the fact that when he exercises a nonqualified stock option and makes a timely IRC Section 83(b) election, he recognizes ordinary compensation income in the amount of the excess of the fair market value of the stock on the date of option exercise over the option exercise price. In short, Regulation 1.83-2(a) provides that, in the event of forfeiture, the optionee does *not* receive additional basis for any ordinary compensation income that he may have recognized on the date of option exercise.

Example: Optionee exercises unvested nonqualified stock options and, if she forfeits shares because they have not vested, her basis in such forfeited shares is her purchase price: Lauren, an executive at Company A, makes an early exercise of *unvested* nonqualified stock options because she expects the fair market value of the stock to increase substantially. On the date of option exercise, the fair market value of the stock is $3 per share. Lauren's exercise price is $1 per share. Company A has the right to repurchase unvested shares at $1 per share (her *original* purchase price) if Lauren's employment terminates. The shares are not transferable. Further, they are subject to a substantial risk of forfeiture because Company A has the right to repurchase unvested shares at Lauren's *original* purchase price if her employment terminates before the vesting date. Lauren files a timely IRC Section 83(b) election and therefore recognizes $2 per share of ordinary compensation income on the date of option exercise. That $2 equals the excess of the fair market value of the stock on the date of option exercise over the option exercise price. Despite the fact that Lauren's *basis* in the shares that have *vested* is $3 per share, Regulation 1.83-2(a) provides that her basis in any *unvested* shares that she sells to the corporation upon termination is only *$1* per share.

WHEN TO MAKE THE 83(b) ELECTION

The IRC Section 83(b) election, *irrevocable* unless the optionee receives consent from the Internal Revenue Service (IRS), must be filed not later than 30 days after the date of option exercise.

CONSENT TO REVOKE ELECTION IS NOT GRANTED

In Private Letter Ruling 200212021, the taxpayer requested that the Section 83(b) election he filed be revoked, arguing ignorance of the tax implications of such election. The IRS denied the request, and, citing another case, wrote: "It should be noted that mere 'oversight, poor judgment, ignorance of the law, misunderstanding of the law, unawareness of the tax consequences of making an election, miscalculation, and unexpected subsequent events have all been held insufficient to mitigate the binding effect of elections made under a variety of provisions of the Code'."

CONSENT TO REVOKE ELECTION IS GRANTED

In Private Letter Ruling 200229004, the taxpayer exercised stock options – granted to him by his employer – on September 17, 2001. The stock he received upon exercise was not vested. On October 8, 2001, the optionee filed a Section 83(b) election with respect to the stock he received. On October 17, 2001, he sent a letter to the IRS, asking for consent to revoke the election.

The IRS gave the taxpayer consent to revoke a Section 83(b) election because the taxpayer filed his request to revoke such election within the 30-day time period allowed for making the election.

THE 29-DAY WINDOW

The Section 83(b) election is a tax strategy, generally used when the stock price is expected to be substantially higher when the stock vests.

But stock prices are not always higher on vesting date. Occasionally, they crash violently and unexpectedly, and a Section 83(b) election that appears to be a sound strategy on the date of option exercise, may not appear to be a sound strategy 30 days later.

With this in mind, anyone who intends to make a Section 83(b) election should prepare the election statement (discussed below) as soon as possible, and – *if* he decides to make such election – file it on the last day allowed by law. That will save him the trouble of asking for consent from the IRS to revoke the election if he changes his mind, as the taxpayer did in Private Letter Ruling 200229004, discussed above.

How to Make the Election

Under U.S. Treasury Regulation 1.83-2(c), the optionee makes an election under IRC Section 83(b) by filing two copies of a written statement with the Internal Revenue Service office where he files his individual income tax return (IRS Form 1040). He files the first copy, preferably via certified mail return receipt requested, not later than 30 days after the date of option exercise. He attaches the second copy to his income tax return for the taxable year in which the option is exercised.

Under U.S. Treasury Regulation 1.83-2(d), the optionee must also submit a copy of the statement to the corporation *for which he performed services* that led to the granting of the option.

In some cases, the corporation that *grants* the option is different from the corporation that engages the services of the optionee. If so, the optionee must also submit a copy of the statement to the corporation that *granted* the option.

The optionee should request a written statement from the corporation(s) acknowledging that a copy of the Section 83(b) election has been received.

Example: Susan performs services for ABC Corporation, a subsidiary of DEF Corporation. DEF Corporation grants an option to Susan as compensation for services that she provides to ABC Corporation. Susan must submit a copy of the statement to ABC Corporation (the corporation for which she performed services) *and* to DEF Corporation (the corporation that granted the option).

Important

Optionees need to be aware that the IRC Section 83(b) election *accelerates* the recognition of ordinary compensation income and the time for withholding of taxes on such income.

The Statement

U.S. Treasury Regulation 1.83-2(e) provides that the statement must be signed by the person making the election and that it state that an election is being made under Internal Revenue Code

Section 83(b). The statement must also contain the following information:

- The name, address and taxpayer identification number (social security number) of the taxpayer

- A description of each property with respect to which the election is being made

- The date or dates on which the property is transferred and the taxable year (for example, "calendar year 2000") for which such election is made

- The nature of the restriction or restrictions to which the property is subject

- The fair market value at the time of transfer (determined without regard to any lapse restriction, as defined in Regulation 1.83-3(i)) of each property with respect to which the election is being made

- The amount (if any) paid for such property

- A statement to the effect that copies have been furnished to other persons as provided in Regulation 1.83-2(d)

ELECTION STATEMENT
UNDER INTERNAL REVENUE CODE SECTION 83(b)

I elect, under Internal Revenue Code Section 83(b), to include in gross income as compensation for services the excess of the fair market value on the date of transfer of property that I received from [NAME OF CORPORATION] over the amount paid for such property.

Taxpayer name: Lauren Optionee
Address: 111 Apple Court
                    San Rafael, CA. 94903

Taxpayer ID number: 012-34-5678

Description of property: One share of common stock of XYZ Corporation acquired by exercising a nonqualified stock option on July 15, Year 1.

Date of property transfer: July 15, Year 1

Taxable year for which election is being made: Calendar Year 1

Nature of the restriction: On July 15, Year 1, restrictions under Section 16(b) of the Securities Exchange Act of 1934 applied to the stock that I acquired by exercise of a nonqualified stock option.

Fair market value of stock on date of transfer (determined without regard to any lapse restriction): $15

Amount paid to purchase the stock: $10

I have furnished copies of this statement to persons as required by U.S. Treasury Regulation 1.83-2(d).

_____   _____

Lauren Optionee   Date

OPTIONS WITH A RELOAD FEATURE

In Chapter 1, Julia exercises a nonqualified stock option that has a reload feature (the example is reproduced below). She pays the exercise price using mature shares of stock that she already owns.

Example: The outstanding stock of Company A consists of one class of common stock. Julia owns one share of Company A stock that she bought (on the open market) on January 5, Year 1 for $5 (her basis in the share is $5). The current market price is $20. Julia owns nonqualified stock options to buy two shares of Company A stock at an exercise price of $10 per share. The options expire on January 5, 2007. They contain a reload provision. On November 1, Year 2, Julia exercises the options to buy two shares of stock and pays the $20 exercise price by transferring to Company A (or, in some cases, merely certifying that she owns one share of Company A stock) the one share of Company A stock that she bought on the open market. She receives two shares of Company A stock *and* a new nonqualified stock option (the reload option). The new option has an exercise price of $20, the fair market value of Company A's stock on the date the corporation grants the reload option. The reload option expires on January 5, 2007, the same date that the original option would have expired.

TAX-DEFERRED EXCHANGE

Julia transfers, or merely certifies that she owns, one share of Company A stock (the "old" share) to Company A as payment of the $20 exercise price. That transfer qualifies as a stock-for-stock *tax-deferred exchange* under IRC Section 1036.

In other words, Julia does *not* recognize a $15 taxable capital gain, the difference between the $20 fair market value of the stock transferred and her $5 original purchase price, upon transfer of the old share. Taxation of the $15 gain is *deferred*.

INCOME RECOGNITION

Julia has exercised a nonqualified stock option. The exercise of a nonqualified stock option, whether or not such option contains a reload feature, results in the recognition of ordinary compensation income on the date of option exercise.

Julia recognizes $20 of ordinary compensation income on November 1, Year 2, the date of option exercise. That $20 equals the excess of the $40 fair market value of the two shares of stock acquired over Julia's $20 exercise price ($10 per share times two shares).

BASIS AND HOLDING PERIOD

After option exercise, Julia owns two "new" shares.

In accordance with IRS Revenue Ruling 80-244, Julia's basis in *one* new share equals $5, which is the *same* as her basis in the old share she transfers to Company A as payment of the exercise price. The new share is considered to have been acquired on January 5, Year 1, the date Julia bought the old share.

Julia's basis in the *other* new share equals $20, the amount of ordinary compensation that she recognizes on the date of option exercise. The holding period for that share begins on November 2, Year 2, the day after option exercise.

Julia's total basis in the two shares is $25. It equals the $5 she paid for the old share, plus the $20 of ordinary compensation income she recognizes on the date of option exercise.

WITHHOLDING AND EMPLOYMENT TAXES

Ordinary compensation income that the optionee recognizes is subject to income tax withholding, in addition to social security and Medicare tax withholding.

Withholding is required by U.S. Treasury Regulation 31.3402(a)-1, *even if the optionee does not sell the stock.* Consequently, those who intend to exercise NQSOs, and *hold* the stock, must be prepared to pay *not only* the exercise price to effect the stock purchase, but also the required withholding taxes.

TRANSFERS OF INTERESTS INCIDENT TO DIVORCE

In Revenue Ruling 2002-22, the IRS held that – under the facts listed below – a taxpayer who transferred interests in nonstatutory stock options to his former spouse incident to divorce was not required to recognize income upon such transfer (such transfer was treated by the IRS as a transfer of property for purposes of IRC Section 1041, and entitled to nonrecognition treatment under that section of tax law):

- Prior to their divorce in 2002, taxpayers used the cash method of accounting.

- Prior to the divorce, the taxpayer's employer issued him nonstatutory employer stock options as part of his compensation.

- The stock options did not have a readily ascertainable fair market value at the time of grant and thus no amount was included in taxpayer's gross income with respect to those options at the time of grant.

- Under state law, stock options earned by a spouse during the period of marriage are marital property subject to equitable division between the spouses in the event of divorce.

- Pursuant to the property settlement incorporated into their judgment of divorce, taxpayer (the "transferor") transferred a portion of the nonstatutory stock options to his (now) former spouse (the "transferee").

- The stock options were vested at the time of transfer.

IRC Section 1041(c) provides that a transfer of property is incident to the divorce if such transfer occurs:

- within 1 year after the date on which the marriage ceases,

    or,

- is related to the cessation of the marriage.

Temporary Regulation 1.1041-1T(b) provides guidance with respect to the terms mentioned above.

> A taxpayer contemplating divorce should not take any action without having received legal and tax advice from an experienced and competent attorney who specializes in family and tax law.

The IRS also concluded in Revenue Ruling 2002-22 that the transferee, not the transferor, recognizes gross income – at the time of option exercise – to the extent determined under IRC Section 83(a), as if the transferee actually performed the services to the grantor of the option. In short, the transferee reports such income as ordinary income on IRS Form 1040.

Revenue Ruling 2004-60, which has an effective date of January 1, 2005, assumed the same facts as those in Revenue Ruling 2002-22, and addressed:

- Income tax withholding,

- FICA (that is, social security tax, and Medicare tax),

- FUTA, a tax that is paid by the employer, not by the employee

The IRS ruled that the transferee is subject to income tax withholding on such income, under IRC Section 3402, and the transferee is entitled to report the amount of income tax withheld as a credit against tax, under IRC Section 31, on IRS Form 1040.

Revenue Ruling 2004-60 states that the amount of ordinary income that was triggered by the option exercise, and the amount of income tax withheld is reportable to the transferee on IRS Form 1099-MISC.

Example: *Transfer of vested nonqualified stock options is not a taxable event:* Henry and Lisa marry on January 1, Year 1 and are cash basis taxpayers. Henry is an employee of ABC Corporation. On January 1, Year 2, ABC Corporation grants to Henry nonqualified stock options to buy 200 shares of ABC stock. The options do not have a readily ascertainable fair market value on grant date. The options vest on January 1, Year 4. The option exercise price is $10. On January 1, Year 5, Henry and Lisa divorce and, incident to the divorce, Henry transfers his rights in vested stock options to Lisa, giving her the right to buy 100 shares of ABC stock at $10 per share. Under Revenue Ruling 2002-22, Henry's transfer of such rights to Lisa is not a taxable event.

SOCIAL SECURITY AND MEDICARE TAX

Revenue Ruling 2004-60 also provides that the transfer of the interests in the stock options does not constitute a payment of wages for purposes of social security and Medicare tax. In short, the transfer is a nonevent for such purposes.

Revenue Ruling 2004-60 also stated that the transferee's *exercise* of the options results in wages to the transferor – for purposes of social security and Medicare tax, but not for purposes of income tax – in the amount of the excess of the fair market value of the stock on the date of option exercise over the option exercise price.

Such wages are subject to social security tax and Medicare tax to the same extent they would have been if the transferor had never transferred his interest in the options and, instead, exercised them himself. That means, for example, if the transferor's employer previously paid to the transferee in that calendar year an amount of wages that exceeded the maximum social security wage base under IRC Section 3121(a)(1) – in calendar year 2005, the maximum amount of wages subject to social security tax is $90,000 – then the transferee's exercise of the option would not trigger any social security tax. But the option exercise would trigger Medicare tax because 100 percent of wages are subject to such tax (that is, there is no ceiling on wages subject to Medicare tax). Revenue Ruling 2004-60 provides that the transferor's portion (that is, the employee's portion) of social security tax or Medicare tax is to be deducted from the payment to the transferee.

Revenue Ruling 2004-60 states that the amount of social security wages, Medicare wages, social security tax withheld, and Medicare tax withheld (if any) – that was triggered by the option exercise – is reportable to the transferor on IRS Form W-2. Since Revenue Ruling 2002-22 provides that the transferee, and not the transferor, recognizes gross income for purposes of income tax and Revenue Ruling 2004-60 requires income tax withholding from the transferee, no amount is included in Box 1 "Wages, tips, other compensation" and no amount is included in Box 2 "Federal income tax withheld" on the transferor's IRS Form W-2.

Example: Transferee exercises the options, which triggers ordinary income to the transferee for purposes of income tax, and wages to the transferor for purposes of social security and Medicare tax (but any social security tax withholding and Medicare tax withholding is deducted from the payment to the transferee): The facts are the same as in the previous example. On July 1, Year 6, Lisa exercises the nonqualified stock options. The fair market value of ABC stock is $30 on the date of option exercise. Lisa recognizes ordinary income on the date of exercise, in the amount of $2,000. That $2,000 equals 100 shares multiplied by $20, the excess of the $30 fair market value on exercise date over the $10 option exercise price. Under Revenue Ruling 2004-60, the $2,000 of ordinary income is subject to income tax withholding, and such withholding will be deducted from the payment to the transferee. The entire $2,000 is subject to Medicare tax withholding because 100 percent of wages are subject to such tax. Up to $2,000 is subject to social security tax, with the exact amount dependent upon whether, or to what extent, the transferor's wages exceed the maximum social security wage base. The transferor's portion of such social security tax, if any, and Medicare tax is to be deducted from the payment made to the transferee.

APPLICATION OF REVENUE RULING 2002-22

Revenue Ruling 2002-22, which has limited application, states:

- The ruling does not apply to transfers of property between spouses other than in connection with divorce.

- The ruling does not apply to transfers of nonstatutory stock options, or other future income rights to the extent such options or rights are *unvested* at the time of transfer or to the extent that the transferor's rights to such income are subject to substantial contingencies at the time of the transfer.

- The same conclusion would apply in a case in which an employee transfers a statutory stock option (for example, an incentive stock option) contrary to its terms to a spouse or former spouse in connection with divorce; that is because Regulation 1.421-1(b)(2) states that if a statutory option is transferred incident to divorce (within the meaning of IRC Section 1041) or pursuant to a domestic relations order, the option does not qualify as a statutory option as of the day of such transfer. In other words, the ISO becomes a nonstatutory option.

- The same conclusion would apply whether the taxpayers live in a community property state or a non-community property state.

GIFTS OF OPTIONS

Many stock option plans allow optionees to gift nonqualified stock options to certain family members, family limited partnerships, and trusts that provide for certain family members. *Tax law prohibits a gift of incentive stock options.*

In Revenue Ruling 98-21, the IRS ruled that the transfer to a family member, for no consideration, of a nonstatutory stock option, is a completed gift under IRC Section 2511 on the *later* of:

(i)   the transfer of the option,

or,

(ii) the date that such option vests

Example: Optionee gifts unvested options and the gift is complete when they vest: ABC Corporation's stock option plan permits the transfer of nonqualified stock options to a member of an optionee's immediate family or to a trust for the benefit of those individuals. The effect of such a transfer is that the transferee (after the required service is completed and before the option's expiration date) will determine whether and when to exercise the stock option and will also be obligated to pay the exercise price. On January 15, Year 1, Tara, an employee of ABC, gifts *unvested* options to buy 100 shares of ABC stock to her daughter, Jackie (the "donee"). The option exercise price is $10 per share. The fair market value of the stock is $10 on January 15, Year 1. On January 15, Year 2, the options vest, at which time the fair market value of the stock is $25. The gift is complete on January 15, Year 2, the later of the January 15, Year 1 transfer date or the vesting date. The amount of the gift, which may be large enough to trigger a gift tax liability for Tara, is computed based on the $25 fair market value of the stock on the date that the gift is complete, not the $10 fair market value when the option was transferred. As discussed below, neither the transfer nor the vesting of the option triggers taxable compensation income; instead, such income is triggered when Tara's daughter exercises the option.

OPTION VALUATION

IRS Revenue Procedure 98-34 sets forth a methodology to value — for gift, estate, and generation-skipping transfer tax purposes — non-publicly traded compensatory stock options on stock that, on the valuation date, is publicly traded on an established securities market. While this methodology is not the only methodology acceptable to the IRS for determining the value of such option, the procedure states that "The Internal Revenue Service will treat the value of a compensatory stock option as properly determined for transfer tax purposes, provided that the requirements of this revenue procedure are met." A copy of Revenue Procedure 98-34 may be found in Internal Revenue Bulletin 1998-18 at www.irs.gov.

Since the optionee has no idea how much the stock will be worth on the date the option vests, he has no idea how high (or low) the value of the option will be on such date. In short, when he gifts an unvested option, he does not know the amount of gift tax, if any, that will be triggered when the option vests. If, instead, he gifts a *vested* option, he knows the amount of the gift on the date the option is transferred to the donee.

OPTION EXERCISE BY DONEE

In the previous example, Tara gifts a nonqualified stock option to her daughter, Jackie. When Jackie exercises that option, Tara (not Jackie) recognizes ordinary income under IRC Section 83. The amount of such income equals the excess of the fair market value of the stock on the date of option exercise over the option exercise price.

Obviously, the fair market of the stock on the date that such option will be *exercised* by the donee is highly uncertain at the time the option is transferred by the donor. It means that the donor has no idea how much compensation income he will recognize, until the donee exercises the option. In short, gifting options (whether unvested or vested on the date of transfer) entails risk to the donor.

Proceeds from the eventual sale of stock acquired by the exercise of such option are tax-free to the donee, except to the extent that such proceeds exceed the donee's basis in the stock as discussed below.

The donee's basis in the stock he acquires by exercising the option equals the option exercise price plus the amount of compensation income recognized by the donor (that is, basis generally equals fair market value on date of exercise). The option exercise starts the donee's holding period. Any gain or loss on the eventual sale of stock is short-term capital gain or loss if the holding period is not more than 12 months, and long-term capital gain or loss if the holding period is more than 12 months.

Example: Option exercise by the donee triggers compensation income to the donor: The facts are the same as the previous example. Jackie exercises the options on July 1, Year 3 and the fair market value of the stock is $100 per share. Tara, the donor, recognizes ordinary compensation income in the amount of $90 per share, which equals the $100 fair market value on the date of exercise over the $10 option exercise price. Jackie's basis in the stock is $100. Jackie recognizes no income on the date of exercise. Jackie sells the stock for $110 per share on August 1, Year 4, which results in a capital gain in the amount of $10, computed as $110 of proceeds minus her $100 basis. The gain is long-term capital gain because Jackie's holding period is more than 12 months. In short, Tara recognizes $90 of compensation income on option exercise date, while Jackie later reaps $100 of tax-free sales proceeds, plus $10 of sales proceeds on which she pays income tax.

4

Incentive Stock Options

This chapter explains the *federal* income tax consequences for calendar year taxpayers (which applies to most individuals). A calendar year taxpayer is one whose taxable year begins January 1 and ends December 31.

The optionee is *not* taxed on the date that a corporation *grants* him an ISO. He is *not* taxed on the date of ISO *exercise* – for purposes of the regular income tax. Generally, he *is* taxed on the date of option exercise – for purposes of alternative minimum tax (AMT).

The mere exercise of an ISO does *not* trigger federal income tax withholding because the excess of the fair market value of the stock on the date of option exercise over the exercise price is not considered "wages" for purposes of *federal income taxation*. Neither is the optionee subject to federal income tax withholding on the date that he sells stock previously acquired by ISO exercise.

For regular income tax purposes, the optionee recognizes gain (or loss, in the event that the stock price on the date of sale is less than the option exercise price) on the date that he *sells* the stock. On the date that he sells the stock, he also realizes some sort of income tax consequences for purposes of AMT.

If he sells the stock in the *same* calendar year that he exercises the ISO, the income tax consequences are the same for regular income tax purposes as they are for purposes of alternative minimum tax (and no amount is reported on IRS Form 6251). If the sale of stock does *not* occur in the calendar year that he exercises the ISO, the amount of income subject to tax in the year of sale for purposes of regular tax is greater than or equal to the amount subject to tax in the year of sale for purposes of AMT.

In order to receive preferential income tax treatment on long-term capital gain from the sale of stock that was previously acquired by exercise of an incentive stock option, the optionee must satisfy two holding period requirements. The date of disposition must be more than 12 months after the date of ISO exercise, *and* more than two years after the option's grant date.

Under current tax law, individuals pay the *greater* of the regular income tax or the tentative minimum tax. The alternative minimum tax is an important issue for optionees that exercise ISOs but do *not* sell the stock during the same calendar year.

If the exercise of an ISO *does* trigger AMT, however, tax law provides an AMT *credit* against regular tax in years subsequent to the year of ISO exercise – but only to the extent that regular tax exceeds tentative minimum tax. The AMT credit changes the conventional approach to AMT planning.

This chapter discusses the following sections:

- *Important Dates*

- *Non-disqualifying Disposition*

- *Disqualifying Disposition*

- *Alternative Minimum Tax*

- *Exercising Unvested Options*

IMPORTANT DATES

GRANT DATE

The recipient of an ISO does *not* recognize taxable income for purposes of either the regular tax or the alternative minimum tax (AMT) on the date that the option is granted.

FAIR MARKET VALUE AND IRC SECTION 409A

As discussed in Chapter 3, IRC Section 409A is especially challenging for companies (and that challenge could ultimately have an adverse impact on employees of those companies) that grant *nonqualified* stock options when the underlying stock is not publicly traded – because the IRS may argue that the fair market value of such stock on option grant date exceeded the option exercise price (and that would generally result in a taxable event, under IRC Section 409A, when the option vests, instead of when the option is exercised).

The Conference Report with respect to the *American Jobs Creation Act of 2004* states that IRC Section 409A "...is not intended to change the tax treatment of incentive stock options meeting the requirements of [section] 422..." And IRC Section 422(c)(1) provides that the option exercise price will be treated as meeting the requirements of IRC Section 422(b)(4) – which states that the option exercise price of an ISO must not be less than the fair market value of the stock on option grant date – if the attempt to set the option exercise price at not less than fair market value on grant date "was made in good faith."

Consequently, the IRC Section 409A issue of option exercise price being not less than the fair market value of the stock on option grant date is far less worrisome (as compared to the grant of nonqualified options) when the employer grants ISOs and the underlying stock is not publicly traded – because the company does not necessarily have to be "correct" in its valuation of the stock on grant date (and in setting the option exercise price not less than fair market value on grant date) as long as it can demonstrate, if need be, that it made a good faith effort to set the option exercise price not less than fair market value.

EXERCISE DATE

The optionee does *not* recognize taxable income, for purposes of the *regular* income tax, when he exercises an ISO. Generally, for purposes of AMT, however, the excess of the fair market value of the stock acquired by ISO exercise over the exercise price *is* treated as an item of adjustment and included in the computation of the optionee's alternative minimum taxable income in the year of exercise.

Example: See Table 4.1. On January 10, Year 1, Carol exercises ISOs. The exercise price is $1,000. The fair market value of the stock on the date of exercise is $3,000. Carol does *not* sell the stock in Year 1.

For purposes of AMT, Carol recognizes $2,000 of taxable income in Year 1, the excess of the fair market value of the stock over the exercise price. She reports that income on IRS Form 6251, because she does not sell the stock in Year 1. She does *not* recognize *any* income in Year 1 for purposes of the regular income tax.

Table 4.1

Income Tax Consequences in Year 1
For Purposes of AMT Only

Exercise Date:	**January 10, Year 1**
Exercise Price:	**$1,000**
FMV on Exercise Date:	**$3,000**

Fair market value of stock on exercise date	$3,000
Less: exercise price	1,000
AMT taxable income in Year 1	$2,000
Basis in 100 shares of stock for AMT purposes	$3,000[1]

[1] For AMT purposes, the basis of the stock equals fair market value on date of option exercise ($3,000). For regular tax purposes, the basis equals the exercise price of the option ($1,000).

This book often refers to the basis of stock acquired by exercise of an incentive stock option – for purposes of alternative minimum tax – as being fair market value on the date of option exercise, because that is almost always the case. That is almost always the case because AMT basis equals the amount paid to buy the stock (the exercise price), plus the amount of AMT taxable income recognized by the optionee.

As explained in Chapter 3, the basis of stock acquired by nonresident alien individuals is not always fair market value on date of option exercise – because of IRC Section 83(c)(4). That section of law is relevant to the AMT basis of ISO-stock because Section 83 applies to the exercise of an incentive stock option, for purposes of AMT.

DISPOSITION DATE

The *sale* of stock previously acquired by exercise of an ISO is a taxable event for both the regular income tax and the alternative minimum tax.

The disposition *date* is important because it is used to determine whether the disposition is classified under the Internal Revenue Code as *non-disqualifying* or *disqualifying.* The income tax consequences of this important distinction are discussed later in this chapter.

If the disposition date is more than two years after the option's grant date *and* more than 12 months after the date of option exercise, the disposition is *non*-disqualifying (a non-disqualifying disposition is also called a *qualifying* disposition). The disposition is disqualifying if the disposition does *not* satisfy *both* holding period requirements (it is a disposition of *immature* ISO-stock).

INCOME TAX CONSEQUENCES IN TWO DIFFERENT YEARS

If the optionee exercises ISOs and sells the stock in the *same* year, there are federal income tax consequences in that one year only.

If the optionee exercises ISOs in one year but sells the stock in *another*, however, there are income tax consequences in *both* tax years – the calendar year of ISO exercise and the calendar year in which the stock is sold. Not only are there income tax consequences in both tax years, but the tax treatment for AMT purposes and for regular tax purposes is *different* for *both* years.

WHAT *IS*, AND *ISN'T*, A DISPOSITION OF ISO-STOCK?

While the *sale* of stock is the most common type of disposition, other transactions involving stock, which was previously acquired by exercise of an ISO, can trigger federal income taxation.

Internal Revenue Code Section 424(c)(1) provides that a disposition includes an *exchange* (with some exceptions), a *gift* or *transfer of legal title*. It also includes the termination of a joint tenancy to the extent that someone other than the optionee acquires ownership of such stock.

The following are *not* dispositions of ISO-stock:

- transfer of the stock from a decedent to an estate or a transfer by bequest or inheritance

- certain exchanges (for example, those that involve exchanges of stock and securities in certain types of corporate reorganizations)

- the mere pledge or hypothecation of the stock

- transfer of the stock to a spouse, or to a former spouse if the transfer is incident to the divorce

- registration of the stock in the name of both spouses if the employee lives in a community property state

Example: Alexa gives immature ISO-stock to her daughter. The gift is a disqualifying disposition.

Example: Alexa gives immature ISO-stock to a charity. The gift is a disqualifying disposition.

Example: Alexa gives ISO-stock to her husband. IRC Section 424(c)(4)(A) provides that a gift to one's spouse is not a disposition. IRC Section 424(c)(4)(B) provides that the same income tax treatment applies to such ISO-stock, now held by her husband, as would have applied to her if she had retained the stock.

Example: Incident to their divorce, Barbara transfers ISO-stock to her ex-husband. IRC Section 424(c)(4)(A) provides that a transfer to an ex-spouse if such transfer is incident to divorce is not a disposition. IRC Section 424(c)(4)(B) provides that the same income tax treatment applies to such ISO-stock, now held by her ex-husband, as would have applied to her if she had retained the stock.

Example: Alexa exercises an ISO and continues to hold such ISO-stock. She dies before satisfying the holding period requirements and the stock is transfered to her heirs. IRC Section 424(c)(1)(A) provides that the transfer is not a disposition of ISO-stock.

Example: Alexa exercises an ISO and holds such ISO-stock in a margin account at a brokerage firm. The terms and conditions of the margin account provide that she is pledging the stock in her account as collateral. That pledge is not a disposition because Regulation 1.424-1(c)(1)(iii) provides that the mere pledge or hypothecation of such stock is not a disposition.

Example: In the previous example, Alexa pledges her ISO-stock as collateral in her margin account and the mere pledge of such stock is not a disposition. Later, the value of the securities in the account falls and Alexa receives a "margin call" – a request from the brokerage firm to deposit more assets into the account to secure her margin loan. Alexa does not deposit more assets into the account and, therefore, the brokerage firm sells her ISO-stock. Alexa has made a disposition of ISO-stock because, while Regulation 1.424-1(c)(1)(iii) states that the mere pledge of such stock is not a disposition, that same regulation also states that a disposition of the stock pursuant to a pledge or hypothecation *is* a disposition.

TRANSFER OF ISO-STOCK "INCIDENT TO DIVORCE"

Regulation 1.424-1(c)(1)(iv) states that a transfer of ISO-stock between spouses or incident to divorce (described in IRC Section 1041(a)) is not a disposition of such stock.

Since IRC Section 424(c)(4)(B) states that the same tax treatment shall apply to the transferee as would have applied to the transferor, the transferee should be aware of Temporary Regulation 1.1041-1T(e), below, because he will need certain information in order to properly report his eventual disposition of the ISO-stock. For reasons that will be evident after reading this book, the transferee should request the following information from the transferor:

- The date of option exercise

- The option exercise price

- Fair market value of the stock on date of option exercise

- If the transferor had exercised an unvested ISO, the date that the stock vested (or the date that it will vest) and the fair market value of the stock on the date that the stock vested

---

Temporary Regulation 1.1041-1T(e) "Notice and Recordkeeping Requirement with Respect to Transactions Under Section 1041"

Temporary Regulation 1.1041-1T(e) includes a requirement that "a transferor of property under IRC Section 1041 must, at the time of transfer, supply the transferee with records sufficient to determine the adjusted basis and holding period of the property as of the date of the transfer."

Any transferee receiving ISO-stock incident to divorce should request that the divorce or separation instrument include language from Temporary Regulation 1.1041-1T(e), Q-14 – to increase the likelihood that the transferor will abide by such regulation.

TRANSFER OF ISO-STOCK TO A TRUST

Regulation 1.421-1(b)(2) states that the transfer of a statutory *option* to a trust does not disqualify the option as a statutory option if, under section 671 and applicable state law, the individual is considered the sole beneficial owner of the option while it is held in the trust.

In PLR 9309027, the IRS ruled that a transfer of an employee's ISO-*stock* to a qualifying grantor trust would not be a disposition if: "The employee will be the sole grantor of the trust. Except in the case of the employee's death or incapacity, either the employee will be the sole trustee of the trust or the employee and spouse will be the sole co-trustee of the trust. The trustee or trustees will not be required, while the grantor is alive, to distribute the income to any person other than the employee or the spouse. The employee will have the ability to revoke all or part of the trust and have the assets revest in himself without the consent of any other person."

A transfer of ISO-stock to an *irrevocable* trust, however, is a disposition of such stock.

CERTAIN TRANSFERS BY INSOLVENT INDIVIDUALS

IRC Section 422(c)(3) provides that if an insolvent individual holds a share of ISO-stock, and if such stock is transferred to a trustee, receiver, or other similar fiduciary in any proceeding under title 11 or any other similiar insolvency proceeding, *neither* such transfer, *nor* any other transfer of such share for the benefit of his creditors in such proceeding, shall be considered a disqualifying disposition of ISO-stock.

SHORT SALE "AGAINST THE BOX" IS A DISPOSITION OF IMMATURE ISO-STOCK

In Revenue Ruling 73-92, the taxpayer held stock that he previously acquired by exercising a *qualified* stock option (the precursor to the *incentive* stock option). He made a short sale of identical stock (known as a "short sale against the box') before having satisfied the special holding period requirement for the stock he had acquired by option exercise. The IRS determined that the short sale constituted a disposition of the stock he had acquired by option exercise.

The IRS made the ruling on the basis that the taxpayer had frozen his economic position on the date of the short sale (and continuing through the date he covered the short sale).

In short, if the stock price would increase (decrease) by $1:

- The value of the ISO-stock would increase (decrease) by $1,

  and,

- The value of the stock he sold short would decrease (increase) by $1.

Example: In January, Year 1, Jennifer exercises an ISO to buy 100 shares of ABC Corporation. She sells short 100 shares of ABC Corporation on June 1, Year 1. Therefore, on June 1, Year 1 her economic position in ABC is frozen until she closes the short sale. In accordance with Revenue Ruling 73-92, Jennifer made a disqualifying disposition of 100 shares of ISO-stock on June 1, Year 1, the date of the short sale.

NO INCOME TAX WITHHOLDING, NO FICA, AND NO FUTA

The *American Jobs Creation Act of 2004* ("2004 Tax Act") added language to IRC Section 421(b), which provides that federal income tax withholding is not required on any increase in income attributable to a disqualifying disposition of ISO-stock.

The 2004 Tax Act also added IRC Section 3121(a)(22), which provides that remuneration on account of the transfer of stock to any individual pursuant to an exercise of an ISO, or remuneration on account of any disposition by the individual of such stock – is not considered "wages" for purposes of social security tax and Medicare tax. In short, neither the ISO exercise nor the disposition of such ISO-stock triggers social security tax or Medicare tax (these two taxes are also called FICA taxes).

Further, the 2004 Tax Act added IRC Section 3306(b)(19), which exempts from the definition of FUTA "wages" any remuneration described in the previous paragraph. It means that such remuneration is exempt from federal unemployment tax.

ESTIMATED TAX PAYMENTS

Since, as described above, federal income tax is not withheld on gain from the disposition of ISO-stock, optionees may need to make estimated tax payments (with IRS Form 1040ES), or request that employers withhold additional income tax on or before December 31 of the year of disposition – in order to avoid a penalty for underpayment of estimated tax. IRS Publication 505, available free at www.irs.gov, offers guidance on making estimated tax payments.

Example: Marilyn exercises ISOs and makes a same-day sale that triggers $100 of ordinary compensation income. No federal income tax is withheld by her employer. Marilyn's marginal tax rate on ordinary income is 35 percent. The stock sale triggers income tax in the amount of $35 (35 percent x $100 of ordinary income). If she does not make estimated tax payments, or request that her employer withhold additional income tax on or before December 31 of the year of sale, Marilyn is likely to owe money to the IRS on April 15 of next year when she files IRS Form 1040.

NON-DISQUALIFYING DISPOSITION

As discussed earlier, in order for the sale of stock previously acquired by ISO exercise to be characterized for income tax purposes as a *non-disqualifying disposition*, the date of disposition must be:

- more than two years after the date of option grant,

    and,

- more than 12 months after the date of option exercise

INCOME TAX CONSEQUENCES IN THE YEAR OF SALE

The optionee does not recognize *ordinary* income in the year he sells the ISO-stock *if* the sale is non-disqualifying. Any gain or loss from such sale is taxed as *long-term* capital gain or loss. The *amount* of that gain or loss, however, is computed differently for purposes of the regular tax than for purposes of AMT.

Regular income tax: The optionee recognizes a long-term capital gain or loss in the year of sale. The amount of that gain or loss is equal to the difference between the amount received in the disposition and the *exercise price* (that is, his basis in the stock is the option exercise price). See Table 4.2.

AMT: The optionee recognizes a long-term capital gain or loss in the year of sale. The amount of that gain or loss is generally equal to the difference between the amount received in the disposition and the *fair market value of the stock on the date of option exercise* (that is because his basis in the stock, for purposes of AMT, is generally the fair market value of the stock on the date of option exercise). Consequently, the amount of income that the optionee recognizes in the year of sale, for purposes of the regular income tax, is greater than or equal to the amount of income that he recognizes for purposes of AMT. See Table 4.2.

Table 4.2
Long-term Capital Gain or Loss on Non-disqualifying Disposition of Stock

Regular Income Tax	Alternative Minimum Tax
Amount received Less: *exercise price*	Amount received Less: *fair market value* on exercise date

---

COMPUTATION OF LONG-TERM CAPITAL GAIN (OR LOSS) IN YEAR OF SALE

Example: Carol exercises ISOs on January 10, Year 1 and pays $1,000 to acquire the stock. On January 11, Year 2, she sells the stock for $3,200. The date of sale is more than two years after the option grant date.

The disposition is *non*-disqualifying because Carol has satisfied both holding period requirements. The date of sale occurs more than 12 months after the date of option exercise *and* more than two years after the date of option grant.

Table 4.3 shows the computation of the $2,200 long-term capital gain in Year 2 for *regular income tax* purposes.

Table 4.3
(see Chart 4.3)

Non-disqualifying Disposition
Income Tax Consequences in Year 2
(for Purposes of Regular Income Tax)

Exercise Date:	**January 10, Year 1**
Sale Date:	**January 11, Year 2**
Exercise Price:	**$1,000**
FMV on Exercise Date:	**$3,000**
Sales Proceeds:	**$3,200**

Amount received from sale of stock	$3,200
Less: exercise price	1,000
Long-term capital gain in Year 2	$2,200

Table 4.4 shows the computation of the $200 long-term capital gain in Year 2 for *alternative minimum tax* purposes.

Notice in Table 4.3 that Carol recognizes a $2,200 long-term capital gain for regular tax purposes. That gain is $2,000 more than the $200 long-term capital gain (Table 4.4) that she recognizes for AMT.

Carol's long-term capital gain is $2,000 *less* for AMT purposes than it is for regular tax purposes because she had previously recognized $2,000 of taxable income for purposes of AMT in the year that she exercised the ISOs (see Table 4.1). The recognition of that $2,000 of taxable income increased her basis in the stock by $2,000, for purposes of AMT.

Table 4.4
(see Chart 4.4)

Non-disqualifying Disposition
Income Tax Consequences in Year 2
(for Purposes of Alternative Minimum Tax)

Exercise Date:	**January 10, Year 1**
Sale Date:	**January 11, Year 2**
Exercise Price:	**$1,000**
FMV on Exercise Date:	**$3,000**
Sales Proceeds:	**$3,200**

Amount received from sale of stock	$3,200
Less: FMV of stock on date of exercise	3,000
Long-term capital gain in Year 2	$ 200

The *total* amount of income recognized by Carol is the *same* for regular tax purposes as it is for AMT. The *timing* of income recognition is different, however.

For AMT purposes, the optionee recognizes *more* income in the year of exercise and *less* in the year of sale. For regular tax purposes, he recognizes *less* (none) income in the year of exercise and *more* in the year of sale.

Unless otherwise stated, all references to exercising ISOs and holding such ISO-stock for more than 12 months assume that the date of disposition is also more than two years after option grant date. Therefore, the disposition is characterized for income tax purposes as a non-disqualifying disposition.

Chart 4.3
(see Table 4.3)

Income Tax Consequences in Year 2
(for Purposes of Regular Income Tax)

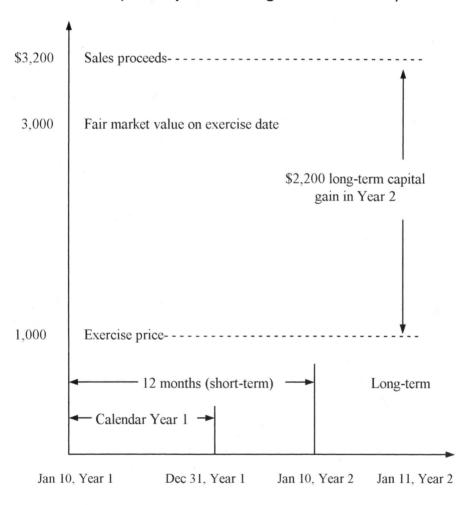

Chart 4.4
(see Table 4.4)

Income Tax Consequences in Year 2
(for Purposes of Alternative Minimum Tax)

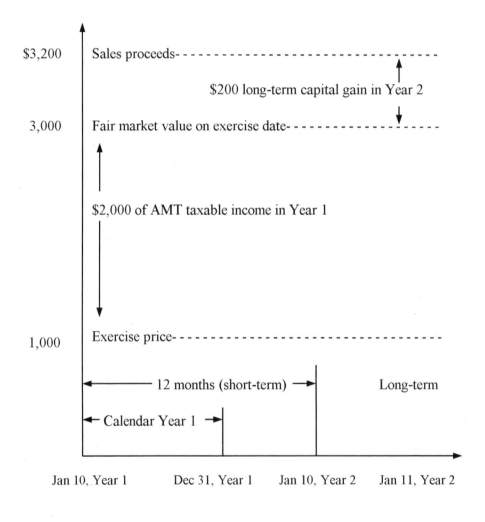

DISQUALIFYING DISPOSITION

If the disposition of stock is *not* a *qualifying* disposition, it is a disqualifying disposition.

If he makes a disqualifying disposition of ISO-stock that was vested on ISO exercise date, IRC Section 83(a) is used to measure the consequences of the disposition, and the special rule under IRC Section 422(c)(2) and Regulation 1.422-1(b)(2)(i) limits compensation income to the amount of actual gain, if any, on the sale. In other words, if he suffers a loss on the sale, he does not recognize any ordinary compensation income.

In short, if he makes a disqualifying disposition, he recognizes *ordinary compensation income*, if any, on the date of such disposition to the extent of the *lesser* of:

(a) the difference between the fair market value of such stock on the date of option exercise and the exercise price (this is the measurement provided by IRC Section 83(a)),

or,

(b) the difference between the amount received in the disposition and the exercise price (that is, compensation income is limited, under the special rule in IRC Section 422(c)(2), to the actual gain on the sale or exchange, if any).

Compensation income cannot be less than zero.

Special Rule that Limits Compensation Income Does Not Always Apply

It is important to note that Regulation 1.422-1(b)(2)(ii) explains that the special rule, which is described in Regulation 1.422-1(b)(2)(i) and which limits the amount of compensation amount to the actual gain on the disposition (if any), does **not** apply if the disposition is a sale or exchange with respect to which a loss (if sustained) would not be recognized by the individual. In other words, if the special rule does not apply, compensation income equals the amount determined under paragraph (a) above. Please see Chapter 7 "*ISO Tax Traps*" for a discussion of this topic.

If the limitation on compensation income does not apply, the optionee recognizes compensation income in the amount of the excess of the fair market value of the stock on the date of option exercise over the option exercise price – regardless of the amount of proceeds he receives from the sale of such stock. That treatment could result in a substantial tax liability, and little or no cash to pay it (that situation can arise, for example, when the stock price collapses after option exercise date, and the optionee sells his ISO-stock at a depressed price, and repurchases the stock within 30 days of the sale date).

In most cases, however, the special rule limiting compensation income *does* apply if an optionee sells his ISO-stock in a disqualifying disposition. That is because, in most cases, an optionee sells ISO-stock on the open market to an unrelated party, and within a period that begins 30 days before the date of sale and ending 30 days after such date (a total of 61 calendar days), the optionee has *not* acquired, nor entered into a contract or option to acquire, substantially identical stock or securities.

EXERCISE ISO AND SELL STOCK IN SAME CALENDAR YEAR - COMPUTATION OF TAXABLE GAIN IN YEAR OF SALE

When the optionee exercises an ISO and sells the stock in the same calendar year:

- the disposition is disqualifying,

  and,

- the income tax consequences for purposes of the regular tax and alternative minimum tax are the *same* (which means that the optionee does not enter an amount on IRS Form 6251)

This section presents two examples. In the first (Table 4.5), the optionee's gain on the sale of stock consists entirely of *ordinary compensation income* because the fair market value of the stock on the date of sale is *less* than it was on the date of exercise (but the fair market value exceeds the exercise price).

In the second example (Table 4.6), a portion of the optionee's gain is taxed as ordinary compensation income, and a portion is taxed as *short-term capital gain* because the fair market value of the stock on the date of sale is *more* than it was on the date of exercise.

Stock Price is Lower on Sale Date than it was on Exercise Date (But the Stock Price is Higher than the Exercise Price)

Example: See Table 4.5. On January 10, Year 1, Carol exercises ISOs to buy 100 shares of stock. The option exercise price is $1,000 ($10 per share) and the fair market value of the stock on the date of exercise is $3,000 ($30 per share). Carol sells the stock for $2,800 on March 5, Year 1.

Disqualifying or non-disqualifying disposition?: The sale of stock is a *disqualifying* disposition because Carol does *not* hold the stock for more than 12 months after the date of option exercise.

Amount of ordinary compensation income: Carol recognizes ordinary compensation income in the amount of the *lesser* of (a) the $2,000 excess of the fair market value ($3,000) of the stock on the date of exercise and the exercise price ($1,000), *and* (b) the $1,800 excess of the amount received in the disposition ($2,800) and the exercise price ($1,000). Consequently, Carol recognizes $1,800 of ordinary compensation income in Year 1.

Amount of capital gain: If the optionee's proceeds from the sale are *more* than what the fair market value of the stock was on the date of ISO exercise, such excess is taxed as capital gain. The gain is taxed as short-term capital gain if the optionee does *not* hold the stock for more than 12 months after the date of option exercise.

In this example, the $2,800 proceeds from the sale are *not* more than the $3,000 fair market value of the stock on the date of exercise. Therefore, Carol does *not* recognize *any* short-term capital gain on the date of sale.

Withholding: Under IRC Section 421(b), federal income tax withholding is not required on any increase in income attributable to a disqualifying disposition of ISO-stock.

Stock Price is Higher on Sale Date than it was on Exercise Date

Example: See Table 4.6. Instead of selling the stock for $2,800 (as shown in Table 4.5), Carol sells the stock for $3,200. Her total gain is $2,200, the excess of the $3,200 received from the sale of stock over the $1,000 exercise price.

Notice in Table 4.6 that Carol recognizes *both* ordinary compensation income *and* capital gain in the year of sale. This occurs because the stock price on the date of sale is *higher* than it was on the date of exercise.

Amount of ordinary compensation income: Carol recognizes $2,000 of ordinary compensation income, the *lesser* of **A** ($2,000) or **B** ($2,200).

Amount of capital gain: Carol also recognizes short-term capital gain in the amount of $200, the excess of his $2,200 total gain over the $2,000 that he recognizes as ordinary compensation income. The gain is short-term because the March 5, Year 1 date of sale is not more than 12 months after the January 10, Year 1 date of ISO exercise.

Stock Price is Lower than the Exercise Price

In the unfortunate circumstance where the stock is sold at a price that is *less* than the exercise price, IRC Section 422(c)(2) provides that the optionee does *not* recognize *any* ordinary income on the disposition.

The optionee realizes a capital *loss*. The loss is taxed as a short-term capital loss because the date of sale is *not* more than 12 months after the date of ISO exercise. The amount of the loss is equal to the difference between the proceeds from the sale and the exercise price (his basis in the stock).

Example: Carol exercises ISOs on January 10, Year 1. The exercise price is $1,000. She sells the stock on December 10, Year 1 for $900.

Carol does not recognize any ordinary compensation income. She realizes a short-term capital loss in the amount of $100, the difference between the $900 proceeds and the $1,000 exercise price.

Table 4.5
(see Chart 4.5)

Disqualifying Disposition
Income Tax Consequences in Year 1

Exercise Date:	January 10, Year 1
Sale Date:	March 5, Year 1
Exercise Price:	$1,000
FMV on Exercise Date:	$3,000
Sales Proceeds:	$2,800

Fair market value of stock on exercise date	$3,000	
Less: exercise price	1,000	
Excess of fair market value over option price	$2,000	A
Amount received from sale of stock	$2,800	
Less: exercise price	1,000	
Excess of amount received over exercise price	$1,800	B
Ordinary compensation income (lesser of A and B)	$1,800	

Regular income tax and AMT: The income tax consequences are the *same* for both regular income tax purposes and for AMT because the ISO exercise and the sale of stock occur during the same calendar year.

EXERCISE ISO IN ONE CALENDAR YEAR AND SELL STOCK IN A DIFFERENT CALENDAR YEAR - COMPUTATION OF TAXABLE GAIN IN YEAR OF SALE

When the optionee exercises an ISO in one calendar year, but sells the stock in *another* calendar year:

- the sale of stock may or may not be a disqualifying disposition

Chart 4.5
(see Table 4.5)

Income Tax Consequences in Year 1
(for Purposes of Regular Income Tax and AMT)

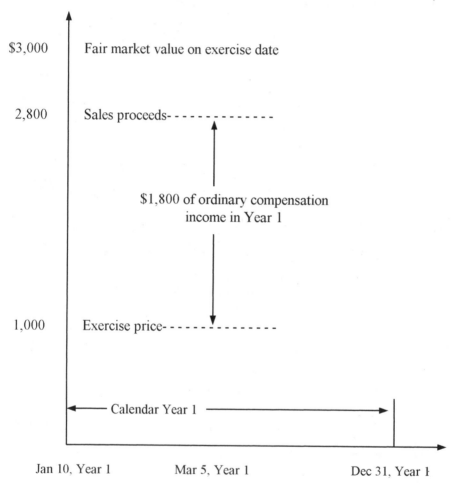

- the tax consequences for purposes of the regular income tax and AMT are different

- the total amount of income recognized in the year of sale for purposes of the regular income tax is always greater than or equal to the amount recognized for AMT

- one hundred percent of any gain or loss in the year of sale, for purposes of AMT, is taxed as *capital* gain or loss – short-term or long-term, depending on the holding period

As discussed earlier, the sale of stock is a disqualifying disposition if *either* of two holding period requirements is *not* satisfied. Either the optionee does not hold the stock for more than 12 months after the date of ISO exercise, *or* the sale date is not more than two years after the option's grant date.

This section describes the federal income tax consequences that result from a disqualifying disposition of stock that occurs in a year *subsequent* to the calendar year of ISO exercise.

The *total* amount of income that the optionee recognizes in the year of sale, for regular income tax purposes, is greater than or equal to the total amount of income that he recognizes for AMT. This occurs because the optionee previously recognized income in the year of ISO exercise, for AMT purposes, in the amount of the excess of the fair market value of the stock on the date of exercise over the exercise price.

Example: Carol exercises ISOs on January 10, Year 1 and pays $1,000 to acquire the stock. The fair market value of the stock on the date of exercise is $3,000. On January 5, Year 2, she sells the stock for $3,200. See Tables 4.7 and 4.8.

The disposition is disqualifying because the January 5, Year 2 date of sale is not more than 12 months after the January 10, Year 1 date of option exercise.

In a disqualifying disposition that occurs *subsequent* to the calendar year of exercise, the amount of income that is subject to tax is *different* for regular tax purposes than for AMT purposes.

Table 4.7 shows the computation of ordinary compensation income, and short-term capital gain, in Year 2 (the year of sale) for *regular income tax* purposes. The total amount of income subject to regular tax is $2,200, some of which is taxed as ordinary income ($2,000) and some as short-term capital gain ($200).

Table 4.8 shows the computation of short-term capital gain in Year 2 for *alternative minimum tax* purposes. Notice that the *total* amount of income subject to AMT in the year of *sale* is only $200 (versus $2,200 for regular tax) because Carol had already recognized $2,000 of taxable income in the year of *exercise,* for purposes of AMT.

Table 4.6

Disqualifying Disposition
Income Tax Consequences in Year 1

Exercise Date:	**January 10, Year 1**
Sale Date:	**March 5, Year 1**
Exercise Price:	**$1,000**
FMV on Exercise Date:	**$3,000**
Sales Proceeds:	**$3,200**

Fair market value of stock on exercise date	$3,000	
Less: exercise price	1,000	
Excess of fair market value over exercise price	$2,000	**A**
Amount received from sale of stock	$3,200	
Less: exercise price	1,000	
Excess of amount received over exercise price	$2,200	**B**
Ordinary compensation income (lesser of **A** and **B**)	$2,000	
Short-term capital gain	200	
Total gain recognized in Year 1	$2,200	

Stock Price is Lower than the Exercise Price

In the unfortunate circumstance where the stock price declines after the date of ISO exercise and the amount received in the disposition is *less* than the exercise price, IRC Section 422(c)(2) provides that the optionee does *not* recognize *any* ordinary income on the disposition. He realizes a *capital loss* in the year of sale.

Table 4.7
(see Chart 4.7)

Disqualifying Disposition
Income Tax Consequences in Year 2
(for Purposes of Regular Income Tax)

Exercise Date:	January 10, Year 1
Sale Date:	January 5, Year 2
Exercise Price:	$1,000
FMV on Exercise Date:	$3,000
Sales Proceeds:	$3,200

Fair market value of stock on exercise date	$3,000	
Less: exercise price	1,000	
Excess of fair market value over exercise price	$2,000	A
Amount received from sale of stock	$3,200	
Less: exercise price	1,000	
Excess of amount received over exercise price	$2,200	B
Ordinary compensation income (lesser of A and B)	$2,000	
Short-term capital gain	200	
Total gain recognized in Year 2	$2,200	

Example: Carol exercises ISOs on January 10, Year 1. The exercise price is $1,000 and the fair market value of the stock on

Chart 4.7
(see Table 4.7)

Income Tax Consequences in Year 2
(for Purposes of Regular Income Tax)

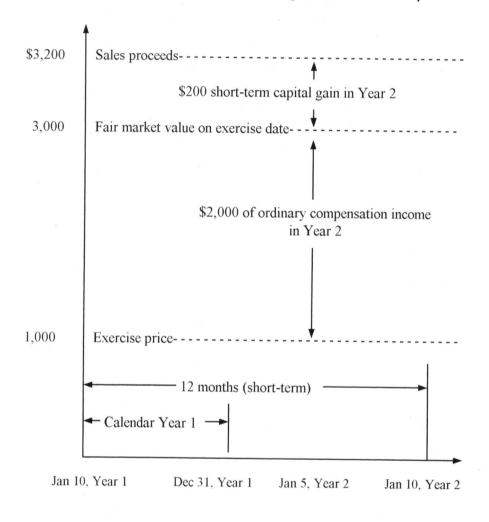

$3,200   Sales proceeds- -

$200 short-term capital gain in Year 2

3,000   Fair market value on exercise date- -

$2,000 of ordinary compensation income
in Year 2

1,000   Exercise price- -

12 months (short-term)

Calendar Year 1

Jan 10, Year 1   Dec 31, Year 1   Jan 5, Year 2   Jan 10, Year 2

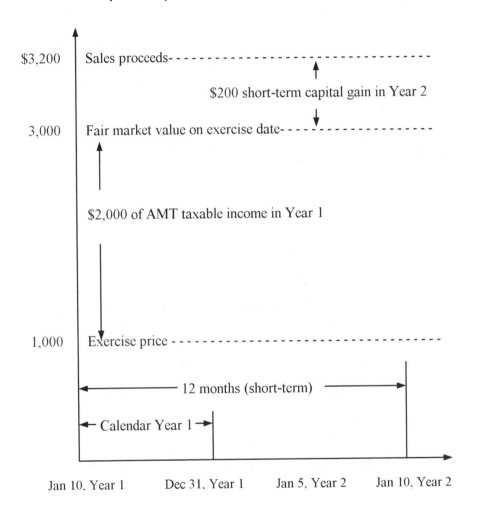

Chart 4.8
(see Table 4.8)

Income Tax Consequences in Year 2
(for Purposes of Alternative Minimum Tax)

$3,200 — Sales proceeds- -

$200 short-term capital gain in Year 2

3,000 — Fair market value on exercise date- - - - - - - - - - - - - - - - - -

$2,000 of AMT taxable income in Year 1

1,000 — Exercise price -

12 months (short-term)

Calendar Year 1

Jan 10, Year 1   Dec 31, Year 1   Jan 5, Year 2   Jan 10, Year 2 the date of exercise is $3,000. She sells the stock on January 5, Year 2 for $900.

Regular income tax: Carol does *not* recognize *any* ordinary compensation income. She realizes a capital *loss* in the year of sale in the amount of $100, the difference between the $900 proceeds from the sale and the $1,000 exercise price (her basis for regular income tax purposes).

The loss is taxed as a *short-term* capital loss because the January 5, Year 2 date of sale is *not* more than 12 months after the January 10, Year 1 date of exercise.

AMT: For purposes of the alternative minimum tax, Carol does not recognize any ordinary compensation income.

She realizes a short-term capital loss in the year of sale in the amount of $2,100, the difference between the $900 proceeds from the sale and the $3,000 fair market value of the stock on the date of ISO exercise (her basis for AMT purposes).

Table 4.8
(see Chart 4.8)

Disqualifying Disposition
Income Tax Consequences in Year 2
(for Purposes of Alternative Minimum Tax)

Exercise Date:	January 10, Year 1
Sale Date:	January 5, Year 2
Exercise Price:	$1,000
FMV on Exercise Date:	$3,000
Sales Proceeds:	$3,200

Amount received from sale of stock	$3,200
Less: basis of stock sold	3,000[1]
Short-term capital gain in Year 2	$ 200

[1] basis for purposes of AMT equals the fair market value of the stock on the date of ISO exercise

CERTAIN SALES OF ISO-STOCK ARE NOT DISQUALIFYING DISPOSITIONS

The *American Jobs Creation Act of 2004* added IRC Section 421(d), which provides that the required sale of ISO-stock (pursuant to a "certificate of divestiture" as defined in IRC Section 1043) by an "eligible person", in order to comply with federal conflict of interest requirements of the federal government, is not a disqualifying disposition, regardless of how long the stock was actually held.

An eligible person is defined in IRC Section 1043(b)(1) and generally includes an officer or employee of the executive branch of the federal government (and any spouse or minor or dependent children whose ownership in property is attributable to the officer or employee). Under the IRC Section 1043(b)(5) special rule for trusts, certain trustees also qualify as an eligible person.

Example: Sale of ISO-stock due to conflict of interest requirements is not a disqualifying disposition: On April 1, Year 1, Patti, the CEO of ABC Corporation, a large defense contractor, exercises ISOs. The fair market value of the stock is $80 on the date of exercise, and her option exercise price is $10. On July 1, Year 1, Patti is asked to serve as the U.S. Secretary of Defense, and she accepts the position. Due of conflict of interest requirements, Patti must sell the ISO-stock she had acquired by ISO exercise. Pursuant to a certificate of divestiture, she sells the ISO-stock for $100 on July 10, Year 1, and realizes a $90 gain. Under IRC Section 421(d), the sale is not a disqualifying disposition, even though Patti does not satisfy the special holding period requirements. Therefore, Patti does not recognize any ordinary compensation income. Her $90 of gain is capital gain.

DEFERRAL OF GAIN ON CERTAIN SALES OF ISO-STOCK

IRC Section 1043(a) provides that the taxpayer may *elect* to defer taxation of the capital gain (that is, he may elect nonrecognition treatment) from the sale of ISO-stock described above, if he buys "permitted property" during the 60-day period beginning on the date of sale.

Gain will only be recognized to the extent the amount realized from the sale exceeds the cost of the permitted property. IRC Section 1043(b)(3) states that permitted property "...means any obligation of the United States or any diversified investment fund approved by regulations issued by the Office of Government Ethics." IRC Section 1043(c) provides that any gain deferred reduces the basis of the permitted property purchased.

Example: Patti buys permitted property within 60 days, and elects nonrecognition treatment: The facts are the same as the previous example. On August 1, Year 1, Patti reinvests the entire $100 – the amount realized from her July 10 sale of ISO-stock – in 10-year U.S. Treasury Notes. She makes a proper election to avoid recognition of (that is, to defer) the $90 gain on her sale of the ISO-stock. Her basis in the U.S. Treasury securities is $10, which equals her $100 cost reduced by $90 of deferred gain on the ISO-stock. Patti will recognize capital gain or loss in the year she sells the Treasury securities (or on maturity date if she does not sell them); it means that Patti could defer income tax on the $90 gain for years. The amount of her eventual taxable gain or loss on the Treasury securities will be measured relative to the $10 basis.

ALTERNATIVE MINIMUM TAX

In the 1970s, Congress passed legislation that established a minimum tax. Under current law, the U.S. Internal Revenue Code provides that the individual taxpayer pays the *greater* of tentative minimum tax or the regular income tax.

THE ISO ADJUSTMENT AND THE AMT CREDIT

The alternative minimum tax *credit* helps to ensure (but does not *guarantee*) that optionees do not pay *both* regular tax *and* AMT on gain that results from an ISO exercise and sale of stock.

AMT becomes an issue when the optionee exercises an ISO but does not sell the stock in the same calendar year. If the optionee exercises ISOs and does *not* sell the stock in the same calendar year, the ISO exercise results in an AMT adjustment that the optionee reports on IRS Form 6251 – for the tax year in which the ISO is exercised.

That ISO adjustment is included in the computation of alternative minimum taxable income. It may, or may not, trigger AMT.

Example: Optionees A, B and C file *joint* income tax returns with their spouses. All three optionees exercise ISOs when the fair market value of the stock on the date of exercise exceeds the option exercise price by $20,000. None of the three sells the stock during the calendar year of exercise.

Since they don't sell the stock during the year of exercise, they each generate a $20,000 AMT adjustment that is reported as taxable income, for AMT purposes, on IRS Form 6251. The $20,000 adjustment affects each taxpayer *differently*. See Table 4.9.

OPTIONEE A

See Table 4.9. The $97,860 of tentative minimum tax does *not* exceed the $100,284 of regular tax. Since tentative minimum tax is *not* greater than regular tax, AMT equals zero. Consequently, the ISO adjustment triggers $0 of AMT for Optionee A and her spouse.

OPTIONEE B

See Table 4.9. Since the $97,860 of tentative minimum tax exceeds the regular tax by $744, AMT equals $744. In other words, AMT is simply the excess of tentative minimum tax over the regular income tax.

If Optionee B did *not* have the $20,000 adjustment, she and her spouse would pay $0 of AMT (see "AMT without ISO adjustment" in Table 4.9). Because of the $20,000 ISO adjustment, however, they incur $744 of AMT. In effect, then, the $20,000 adjustment triggers $744 of AMT.

Optionee B and her spouse receive a $744 AMT credit. They may use it to reduce regular tax in *subsequent* years, but only to the extent that their regular tax liability in those years exceeds tentative minimum tax. They claim the credit on next year's IRS Form 8801. If they can't utilize the entire credit next year, they apply the unused amount to the following year. This process of carrying the credit forward continues indefinitely until the AMT credit is fully utilized.

OPTIONEE C

See Table 4.9. Since the $97,860 of tentative minimum tax exceeds the regular tax by $7,476, AMT equals $7,476. In other words, AMT is simply the excess of tentative minimum tax over the regular income tax.

If C did *not* have the adjustment, she and her spouse would pay $1,876 of AMT (see "AMT without ISO adjustment" in Table 4.9). In effect, then, the $20,000 adjustment triggers $5,600 ($7,476 minus $1,876) of AMT. Optionee C and her spouse pay AMT tax at the rate of 28 percent (28% x $20,000 equals $5,600) on the ISO adjustment.

Optionee C and her spouse receive a $5,600 AMT credit.

DEFERRAL VERSUS EXCLUSION ITEMS

The ISO adjustment is termed a *deferral* item, as opposed to an *exclusion* item. Exclusion items include state income taxes, real estate and personal property taxes, tax consulting and preparation fees, and other miscellaneous itemized deductions that taxpayers report on IRS Form 1040, Schedule A *"Itemized Deductions"*.

While an exclusion item results in a *permanent* difference in taxable income over time, a deferral item does *not* result in a permanent difference in taxable income over time. A deferral item results in a *timing* difference that can cause the taxpayer to pay more income tax now, and less later – by operation of the AMT.

The *disadvantage* of paying more tax now, and less later, is that money has a time value (please see the Appendix *"Time Value of Money"*. One dollar of income tax paid now is more costly than one dollar paid later.

Table 4.9

The $20,000 ISO Adjustment Affects Optionees A, B & C Differently

	A	B	C
Total income	$375,000	$375,000	$375,000
Less:state taxes	31,500	39,500	56,500
Less:other deductions	25,386	25,386	25,386
Less:exemptions	0	0	0
Regular taxable income	318,114	310,114	293,114
Regular tax	100,284	97,116	90,384
Tentative minimum tax	97, 860	97,860	97,860
AMT⇒	0	744	7,476
AMT w/o ISO adjustment⇒	0	0	1,876
AMT credit carryforward⇒	0	744	5,600

Note: tax computations are based upon 1997 income tax rates

With respect to the previous example, Optionee B and her spouse, in effect, make a $744 *interest-free loan* to the U.S. Treasury. That "loan" will be repaid (via the AMT credit) when, or *if*, and to the extent that their regular income tax liability in tax years subsequent to the year of ISO exercise exceeds their tentative minimum tax. Optionee C and her spouse make a $5,600 loan to the U.S. Treasury under the same unfavorable terms. Please see Chapter 8 "The Cost of AMT".

AMT PLANNING IS DIFFERENT

Corporate executives engage the services of tax professionals and pay them substantial fees to design strategies that minimize or eliminate AMT.

EQUALIZE TENTATIVE MINIMUM TAX AND REGULAR TAX

The *Jobs and Growth Tax Relief Reconciliation Act of 2003* made AMT planning more difficult, and a one-size-fits-all answer to planning does not apply. More often than not, however, when *exclusion* items trigger AMT, the tax planning strategy is to accelerate ordinary income into the current tax year. For example, a sole proprietor who reports taxable income on the cash method of accounting tries to accelerate income by invoicing customers on December 1 (because he wants to be paid *on or before* December 31) rather than waiting until December 15.

The taxpayer tries to accelerate just enough ordinary income so that tentative minimum tax equals regular tax. Since AMT is equal to the *excess* of tentative minimum tax over regular tax, AMT equals *zero* when tentative minimum tax equals regular tax. That's generally the objective of AMT planning – *when exclusion items trigger AMT*.

By accelerating ordinary income into a year when the taxpayer is otherwise subject to AMT, the income that is accelerated is often taxed at the lower AMT rate of either 26 or 28 percent (but "often" is different from "always" and a wise strategy is implemented only after making an income tax projection for the current taxable year, and at least one future taxable year).

This strategy of accelerating income can be particularly attractive when the taxpayer's marginal federal rate for regular tax purposes is substantially higher than the marginal tax rate on alternative minimum taxable income.

TAX PLANNING DIFFERS WHEN AN ISO EXERCISE TRIGGERS AMT

The AMT credit that arises when an ISO adjustment triggers AMT *changes* the approach to conventional AMT planning.

In the example that follows, Optionee B does *not* use the conventional strategy of AMT planning. Optionee B does *not* accelerate income into Year 1 in order to avoid AMT in Year 1.

Instead, she wisely chooses to pay AMT in Year 1. The $744 of AMT that she and her spouse incur, results in a $744 AMT tax *credit*. They utilize that $744 AMT credit in Year 2 to reduce their *regular* income tax liability.

Example: Recall from Table 4.9 that Optionee B exercises ISOs in Year 1. The exercise results in $744 of AMT in Year 1 and a $744 AMT credit carryforward to Year 2.

Table 4.10 shows the federal income tax consequences in Years 1 and 2 if Optionee B *accelerates* $6,258 of income from her sole proprietorship into Year 1 in order to avoid AMT in Year 1.

Table 4.11 shows the federal income tax consequences in Years 1 and 2 if Optionee B does *not* accelerate income into Year 1. Instead, she receives the income that she *could* have received in Year 1, if she had sent invoices to clients early in December, in Year 2.

Table 4.12 compares the cash flows that result from each of the two alternatives.

Whichever strategy she chooses, Optionee B and her spouse pay $197,488 in *total* federal tax over the two-year period. If she accelerates income, they pay *more* tax in Year 1 ($100,372) and *less* in Year 2 ($97,116). If she does *not* accelerate income, they pay *less* tax in Year 1 ($97,860) and *more* in Year 2 ($99,628).

An analysis of the differential cash flows (column 3 of Table 4.12) reveals that *not* accelerating income is the wiser strategy. In fact, it would be difficult to find many rational, informed investors that *would* choose to receive the cash flows associated with Table 4.12 column A over those in column B. The higher the rates of return on alternative investment opportunities, the less attractive it is for Optionee B to accelerate income into Year 1.

Table 4.10

Optionee B Accelerates $6,258 of Schedule C Income into Year 1 to Avoid AMT in Year 1

	Year 1	Year 2
Total income	$381,258	375,000
Less: 1/2 of self-employment tax	442	0
Adjusted gross income	$380,816	375,000
Less:itemized deductions	64,712	64,886
Regular taxable income	$316,104	310,114
Regular income tax	99,488[1]	97,116[2]
Self-employment tax	884	0
Alternative minimum tax	0[1]	0[2]
Total federal tax	$100,372	97,116
Less: federal withholding	100,000	100,000
Refund (balance due) per Form 1040	(372)	2,884

[1] tentative AMT equals $99,488; regular income tax equals $99,488; Optionee pays the *greater* of tentative AMT or regular income tax. Therefore, AMT equals $0, the excess of tentative AMT over regular income tax

[2] tentative AMT equals $92,260; regular income tax equals $97,116; Therefore, AMT equals $0, the excess of tentative AMT over regular income tax

Assumptions:

a) 1997 income tax rates
b) income tax rates in Years 1 and 2 are the same
c) $6,258 of Schedule C income is received on December 15, Year 1 and no Schedule C income is received during Year 2

Table 4.11

Optionee B Does Not Accelerate Any Schedule C Income into Year 1. She Pays AMT in Year 1 and Receives an AMT Credit That Reduces Regular Tax in Year 2

	Year 1	Year 2
Total income	$375,000	381,258
Less: 1/2 of self-employment tax	0	442
Adjusted gross income	$375,000	380,816
Less:itemized deductions	64,886	64,712
Regular taxable income	$310,114	316,104
Regular income tax	97,116[1]	99,488[2]
Less: AMT credit against regular tax	0	744
Regular income tax after credits	97,116	98,744
Plus: self-employment tax	0	884
Plus: alternative minimum tax	744[1]	0[2]
Total federal tax	$ 97,860	99,628
Less: federal withholding	100,000	100,000
Refund (balance due) per Form 1040	2,140	372

[1] tentative AMT equals $97,860; regular income tax equals $97,116; Optionee pays the *greater* of tentative AMT or regular income tax. Therefore, AMT equals $744, the excess of tentative AMT over regular income tax

[2] tentative AMT equals $93,888; regular income tax equals $99,488; Therefore, AMT equals $0, the excess of tentative AMT over regular income tax

Assumptions:

a) 1997 income tax rates
b) income tax rates in Years 1 and 2 are the same
c) Optionee B does not receive any Schedule C income during Year 1. He receives $6,258 of Schedule C income on January 15, Year 2.

Table 4.12

Comparison of Cash Flows (See Tables 4.10 and 4.11)
Accelerate versus <u>Not</u> Accelerate Income into Year 1

Date	(A) Accelerate	(B) Not Accelerate	(A) - (B) Difference
Dec 15, Year 1	$6,258[1]	0	$6,258
Jan 15, Year 2	0	6,258[1]	(6,258)
Apr 15, Year 2	(372)[2]	2,140[3]	(2,512)
Apr 15, Year 3	2,884[4]	372[4]	2,512
	$8,770	8,770	0

[1] Optionee B's sole proprietorship receives $6,258 for services provided
[2] Payable to Internal Revenue Service per IRS Form 1040 for the year ended December 31, Year 1
[3] Refund from the Internal Revenue Service per IRS Form 1040 for the year ended December 31, Year 1
[4] Refund from the Internal Revenue Service per IRS Form 1040 for the year ended December 31, Year 2

EXERCISING UNVESTED ISOs

While options are typically *exercisable* on or after the vesting date, some optionees have the opportunity to exercise options, nonqualified as well as incentive stock options, *before* they vest.

Generally, on the date he exercises an *unvested* option (either a nonqualified stock option or an incentive stock option), the stock acquired upon such exercise is:

(A) subject to a substantial risk of forfeiture

and

(B) not transferable.

Table 4.13

Comparison of Income Tax Treatment on Incentive and Nonqualified Stock Options

Example:

Assumes the eventual sale of ISO-stock is a *qualifying disposition*. Therefore, for purposes of the regular income tax, 100 percent of the $90 economic gain ($100 proceeds from sale minus $10 exercise price) is *long-term* capital gain.

Exercise price $ 10
Fair market value (FMV) of the stock on option grant date 10
Fair market value (FMV) of the stock on option exercise date 110
Proceeds from the eventual sale of stock 100 (optionee realizes a $90 gain)

The options do not have a readily ascertainable fair market value on grant date. Therefore, no tax consequences on option grant date.

	Type of Option	Grant Date	Vesting Date	Exercise Date	Holding Period Begins	Basis of Stock Acquired by Exercise of the Option	Capital Gain (loss) on Eventual Sale of Stock
A	Nonqualified stock option	No tax consequences	No tax consequences	$100 compensation income = $110 FMV on exercise date minus $10 exercise price	Option exercise date	$110 = $10 exercise price + $100 compensation income that was reported on IRS Form 1040	($10) long-term capital loss = $100 proceeds minus $110 basis
B	Incentive stock option (for purposes of the regular income tax)	No tax consequences for regular tax	No tax consequences for regular tax	No tax consequences for regular tax	Generally, date of option exercise	Basis for regular tax = $10 = option exercise price	$90 long-term capital gain = $100 proceeds minus $10 basis
	Incentive stock option (for purposes of the alternative minimum tax)	No tax consequences for AMT	No tax consequences for AMT	$100 of AMT income = $110 FMV minus $10 exercise price	Generally, date of option exercise	Basis for AMT = $110 = FMV on option exercise date	($10) AMT long term capital loss = $100 proceeds minus $110 basis

Table 4.14
Comparison of Income Tax Treatment Where Optionee Exercises an ISO in Year 1 and Sells the Stock in a Disqualifying Disposition in Year 2

Example: (see Tables 4.7 and 4.8)

Exercise price	$1,000
Fair market value (FMV) of stock on date of option exercise	$3,000
Exercise date	January 10, Year 1
Sale date	January 5, Year 2

Note 1: Any capital gain or loss shown below is *short-term* because the sale date is not more than 12 months after exercise date.

Note 2: If column (C) below shows a loss, basis of the stock for regular tax purposes (column F) = exercise price (column B).

	(A) Proceeds from Sale of Stock	(B) Exercise Price	(C) Economic Gain (loss) = (A) minus (B)	(D) FMV of Stock on Date of Exercise	(E) Spread on Date of Exercise = (D) minus (B)	(F) Basis for Reg. Tax = (B) plus lesser of (C) or (E)	(G) Basis for AMT = (D)	(H) Year 1 Income for Regular Tax	(I) Year 1 Income for AMT = (E)	(J) Year 2 Income for Regular Tax: Compensation = Lesser of (C) or (E)* and Capital Gain = (A) minus (F)	(K) Year 2 AMT Income = (A) - (G)
Three Possible Scenarios Re: Proceeds from the Eventual Sale of Stock											
Proceeds *greater than* exercise price	$3,200	$1,000	$2,200	$3,000	$2,000	$3,000	$3,000	No tax consequences	$2,000	$2,000 compensation and $200 short-term capital gain	$200 short-term capital gain
Proceeds *equal to* exercise price	$1,000	$1,000	$0	$3,000	$2,000	$1,000	$3,000	No tax consequences	$2,000	$0 compensation, and $0 short-term capital gain	$0 short-term capital gain
Proceeds *less than* exercise price	$900	$1,000	($100)	$3,000	$2,000	$1,000 See Note 2	$3,000	No tax consequences	$2,000	$0 compensation, and $100 short-term capital loss	$2,100 short-term capital loss

* Compensation income is never less than zero. If the lesser of column (C) or (E) yields a negative result, then compensation = zero.

Table 4.15
Comparison of Income Tax Treatment Where Optionee Exercises an ISO in Year 1 and Sells the Stock in a Disqualifying Disposition in Year 2

Example:

Exercise price — $1,000

Fair market value (FMV) of stock on date of option exercise — $3,000

Grant date — January 2, Year 1

Exercise date — January 10, Year 1

Sale date (disqualifying disposition because not more than 2 years after grant date) — January 15, Year 2

Note 1: Any capital gain or loss shown below is *long-term* because the sale date is more than 12 months after exercise date.

Note 2: If column (C) below shows a loss, basis of the stock for regular tax purposes (column F) = exercise price (column B).

	(A)	(B)	(C)	(D)	(E)	(F)	(G)	(H)	(I)	(J)	(K)
Three Possible Scenarios Re: Proceeds from the Eventual Sale of Stock	Proceeds from Sale of Stock	Exercise Price	Economic Gain (loss) = (A) minus (B)	FMV of Stock on Date of Exercise	Spread on Date of Exercise = (D) minus (B)	Basis for Reg. Tax = (B) plus lesser of (C) or (E)	Basis for AMT = (D)	Income for Regular Tax — Year 1	Income for AMT = (E) — Year 1	Income for Regular Tax: Compensation = Lesser of (C) or (E)* and Capital Gain = (A) minus (F) — Year 2	Income for AMT = (A) minus (G) — Year 2
Proceeds greater than exercise price	$3,200	$1,000	$2,200	$3,000	$2,000	$3,000	$3,000	No tax consequences	$2,000	$2,000 compensation, and $200 long-term capital gain	$200 long-term capital gain
Proceeds equal to exercise price	$1,000	$1,000	$0	$3,000	$2,000	$1,000	$3,000	No tax consequences	$2,000	$0 compensation, and $0 long-term capital gain	$0 long-term capital gain
Proceeds less than exercise price	$900	$1,000	($100)	$3,000	$2,000	$1000 see Note 2	$3,000	No tax consequences	$2,000	$0 compensation, and $100 long-term capital loss	$2,100 long-term capital loss

* Compensation income is never less than zero. If the lesser of column (C) or (E) yields a negative result, then compensation = zero.

Table 4.16
Comparison of Income Tax Treatment on Disqualifying Disposition of Stock Acquired by ISO Exercise Optionee Exercises the ISO and Sells the ISO-Stock in the <u>Same</u> Calendar Year

Example:

Exercise price	$ 1,000
Fair market value (FMV) of stock on exercise date	3,000
Exercise Date	January 10, Year 1
Sale Date	March 5, Year 1

(1) The options do not have a readily ascertainable fair market value on grant date. Therefore, no tax consequences on grant date.

Three Different Scenarios	(A) FMV on Exercise Date	(B) Exercise Price	(C) (A) - (B)	(D) Proceeds from Sale of Stock	(E) (D) minus (B) Economic Gain (loss)	(F) Compensation Income Lesser of (C) or (E)	(G) Short-term Capital Gain (loss) on Sale of Stock
A Proceeds from sale of stock are *lower* than the FMV of the stock on exercise date but *higher* than the exercise price (see Table 4.5)	$3,000	$1,000	$2,000	$2,800	$1,800	$1,800 compensation in Year 1	None
B Proceeds from sale of stock are *higher* than the FMV of the stock on exercise date (see Table 4.6)	$3,000	$1,000	$2,000	$3,200	$2,200	$2,000 compensation in Year 1	$200 in Year 1
C Proceeds from sale of stock are *lower* than the exercise price (optionee suffers an economic *loss*)	$3,000	$1,000	$2,000	$900	($100)	None	($100) in Year 1

If the stock acquired is *both* (A) *and* (B) on the date of option exercise (that is, the stock is not vested), the recognition of income is *delayed* until the first time the rights in such stock are *either* not subject to a substantial risk of forfeiture *or* transferable (that is, recognition of income occurs on the vesting date).

Please see Chapter 3 for a discussion of the terms "substantial risk of forfeiture" and "transferable."

INCOME RECOGNITION

REGULAR INCOME TAX

For purposes of regular income tax, the income tax treatment that applies to ISOs does *not* change merely because, on the date of option exercise, the stock acquired by such exercise is *both* subject to a substantial risk of forfeiture *and* not transferable.

The optionee does *not* recognize taxable income on the date of option exercise. He recognizes taxable income (or a capital loss if the proceeds from his sale of stock are less than his option exercise price) on the date he *disposes* of the stock.

ALTERNATIVE MINIMUM TAX

For purposes of AMT, the optionee does *not* recognize taxable income on the date of option exercise if the stock is not vested on the date of exercise. He recognizes taxable income on the first day that his rights in the stock that he acquires by exercise of an ISO are *either* not subject to a substantial risk of forfeiture *or* are transferable (that is, he recognizes taxable income on the vesting date).

The amount of income he recognizes on the vesting date equals the excess of the fair market value of the stock on the vesting date over the option exercise price.

Example: Anna exercises an *unvested* incentive stock option. On the date of option exercise, the stock acquired by such exercise is *both* subject to a substantial risk of forfeiture *and* not transferable. Anna forgets to make a timely IRC Section 83(b) election and therefore does *not* recognize taxable income, for purposes of AMT, on the date of option exercise. The option exercise price is $1. The fair market value of the stock on the date of option exercise is $3. The fair market value of the stock on September 2, Year X, the first day that Anna's rights in the stock are *either* not subject to a substantial risk of forfeiture *or* transferable, is $50. For purposes of AMT, Anna recognizes $49 of taxable income on September 2, Year X.

THE IRC SECTION 83(b) ELECTION

Recall from Chapter 3 that the early exercise of an *unvested* compensatory stock option is effectively an IRC Section 83(b) tax strategy when, on the date of option exercise, the stock acquired by the exercise of such option is *both* subject to a substantial risk of forfeiture *and* not transferable. The optionee exercises the option *and* generally makes a timely Section 83(b) election.

REGULAR INCOME TAX

The IRC Section 83(b) election does *not* change an incentive stock option's *character*. It remains an incentive stock option. Therefore, the option exercise followed by a Section 83(b) election does not result in taxable income for purposes of regular tax.

To summarize, if the optionee exercises an unvested incentive stock option, the Section 83(b) election does *not* trigger the recognition of taxable income, for purposes of the regular income tax, on the date of option exercise. That is because IRC Section 83 does not apply to an ISO for regular income tax purposes on the date of ISO exercise. The legal authority for this tax treatment is found in Regulation 1.422-1(b)(3), issued by the Internal Revenue Service in 2004 (in Treasury Decision 9144).

For regular income tax purposes, the optionee recognizes taxable income (or a capital loss if the proceeds from his sale of stock are less than his option exercise price) on the date he *disposes* of the stock.

QUALIFYING DISPOSITION

The "Explanation of Provisions" that accompanies Treasury Decision 9144 states that "...there is a transfer (as defined in Section 1.421-1(g) of the final regulations) of the stock on the date of exercise for purposes of the holding period requirement of section 422(a)(1). Thus, the holding period for the transfer of the stock for purposes of section 422 and the holding period requirements begins on the date of exercise (rather that the date of vesting)."

In short, the optionee makes a qualifying disposition of ISO-stock, which was not vested on the date of option exercise because the ISO was not vested at that time, if the sale date is:

- more than two years after the option grant date,

  and,

- more than 12 months after the date of option *exercise* (in other words, the sale date does *not* have to be more than 12 months after the stock *vests*).

DISQUALIFYING DISPOSITION

If he makes a disqualifying disposition of ISO-stock that was not vested on option exercise date, IRC Section 83(a) is used to measure the consequences of the disposition, and the special rule under IRC Section 422(c)(2) limits compensation income to the amount of actual gain, if any, on the sale.

In short, if he makes a disqualifying disposition, he recognizes ordinary compensation income, if any, on the date of such disposition to the extent of the *lesser* of:

(a) the difference between the fair market value of such stock on the date the stock *vested* and the exercise price (this is the measurement provided by IRC Section 83(a)),

  or,

(b) the difference between the amount received in the disposition and the exercise price (that is, compensation income is limited, under the special rule in IRC Section 422(c)(2), to the actual gain on the sale, if any).

Compensation income cannot be less than zero, however.

The next example is adapted from Regulation 1.422-1(b)(3) Example 2 and shows the income tax treatment that applies if the optionee sells the ISO-stock, after the stock vests, in a disqualifying disposition.

Example: *Disqualifying disposition of ISO-stock that was not vested on the date of ISO-exercise:* On June 1, 2006, X Corporation grants an incentive stock option to Tina, an employee of X Corporation, entitling Tina to purchase one share of X Corporation stock. On August 1, 2006, Tina exercises the option and the share of X Corporation stock is transferred to her on that date. The option exercise price is $100, which is the fair market value of the stock on the June 1, 2006 grant date, and the fair market value on the August 1, 2006 exercise date and date of transfer is $200. The share of X Corporation stock received by Tina is subject to a substantial risk of forfeiture and not transferable (that is, the stock is not vested) for a period of six months after the date of exercise. On February 1, 2007, the six-month restriction lapses (that is, the stock vests), and the fair market value at that time is $225. Tina makes a disqualifying disposition by selling the share on June 1, 2007 for $250. That disposition triggers compensation income in the amount of $125, which is the *lesser* of:

(a) $125, computed as the $225 fair market value on the date the stock *vested* over the $100 amount paid for the stock, *or,*

(b) $150, which equals the $250 proceeds from the sale minus the $100 amount paid (in other words, $150 is the actual gain on the sale of stock)

The ISO-stock basis is $225, which consists of the $100 amount paid plus $125 of compensation income recognized. Tina also recognizes a $25 capital gain, which equals the $250 proceeds from the sale minus her $225 basis.

HOLDING PERIOD FOR CAPITAL GAIN PURPOSES

Regulation 1.422-1(b)(3) Example 2, as corrected and published in the *Federal Register* on December 7, 2004, addresses the regular income tax and states that "...the holding period for capital gain purposes begins on the vesting date..." if the sale is a disqualifying disposition.

Example: Holding period of ISO-stock (for determining whether any capital gain from a disqualifying disposition is short-term or long-term), that was not vested on the date of ISO-exercise, begins on vesting date: In the previous example, Tina's ISO-stock vested on February 1, 2007. In accordance with Regulation 1.422-1(b)(3) Example 2, her holding period starts on that day. Consequently, the June 1, 2007 sale, which is a disqualifying disposition, results in a $25 *short-term* capital gain because the sale date is not more than 12 months after February 1, 2007.

The next section uses the facts from the example above to illustrate the income tax treatment for purposes of AMT.

ALTERNATIVE MINIMUM TAX

Regulation 1.422-1(b)(3) Example 2 states that an optionee is permitted to make an IRC Section 83(b) election – for purposes of AMT only – if he exercises an unvested ISO. In the example above, Tina's election triggers taxable income on the date of option exercise, for purposes of AMT.

The amount of taxable income that she recognizes in the year of ISO exercise, for purposes of AMT, equals the fair market value of the stock on the date of option exercise over the option exercise price. Consequently, Tina recognizes $100 of AMT income in Year 2006, which is computed as the $200 fair market value of the stock on the August 1, 2006 option exercise date over her $100 option exercise price.

Tina's basis in the stock for purposes of AMT is $200, which equals her $100 option exercise price plus the $100 of AMT taxable income she recognizes (that is, basis equals the fair market value of the stock on the date of option exercise). Therefore, Tina's sale of stock for $250 on June 1, 2007 results in a capital gain in the amount of $50, computed as $250 of proceeds minus her $200 basis.

$100,000 LIMIT UNDER IRC SECTION 422(d)

Under Internal Revenue Code Section 422(d), an individual cannot receive an unlimited amount of incentive stock options. Tax law says that to the extent the aggregate fair market value of stock with respect to which incentive stock options are exercisable for the first time during any *calendar* year (under all plans of the individual's employer corporation and its parent and subsidiary corporations) exceeds $100,000, such options shall be treated as options that are not incentive stock options. It also provides that the $100,000 amount is determined as of the time the option is *granted*.

Example: *The $100,000 annual limit is based on the fair market value of the stock on the date of option grant:* ABC Corporation makes an ISO grant to Lilian on January 2, Year 1, that allows her to buy 100,000 shares of ABC stock at $1 per share. The fair market value of ABC stock is $1 per share on option grant date (the fair market value of the stock on the date of ISO exercise is *irrelevant* for purposes of the $100,000 limit). The options vest over 4 years, such that options on 25,000 shares are first exercisable in calendar Year 1, options on 25,000 shares are first exercisable in calendar Year 2, options on 25,000 shares are first exercisable in calendar Year 3, and options on 25,000 shares are first exercisable in calendar Year 4. The $100,000 annual limit has not been reached for any of the four years, because 25,000 shares multiplied by the $1 fair market value on the date of grant is only $25,000. In fact, on January 2, Year 1, ABC could have granted options on 400,000 shares (instead of only 100,000 shares) and all of the options would have been ISOs.

In short, IRC Section 422(d) effectively limits the number of incentive stock options that may become *exercisable* by an individual during any calendar year. It provides that if this number is exceeded, such "excess" options "..shall be treated as options which are not incentive stock options". In other words, the incentive stock options become *nonqualified stock options*.

$100,000 ANNUAL LIMIT AND UNVESTED ISOS

The Internal Revenue Service would likely argue that the mere *opportunity* to exercise unvested ISOs makes such ISOs *exercisable.* The optionee needs to be aware of this *before* he applies to the optionor corporation requesting the opportunity to make an early exercise of unvested ISOs. He needs to be aware because, if the corporation grants the opportunity to exercise early, some of his ISOs could become NQSOs *even if* he later decides *not* to exercise such unvested ISOs.

T.D. 9144 Final Regulations for Statutory Options

In Treasury Decision 9144, the Internal Revenue Service stated that the effective date for the final regulations on statutory options is August 3, 2004. It also stated there is a transition period, which expires on or before January 1, 2006, during which taxpayers may rely on certain previously published Proposed Regulations, or the final regulations under T.D. 9144 – but whichever they choose, such choice "...must be in its entirety." For example, taxpayers cannot choose to rely on the 2003 Proposed Regulations for one item, and rely on the final regulations for another.

The IRS wrote "For rules concerning reliance and transition period, see regulations sections 1.421-1(j)(2), 1.421-(2)(f)(2), 1.422-5(f)(2), and 1.424-1(g)(2)." A discussion of the transition rules, or how to make a wise choice of regulations on which to rely, is beyond the scope of this book.

5

Tax-deferred Exchanges

At the time of ISO exercise, the optionee may pay for shares in cash. Tax law also permits a cashless exercise (followed by a same-day sale of stock) and a tax-deferred exchange under Internal Revenue Code Section 1036.

The general rule under IRC Section 1036 is that "No gain or loss shall be recognized if common stock in a corporation is exchanged solely for common stock in the same corporation...". IRC Section 422(c)(4)(A) provides that "the employee may pay for the stock with stock of the corporation granting the option".

If the employer's plan permits, optionees who already own shares, including shares previously purchased on the open market, may exchange them for shares of the same corporation without triggering income tax on unrealized capital gain that exists in the shares already owned. In effect, optionees use "old" shares (instead of cash) to pay for "new" shares to be acquired by exercising options – in a *tax-deferred exchange*.

EXERCISING <u>NQSO</u>S AND PAYING WITH STOCK THAT HAD BEEN ACQUIRED BY EXERCISE OF A NONQUALIFIED STOCK OPTION

The following example shows how an optionee exercises vested nonqualified stock options (NQSOs) using shares of stock that he already owns as payment of the exercise price – *without* triggering an income tax liability on any of the appreciation in the shares that he already owns.

Example: The current price of ABC stock is $5 per share. On December 10, Year 1, Patricia wants to exercise vested *NQSOs* that give her the right to purchase 100 shares of her employer's stock (ABC Corporation) at an exercise price of $1 per share. She prefers to exercise without using cash.

She already owns shares: Pat owns 20 shares of ABC stock that have a current fair market value of $100. She acquired the shares on January 2, Year 1 by exercising *NQSOs*. Her exercise price was $1 per share ($20). The fair market value of ABC stock on the date of exercise was $3 per share ($60).

Basis of 20 "old" shares: The basis of the 20 shares is $60, the fair market value on the date she exercised the NQSOs.

If she sells 20 "old" shares to raise cash: If she sells the 20 old shares at $5 per share, her gross proceeds are $100. Her basis is $60. She pays income tax on a $40 short-term capital gain. The gain would be short-term because the December 10, Year 1 date of sale is not more than 12 months after the January 2, Year 1 date of acquisition. She doesn't like this alternative because the sale of stock triggers an income tax liability. Instead, she makes a tax-deferred exchange of 20 "old" shares for 100 "new" shares.

Tax-deferred exchange: On December 10, Year 1, Patricia exercises NQSOs on 100 shares of stock (at an exercise price of $1 per share). She pays the $100 exercise price by surrendering 20 "old" shares, which have a fair market value of $100, to ABC Corporation. In exchange for the 20 "old" shares, she receives 100 "new" shares from ABC Corporation. No cash is required.

Taxable gain: Patricia recognizes $400 of ordinary compensation income on December 10, Year 1, the date of NQSO exercise. That taxable gain is equal to the excess of the $500 ($5 per share) fair market value of the shares on the date of exercise over the $100 ($1 per share) exercise price.

Basis of 100 "new" shares: She now holds 100 "new" shares. IRC Section 1031(d) provides that if property is acquired in an exchange described in IRC Section 1036(a), the basis of that property shall be the same as that of the property exchanged. Therefore, as discussed in IRS Private Letter Ruling 9629028, Patricia's basis in 20 of the "new" shares is $60 (the same as her basis in the 20 "old" shares that she surrenders). Patricia's basis in 80 of the "new" shares is $400, the amount of taxable compensation income she recognizes on the exercise of the nonqualified stock options. Her total basis in the 100 shares is $460.

Acquisition date for computing holding period: Under IRC Section 1223, the date of acquisition on 20 of the "new" shares, for purposes of computing her holding period, is January 2, Year 1, the date she originally acquired the 20 "old" shares. The date of acquisition on 80 of the "new" shares begins on December 10, Year 1, the date she exercises the NQSOs on 100 shares of stock.

Summary: The stock-for-stock exchange under Internal Revenue Code Section 1036 allows Patricia to use the $100 fair market value of stock she currently owns to pay the $100 exercise price to acquire the 100 new shares – without paying income tax on the $40 of unrealized appreciation in the "old" shares.

SURRENDERING SHARES PREVIOUSLY ACQUIRED THROUGH THE EXERCISE OF AN ISO OR THROUGH PARTICIPATION IN A QUALIFIED STOCK PURCHASE PLAN

In the above stock-for-stock example, Patricia exchanges 20 "old" shares of stock which she previously acquired by exercising a *nonqualified* stock option.

The federal income tax consequences are different if the 20 "old" shares had been acquired (1) by exercising an incentive stock option *or* (2) via participation in a qualified stock purchase plan, *and* (3) applicable holding period requirements are *not* met *before* surrendering the "old" shares. In this situation, the surrender of the "old" shares is treated as a disqualifying disposition.

If the applicable holding periods for stock acquired by ISO exercise (more than 12 months after exercise date *and* more than two years after grant date) on the 20 shares *have* been satisfied, however, the stock-for-stock exchange defers the recognition of the $40 of appreciation in the 20 shares which are surrendered.

EXERCISING ISOS AND PAYING WITH STOCK

Regulation 1.422-5(b)(1) states that an option does not fail to be an ISO merely because the optionee may exercise it using previously acquired stock of the grantor of such ISO. Generally, however, unpleasant tax consequences arise if the optionee uses *immature* ISO-stock because that is a disqualifying disposition. Unpleasant tax consequences also arise if the optionee uses previously acquired stock to pay the exercise price and later makes a disqualifying disposition – because Regulation 1.422-5(b)(2) states that the "...disqualifying disposition of any stock acquired through such exercise is treated as a disqualifying disposition of the shares with the lowest basis."

The following example shows how an optionee exercises incentive stock options (ISOs) using *mature* ISO-stock.

Example: The current price of ABC stock is $5 per share. On December 10, Year 3, Patricia wants to exercise *ISOs* that give her the right to purchase 100 shares of her employer's stock (ABC Corporation) at an exercise price of $1 per share. She prefers to pay the exercise price without using cash.

She already owns shares: Pat owns 20 shares of ABC stock that she acquired on January 2, Year 1 by exercising *ISOs*. Her exercise price was $1 per share ($20). The fair market value on the date of exercise was $3 per share ($60).

Basis of 20 "old" shares: Patricia's basis for regular tax purposes is $20, the exercise price. Her basis for AMT purposes is $60, the fair market value of the stock on the date of ISO exercise.

Tax-deferred exchange: On December 10, Year 3, Patricia exercises ISOs on 100 shares of stock (at an exercise price of $1 per share). She pays the $100 exercise price by surrendering 20 old shares, which have a fair market value of $100, to ABC Corporation. The surrender of the 20 ISO-shares is *not* a disqualifying disposition because *prior* to the date of surrender she had already satisfied holding period requirements. In exchange for the 20 old shares, she receives 100 new shares.

Taxable gain for regular tax purposes: The December 10, Year 3 exercise does not trigger the recognition of taxable income.

Taxable gain for AMT purposes: Patricia recognizes $400 of income in Year 3, which equals the $500 fair market value on exercise date over the $100 ($1 per share) exercise price.

Basis of 100 "new" shares for regular tax purposes: Under Regulation 1.422-5(b)(3)(ii) (consistent with IRS Private Letter Ruling 9629028), Patricia's basis in 20 of the "new" shares is $20 (the same as her basis in the 20 "old" shares that she surrenders). Patricia's basis in 80 of the "new" shares is $0.

Basis of 100 "new" shares for AMT purposes: In accordance with IRC Section 1031(d) and guidance from IRS Private Letter Ruling 9629028, it appears that Patricia's basis in 20 of the "new" shares is $60 (the same as her basis in the 20 "old" shares that she surrenders), and her basis in 80 of the "new" shares is $400, which equals the cash she pays (zero) plus $400 of AMT income she recognizes on the date that she exercises the ISOs.

Acquisition date for computing holding period: Under IRC Section 1223, the date of acquisition on 20 of the "new" shares, for purposes of computing her holding period, is January 2, Year 1, the date she acquired the 20 "old" shares. The date of acquisition on 80 of the "new" shares begins on December 10, Year 3, the date she exercises the ISOs on 100 shares of stock.

Acquisition date for determining qualifying versus disqualifying disposition: As discussed in Private Letter Ruling 9629028, the holding period for purposes of determining whether the eventual disposition of the 100 shares of "new" stock acquired by ISO exercise is a qualifying or disqualifying disposition begins on December 10, Year 3, the date of ISO exercise. Regulation 1.422-5(b)(2) provides that date applies to *all* 100 shares. Consequently, if Pat disposes of shares before December 11, Year 4 the disposition will be treated as disqualifying.

DISQUALIFYING DISPOSITION OF ISO-STOCK

The next two examples are adapted from Regulation 1.422-5(e) Examples 1 and 2. Example 1 illustrates the exercise of a vested ISO, using shares previously purchased on the open market. Example 2 illustrates the unpleasant tax consequences (shares with the *lowest* basis treated as sold) that arise under Regulation 1.422-5(b)(2) if the optionee later makes a disqualifying disposition.

Example 1: On June 1, 2004, X Corporation grants an ISO to A, an employee of X Corporation, entitling A to purchase 100 shares of X Corporation common stock at $10 per share. The option provides that A may exercise the option with previously acquired shares of X Corporation common stock. X Corporation has only one class of common stock outstanding. Under the rules of section 83, the shares transferable to A through the exercise of the option are vested. On June 1, 2005, when the fair market value of an X Corporation share is $25, A uses 40 shares of X Corporation common stock, which A had purchased on the open market on June 1, 2002, for $5 per share, to pay the full option price. After exercising the option, A owns 100 shares of ISO-stock. Forty of the shares have a $200 aggregate carryover basis (the $5 purchase price x 40 shares) and a three-year holding period for purposes of determining capital gain, and 60 of the shares have a zero basis and a holding period beginning on June 1, 2005, for purposes of determining capital gain. All 100 shares have a holding period beginning on June 1, 2005, for purposes of determining whether the special holding period requirements are satisfied.

Example 2: Assume the same facts as in Example 1. Assume further that, on September 1, 2005, A sells 75 of the shares that A acquired through exercise of the incentive stock option for $30 per share. Because the holding period requirements were not satisfied, A made a disqualifying disposition of the 75 shares on September 1, 2005. Under Regulation 1.422-5(b)(3), A has sold 60 shares that have a zero basis, and 15 shares that have a $25 basis. The amount of compensation attributable to A's exercise of the option and subsequent disqualifying disposition of 75 shares is $1,500 (the difference between the fair market value of the stock on the date of transfer, $1,875 (75 shares at $25 per share), and the amount paid for the stock, $375 (60 shares at $0 per share plus 15 shares at $25 per share)). In addition, A must recognize a capital gain of $675, which consists of $375 ($450, the amount realized from the sale of 15 shares, less A's basis of $75) plus $300 ($1,800, the amount realized from the sale of 60 shares, less A's basis of $1,500 resulting from the inclusion of that amount in income as compensation). Accordingly, A must include in gross income for the taxable year in which the sale occurs $1,500 as compensation and $675 as capital gain.

6

Two Tax-saving Strategies (but are they right for you?)

Two of the more common tax-saving strategies that involve compensatory stock options are examined in this chapter. One is the exercise of ISOs and sale of stock 12 months and one day later, the objective of which is to convert ordinary income into long-term capital gain. The other is the early exercise of vested NQSOs, the objective of which is to convert anticipated appreciation in the stock price after the date of exercise into long-term capital gain.

I. EXERCISE ISOs AND HOLD THE STOCK

In most cases, the relevant question for the ISO holder is: Which projected series of cash flows is likely to offer more value, those that result from:

- Exercising ISOs and selling the stock on the same day,

  or,

- Exercising ISOs and selling the stock 12 months and one day after exercise?

Two Critical Conditions

As a *general rule*, exercising ISOs and selling the stock 12 months and one day after exercise is most appropriate where two conditions are present:

- the optionee is subject to a marginal income tax rate on ordinary income that is *substantially* in *excess* of the tax rate on long-term capital gains, *and*

- the option exercise price is relatively *low* in relation to the fair market value of the stock on the date of exercise.

One should observe that the optionee who is subject to higher marginal income tax rates on ordinary income reaps more of an income tax savings when he converts ordinary income into long-term capital gain than the optionee who is subject to a lower marginal income tax rate on ordinary income.

One should also observe that if the exercise price is relatively low in relation to the fair market value of the stock on the date of exercise it means that the gain is larger. Naturally, the larger the gain, the more the income tax savings on the conversion of that gain from ordinary income into long-term capital gain.

As the excess of the marginal rate on ordinary income over the rate of tax on long-term capital gain *declines*, <u>or</u> as the exercise price as a percentage of the fair market value of the stock *increases*, exercising ISOs and holding the stock for 12 months and one day becomes a less attractive alternative.

In fact, exercising ISOs and holding the stock for 12 months and one day is not a wealth-maximizing strategy for many optionees because the internal rate of return that results from this strategy is sometimes less – and often substantially less – than rates of return on alternative investments of equivalent risk.

Same-Day Sale

The *advantages* of an ISO exercise and same-day sale of stock, relative to exercising the ISO and holding the stock for 12 months and one day, are that (1) the same-day sale *generates* cash on the date of exercise, while exercising and holding the stock *requires* cash on the date of exercise, *and* (2) the optionee eliminates the possibility of a decline in the stock price over the next 12 months.

The *disadvantages* of exercising an ISO and selling the stock on the same day is that the sale is a disqualifying disposition that triggers recognition of ordinary income, *and* it eliminates the potential for appreciation in the stock price over the next 12 months.

ANALYSIS OF THE TWO ALTERNATIVES

In order to project the future cash flows that will result *exclusively* from one alternative versus the other, the optionee first prepares three *income tax projections* for *every* tax year that will be affected by either one of the two mutually exclusive alternatives:

- Tax projection #1 assumes that No ISOs are exercised

- Tax projection #2 assumes that ISOs are exercised and the stock is sold on the same-day

- Tax projection #3 assumes that ISOs are exercised and the stock is sold 12 months and one day later

All three projections assume that, 12 months and one day after the date of ISO exercise, the stock price will be equal to the exercise price. By assuming a constant stock price, the optionee isolates the cash flow effects that are associated exclusively with income taxation. But optionees must remember from Table 2.5 that, in most cases (depending on stock price volatility), the probability is *greater than 50 percent* that the stock price 12 months later will be *lower* than it is today.

Second, the optionee prepares a schedule of the *projected future cash flows* under each alternative. That schedule shows the amount and date of each projected cash flow.

Third, using the schedule from step two, he computes the *differential cash flows* associated with one alternative relative to the other. From those differential cash flows, he computes the *projected internal rate of return (IRR)* that he earns from the decision to exercise ISOs and hold the stock for 12 months and one day.

THE ELEMENTS OF A WISE DECISION

Four sections, labeled A through D, follow this subsection:

- *Section A "Exercise ISOs and Sell the Stock on Same-Day"* shows the income tax and cash flows that result from a same-day sale of stock

- *Section B "Exercise ISOs and Sell Stock 12 Months and One Day Later"* shows the income tax and cash flows that result from holding the stock for 12 months and one day

- *Section C "Comparison of Same-Day Sale to Holding for 12 Months and One Day"* compares the cash flows from Sections A and B

- *Section D "Investment Analysis"* offers investment analysis and commentary

Sections A through D are based upon one simplified example that assumes (1) no state income taxes, (2) that exercising ISOs and holding the stock does not trigger alternative minimum tax, *and* (3) that the optionee's federal marginal income tax rate remains constant every year.

Example: Employees A and B hold ISOs on 1,000 shares of stock. The exercise price is $60 per share. The fair market value of the stock is $100 per share. The stock does not pay a dividend. Employee A's federal marginal income tax rate is 28 percent and B's is 35 percent. Both employees exercise options on January 15, Year 1. *Which is more advantageous – the same-day sale, or exercising and holding the stock for 12 months and one day?*

A: EXERCISE ISOs AND SELL THE STOCK ON SAME-DAY

FEDERAL INCOME TAXATION

When they exercise ISOs and sell the stock on the same day, Employees A and B make disqualifying dispositions because they do not hold the stock for more than 12 months.

Consequently, gain is taxed as *ordinary compensation* income to the extent of the *lesser* of (a) the difference between the fair market value of the stock on the date of exercise and the option price, *and* (b) the difference between the amount received in the disposition and the option price. If (b) is greater than (a), such excess is treated as a *short-term capital gain.*

For Employees A and B, (a) equals $40,000 ($100,000 - 60,000) and (b) also equals $40,000. Therefore, both recognize $40,000 of ordinary compensation income from a same-day sale. There is no short-term capital gain because (b) is *not* greater than (a).

Table 6.1 shows (1) computation of the gain, and (2) the amount of federal income tax on that gain.

CASH FLOWS

The cash flows to Employees A and B are shown in Table 6.2.

The exercise and same-day sale produces a $40,000 gain on January 15, Year 1 which is taxed as ordinary compensation income. As discussed earlier, the gain is not subject to federal income tax *withholding,* and not subject to social security tax, or Medicare tax. Consequently, the optionee receives the entire $40,000 gain on *settlement date,* generally not more than three business days after the date of sale.

Employee A incurs a federal income tax *liability* on the date of sale in the amount of $11,200 (28% X $40,000), and Employee B incurs a liability of $14,000 (35% X $40,000). In many situations, however, the tax is not *payable* until April 15, Year 2, the due date for filing IRS Form 1040 for the year ending December 31, Year 1.

Table 6.1

After-tax Gain for Employees A and B from a Same-Day Sale
(Assuming no State Income Tax and no AMT)

	A	B
Proceeds from sale of stock	$100,000	$100,000
Less: ISO exercise price	60,000	60,000
Pre-tax gain	40,000	40,000
Less:federal income tax[1]	11,200	14,000
After-tax gain	$ 28,800	$ 26,000

[1] Employee A's marginal income tax rate is 28% and B's is 35%. The $40,000 taxable gain is *not* subject to income tax *withholding*.

Table 6.2

Cash Flows to Employees A and B if Same-Day Sale
(Assuming no State Income Tax and no AMT)

Date	Event	A	B
Jan 15[3], Year 1	Exercise and sell stock[1]	$40,000	40,000
Apr 15, Year 2	Pay federal income tax[2]	- 11,200	-14,000
Net cash flow		$28,800	26,000

[1] Proceeds from sale of stock = $100,000. Exercise price = $60,000.
[2] Employee A's marginal income tax rate is 28% and B's is 35%.
[3] Cash is actually received on *settlement* date, generally not more than three business days after the date of sale.

Since there is no withholding, Employees A and B have use of the entire $40,000 gain for 15 months – from January 15, Year 1 (date of sale) until April 15, Year 2 (date of tax payment).

In this example, no income tax withholding is required. In some cases, however, the optionee is required to make *estimated tax payments* as a result of gain attributable to ISOs in order to avoid a **penalty** for underpayment of estimated tax.

B. EXERCISE ISOs AND SELL STOCK 12 MONTHS AND ONE DAY LATER

In a world where individuals strive to maximize the value of ISOs, an optionee exercises ISOs well in advance of the option's expiration date because his unique needs or circumstances dictate that, at some point *between* the date of exercise and 12 months and one day later, it is time for him to sell stock. Otherwise, he would follow the general rule discussed earlier and *not* exercise until just prior to option expiration date.

Given that the optionee exercises ISOs because he has decided that it's time to sell stock, there must be an underlying incentive that would entice him to *hold* the stock. That motivating incentive – preferential tax treatment of long-term capital gains – must be strong enough to overcome the fact that if he exercises ISOs and holds the stock, he (1) incurs opportunity costs, *and* (2) assumes the risk of decline in the stock price.

OPPORTUNITY COSTS

When they exercise ISOs and make a same-day sale of stock, Employees A and B both *receive* $40,000 on settlement date (see Table 6.2). When Employees A and B exercise ISOs and *hold* the stock, they *pay* $60,000 to effect the exercise.

The *difference* between the $40,000 that they *would* receive from a same-day sale, and the $60,000 that they must *pay* to exercise and hold, is $100,000. Essentially, then, both optionees invest $100,000 (the fair market value of the stock on the date of exercise) when they exercise ISOs and hold the stock. When they invest $100,000 in the stock, this $100,000 is not available for investment elsewhere.

FEDERAL INCOME TAXATION

See Table 6.3. Recall that Employees A and B exercise ISOs on January 15, Year 1. The assumption in Table 6.3 is that they sell the stock on January 16, Year 2. The price of the stock on January 16, Year 2 (the date of sale) is $100 per share, the same as its price on January 15, Year 1 (the date of ISO exercise)

The sales by Employees A and B are *not* disqualifying dispositions because the sale date is more than 12 months after exercise date. Therefore, the $40,000 gain is taxed as long-term capital gain. Federal income tax on that gain is $6,000 (15% x $40,000 = $6,000) for both optionees.

CASH FLOWS

The cash flows to Employees A and B are shown in Table 6.4.

On January 15, Year 1 both employees exercise ISOs by *paying* $60,000 to acquire 1,000 shares of stock. On January 16, Year 2, they both *receive* $100,000 from the sale of 1,000 shares of stock. They both realize a $40,000 long-term capital gain.

The $40,000 *long-term* capital gain is subject to income tax at the rate of 15 percent, resulting in a $6,000 federal income tax *liability*. That liability is *payable* not later than April 15, Year 3 with IRS Form 1040 for the year ending December 31, Year 2. Net cash flow from the transactions is $34,000 for both employees.

C: COMPARISON OF SAME-DAY SALE TO HOLDING FOR 12 MONTHS AND ONE DAY

The exercise and hold alternative *appears* advantageous in that the optionee pays less income tax. But, the amount of tax savings relative to the amount of money that the optionee must invest to generate that tax savings, *and* the *risk* that he takes to generate that savings might be minimal. Consequently, it is *not* always wise to exercise ISOs and hold the stock in order to strive for favorable tax treatment on long-term capital gain.

Table 6.3

After-tax Gain from Exercising ISOs and Selling the Stock 12 Months and One Day Later in a Non-disqualifying Disposition
(Assuming no State Income Tax and no AMT)

	A	B
Sale of stock at $100 per share	$100,000	$100,000
Less: ISO exercise price	60,000	60,000
Long-term capital gain	40,000	40,000
Less: federal income tax @ 15%	6,000	6,000
After-tax gain	34,000	34,000

Table 6.4

Cash Flows to Employees A and B if They Exercise ISOs and Sell the Stock 12 Months and One Day Later
(Assuming no State Income Tax and no AMT)

Date	Event	A	B
Jan15, Year 1	Exercise ISOs on 1,000 shares[1]	-$ 60,000	- 60,000
Jan16, Year 2	Sell 1,000 shares of stock[2]	+100,000	+100,000
Apr 15, Year 3	Pay federal income tax[3]	-6,000	-6,000
Net cash flow		$ 34,000	34,000

[1] Exercise price = $60 per share.
[2] Selling price = $100 per share.
[3] Both employees pay 15 percent tax on $40,000 long-term capital gain.

In short:

- *What is the projected rate of return on the decision to exercise and hold the stock for 12 months and one day, assuming a constant stock price?* and,

- *How does that projected rate of return compare to projected returns on alternative investments of equivalent risk?*

FEDERAL INCOME TAX

Table 6.5 compares the federal income tax liabilities that result from a same-day sale (see Table 6.1) to those that result from exercising ISOs and selling the stock 12 months and one day later (see Table 6.3).

Employees A and B both pay $6,000 in federal income tax under the exercise and hold strategy. The $6,000 tax liability is $5,200 less than the $11,200 Employee A pays if he makes a same-day sale. The $6,000 tax is $8,000 less than the $14,000 Employee B pays if he makes a same-day sale.

In other words, holding the stock for 12 months and one day is more advantageous for Employee B than for Employee A. This is because Employee B's tax rate on the $40,000 gain is reduced by 20 percentage points – from 35 percent (his marginal rate on ordinary income) to 15 percent (his tax rate on long-term capital gain). Employee A's tax rate is reduced by only 13 percentage points – from 28 percent (his marginal rate on ordinary income) to 15 percent (his tax rate on long-term capital gain).

CASH FLOWS

The cash flows from a same-day sale are presented in Table 6.2. The cash flows from exercising and holding the stock for 12 months and one day are presented in Table 6.4. The difference between the two series of cash flows for Employee A is shown in Table 6.6. The difference between the two series of cash flows for Employee B is shown in Table 6.7.

Table 6.5

**Comparison of Employee A's and B's Federal Income Tax:
Exercise ISOs and Same-Day Sale of Stock vs. Exercise ISOs
and Sell the Stock 12 Months and One Day Later
(Assuming no State Income Tax and no AMT)**

	A	B
Federal tax from a same-day sale[1]	$11,200	14,000
Federal tax from exercise and hold[2]	6,000	6,000
Federal tax savings from exercise and hold	$ 5,200	8,000

[1] from Table 6.1
[2] from Table 6.3

By analyzing the amounts and timing of the *differential* cash flows associated with these two mutually exclusive alternatives, the optionee quantifies the *projected* after-tax internal rate of return that results *exclusively* from the decision to exercise and hold. He then compares that return to expected returns on alternative investment opportunities of *equivalent risk*.

AFTER-TAX IRR

When the optionee exercises ISOs and holds the stock for 12 months and one day, he invests $100,000 for a period of 12 months and one day. He expects to earn a rate of return on that investment, a return that adequately compensates him for the risk he assumes from holding the stock.

The projected income tax savings that result from holding the stock may not be sufficient in relation to the risk that the optionee assumes of a substantial decline in the stock price. The more volatile the stock, the more risky it is to exercise ISOs and hold the stock.

Table 6.6

Differential Projected Cash Flows to Employee A, and Projected IRR from Exercising ISOs and Holding the Stock for 12 Months and One Day

DATE	(A) EXERCISE & HOLD[1]	(B) SAME-DAY SALE[2]	(A) - (B) DIFFERENCE
Jan/Yr 1	($60,000)	40,000	($100,000)
Jan/Yr 2	100,000	0	100,000
Apr/Yr 2	0	(11,200)	11,200
Apr/Yr 3	(6,000)	0	(6,000)
Net cash flow	34,000	28,800	5,200

Projected after-tax IRR from the decision to **exercise and hold**:

Projected after-tax annual IRR = 5.3% (compounded monthly)

[1] from Table 6.4
[2] from Table 6.2

Table 6.8 shows the projected *after-tax annual internal rate of return (IRR)*, compounded monthly, that results *exclusively* from the decision to exercise ISOs and sell the stock 12 months and one day later, as opposed to making an exercise and same-day sale. The returns shown in this table assume a constant stock price, a constant federal marginal income tax rate, no state income tax, no alternative minimum tax, and various other factors as disclosed in the table.

Notice from Table 6.8 that, all things being equal, the higher the federal marginal income tax rate on ordinary income, the higher the projected after-tax return from exercising and holding, relative to the same-day sale. Also notice that, all things being equal, the lower the exercise price of the ISO relative to the stock price on the date of exercise, the higher the projected after-tax return from exercising and holding.

Table 6.7

Differential Projected Cash Flows to Employee B, and Projected IRR from Exercising ISOs and Holding the Stock for 12 Months and One Day

DATE	(A) EXERCISE & HOLD[1]	(B) SAME-DAY SALE[2]	(A) - (B) DIFFERENCE
Jan/Yr 1	($60,000)	40,000	($100,000)
Jan/Yr 2	100,000	0	100,000
Apr/Yr 2	0	(14,000)	14,000
Apr/Yr 3	(6,000)	0	(6,000)
Net cash flow	34,000	26,000	8,000

Projected after-tax IRR from the decision to <u>exercise and hold</u>:

Projected after-tax annual IRR = 8.0% (compounded monthly)

[1] from Table 6.4
[2] from Table 6.2

The exercise and hold strategy becomes increasingly attractive when the optionee's marginal tax rate on ordinary income is higher or when his gain is larger, or both. This is logical because under these two conditions the optionee enjoys more of an income tax savings from converting ordinary income into long-term capital gain.

Since many variables affect the IRR, and since the assumptions used in Table 6.8 are unlikely to fit exactly the unique circumstances of individual optionees, Table 6.8 should be used as a guide only. It is not a substitute for comprehensive planning, particularly when large sums of money are involved.

Example: Debra holds ISOs that have an exercise price equal to 30 percent of the current stock price. Her income is subject to a federal marginal income tax rate of 35 percent. Table 6.8 shows that Debra earns an after-tax return of 13.9 percent if she exercises the options and holds the stock for 12 months and one day, relative to exercising options and making a same-day sale of stock.

Comprehensive planning, however, shows a projected after-tax return of less than 13.9 percent on the decision to exercise and hold. The following factors affect Debra's projected return. First, her income *is* subject to state income taxation. Second, the AMT *does* impact her projected cash flows. Third, she exercises ISOs on August 15, not January 15.

Table 6.8

Projected After-tax Annual Rate of Return from the Decision to Exercise ISOs and Sell the Stock 12 Months and One Day Later When the Tax Rate on Long-term Capital Gain is 15 Percent

EXERCISE PRICE AS A % OF STOCK PRICE	MARGINAL INCOME TAX RATE			
	28%	30%	35%	40%
90%	1.3%	1.5	2.0	2.5
80	2.6	3.0	4.0	5.0
70	4.0	4.6	6.0	7.4
60	**5.3**	6.1	**8.0**	9.8
50	6.7	7.6	10.0	12.2
40	8.0	9.2	12.0	14.6
30	9.4	10.7	**13.9**	17.0
20	10.8	12.3	15.9	19.3
10	12.1	13.8	17.8	21.5

Assumptions:

1. Employee exercises ISO on January 15
2. ISO exercise does not trigger alternative minimum tax
3. Excluding the impact of state income taxes and transaction costs
4. Neither alternative affects estimated tax payment requirements
5. The stock does not pay a dividend
6. Optionee's marginal income tax rate is the same every year

D: INVESTMENT ANALYSIS

Which alternative is more attractive – exercise ISOs and hold the stock for 12 months and one day, or exercise ISOs and sell the stock on the same day? For some optionees, there *isn't* a choice. They don't have the financial resources to exercise the option *and hold* the stock. Consequently, they make a cashless exercise followed by an immediate sale of stock.

For others, it depends. The projected IRR associated with exercising and holding may, or may not, be high enough to justify the risk associated with holding the stock for 12 months and one day. Notice that Employee A's projected IRR is lower than B's.

EMPLOYEE A

Employee A's exercise price ($60 per share) as a percentage of the stock price ($100 per share) on the date of exercise is 60 percent. His marginal income tax rate is 28 percent.

The decision to exercise ISOs and sell the stock 12 months and one day later generates a *projected after-tax* annual rate of return of 5.3 percent (see Table 6.8).

Employee A compares the projected after-tax return with the rate of return he could earn from buying a U.S. Treasury security that has one year remaining until maturity date, and wisely concludes that the 5.3 percent projected IRR does not adequately compensate him for the risk of holding the stock. He exercises the ISO and makes a same-day sale.

EMPLOYEE B

Employee B's exercise price as a percentage of the stock price on the date of exercise is also 60 percent. His marginal income tax rate is 35 percent (7 percentage points higher than Employee A's 28 percent marginal rate).

The decision to exercise ISOs and sell the stock 12 months and one day later generates a *projected after-tax* annual rate of return of 8.0 percent (see Table 6.8).

Employee B invests the *same* amount of money and assumes the *same* stock price risk as Employee A when both exercise ISOs and hold the stock for 12 months and one day. But, Employee B's projected rate of return is substantially higher. His projected return is higher because Employee B enjoys more of an income tax savings (a savings of $8,000 for B and only $5,200 for A – see Table 6.5) when he converts ordinary income into long-term capital gain.

Employee B, like Employee A, compares the projected 8.0 percent projected after-tax IRR to the return available on U.S. Treasury securities with one year remaining until maturity date, and to expected returns on alternative investments of equivalent risk –before deciding whether he should exercise ISOs and hold the stock for 12 months and one day.

CONCLUSION

If he exercises ISOs and holds the stock for 12 months and one day, the optionee invests an amount of money that is equal to the fair market value of the optioned stock on the date of exercise. For example, if he holds ISOs on 1,000 shares of stock and the fair market value of that stock is $100 per share on the date of option exercise, he invests $100,000 (1,000 shares x $100 per share) on the date of option exercise.

Naturally, the risk associated with the investment depends upon the volatility of the stock price. Other things being equal, the less volatile the stock, the more attractive it is to exercise ISOs and hold the stock (holding versus selling ISO-stock is discussed extensively in Chapter 9 "*ISO-Stock: The December 31 Decision*" because optionees, who do exercise ISOs and hold the stock, should evaluate – as the end of December approaches – whether it is wise to hold ISO-stock beyond December 31 of the year of ISO exercise).

The projected rate of return that results *exclusively* from the decision to exercise ISOs and hold the stock for 12 months and one day is different for each optionee. It is a function of several factors, including, (1) the price of the stock at the end of 12 months and one day, (2) the employee's marginal income tax rate on ordinary income, (3) the income tax rate on long term capital gains,

(4) the relationship between the exercise price of the option and the stock price on the date of exercise, (5) whether, or to what extent, the alternative minimum tax impacts the amounts and timing of cash flows, (6) the date of exercise, (7) dividend yield on the stock, *and* (8) whether, or to what extent, either of the two mutually exclusive alternatives affects the amounts and timing of estimated tax payments.

An important lesson learned from the devastating bear market that began in 2000 and lasted into 2002, is that exercising ISOs with the intention of selling the stock 12 months and one day later is not the panacea that many had previously thought.

IIA. EARLY EXERCISE - VESTED NQSOS

Optionees that hold *vested* nonqualified stock options sometimes exercise them well in advance of expiration date. They usually intend to *hold* the stock for more than 12 months, and sometimes for a much *longer* period.

They exercise options well before expiration date with the *expectation* that they will convert *anticipated future appreciation* in the stock price after the date of option exercise, from ordinary income into more favorably taxed long-term capital gain. If they hold the stock for more than 12 months after the date of option exercise, 100 percent of any appreciation in the stock price that occurs *after the date of exercise* is taxed as long-term capital gain.

This strategy comes with risk. It produces inferior returns relative to other investment alternatives when the stock price does *not* appreciate sufficiently. The price of the stock may even decline subsequent to the option exercise.

Obviously, the less risky alternative is to exercise the option *after,* and *if,* anticipated appreciation in the stock price materializes. The *disadvantage,* however, is that this less risky strategy comes with less favorable income tax treatment. One hundred percent of the excess of the fair market value of the stock on the [eventual] exercise date over the exercise price is taxed as *ordinary* income on the date of exercise.

CONVERTING ORDINARY INCOME INTO CAPITAL GAIN

Generally, the *exercise* of a vested NQSO triggers the recognition of *ordinary compensation income* in the amount of the excess, if any, of the fair market value of the stock at the time of exercise over the exercise price.

Table 6.9 shows that the optionee recognizes *no* taxable income if he exercises the option on the date that it is granted *and* the fair market value of the stock is equal to the option's exercise price (which is usually the case). His *basis* in the stock acquired is $100, its fair market value on the date of option exercise.

Table 6.9	
Exercise NQSO on Grant Date (Year 1)	
Fair market value of stock	$ 100[1]
Less: exercise price	100
Ordinary compensation income	None

[1] the optionee's basis in the stock is $100, the stock's fair market value on date of option exercise

Table 6.10 shows that if he sells the stock in Year 6 for $500, he recognizes $400 of long-term capital gain.

Table 6.10	
Sale of Stock Previously Acquired by Exercise of NQSO (Year 6)	
Proceeds from sale of stock	$ 500
Less: fair market value on date of option exercise	100
Long-term capital gain	$ 400

If the optionee would have *waited* until Year 6 to exercise the NQSO (instead of exercising the option in Year 1) and sell the stock, he would *not* have received preferential income tax treatment on long-term capital gain.

The *intended* result of this "exercise early" strategy is that the optionee holds the stock for more than 12 months after the date of option exercise, the stock price increases substantially after the date of option exercise, and the optionee pays income tax at the lower tax rate on *long-term capital gains.* By exercising early, he converts 100 percent of the appreciation in the stock price that occurs after the exercise date, from ordinary income into long-term capital gain.

IS IT WISE TO EXERCISE A VESTED NQSO EARLY?

Whether or not early exercise makes sense depends upon a number of factors, the most important being the future rate of appreciation in the price of the stock. The more rapid the appreciation, the more likely that an early exercise is more advantageous than holding the NQSO and waiting to exercise (other things being equal).

In theory, it is possible to project the *minimum* rate of appreciation in the price of the stock, after the date of option exercise, that makes an early exercise attractive. That rate of appreciation is dependent upon a number of factors, including – the exercise price, the stock price, the optionee's marginal income tax rate on ordinary income, the tax rate on long-term capital gains, dividend yield on the stock, and interest rates. Tables 6.11 and 6.12 illustrate this point.

In Table 6.11 the optionee exercises the NQSO on grant date when the fair market value of the stock *equals* the exercise price of the option. Consequently, he does not recognize any taxable income on the date of exercise (because the fair market value of the stock on the date of exercise does not exceed the exercise price). He recognizes long-term capital gain in Year 6, the year that he sells the stock.

The example shown in Table 6.11 incorporates the following assumptions: (1) the optionee exercises the NQSO in Year 1 at an exercise price of $100 when the fair market value of the stock is $100, (2) long-term capital gains in Year 6 are taxed at 15 percent, (3) the stock price appreciates at a compounded annual rate of 14 percent, from $100 in Year 1 to $193 in Year 6, *and* (5) the stock does not pay a dividend.

In summary, the optionee invests $100 in Year 1. The after-tax terminal value in Year 6 is $179.

In Table 6.12 the optionee does *not* exercise early. He waits until Year 6 to exercise the NQSO and recognizes *ordinary* income in the amount of the excess of the $193 fair market value of the stock on the date of exercise over the $100 option exercise price. He sells the stock *immediately* after option exercise and therefore does not realize any capital gain or loss because the fair market value of the stock on the date of sale is exactly equal to his basis (fair market value on the date of exercise).

The example shown in Table 6.12 incorporates the following assumptions: (1) as an alternative to paying $100 to exercise the NQSO in Year 1, the optionee uses that $100 to buy United States Savings Bonds in Year 1 and redeems them in Year 6, (2) the savings bonds yield 5.20 percent compounded annually, (3) the optionee exercises the NQSO in Year 6, at an exercise price of $100, and immediately sells the stock, (4) the stock price appreciates at a compounded annual rate of 14 percent, from $100 in Year 1 to $193 in Year 6, *and* (5) the optionee's federal marginal income tax rate in Year 6 is 35 percent.

Table 6.11

Exercise NQSO in Year 1
Sell the Stock in Year 6
Terminal Value of the Investment
(Assuming no State Income Tax)

Year⇒	1	2	3	4	5	6
Exercise NQSO	($100)					
Tax on NQSO exercise	0^1					
Sell stock						193
Income tax on LTCG						$(14)^2$
Net cash flow	($100)	0	0	0	0	179

[1] income tax on exercise date is zero because the $100 stock price equals the $100 option exercise price
[2] 15% x ($193 – 100) = $14, payable not later than April 15, Year 7 with IRS Form 1040

In summary, the optionee invests $100 in Year 1. The after-tax terminal value at the end of Year 6 is $179.

CONCLUSION

Under the assumptions presented in Tables 6.11 and 6.12, the after-tax terminal values are equal ($179). From a wealth standpoint, the optionee would be *indifferent* to exercising early versus waiting to exercise the NQSO.

The answer to the question *"Exercise early or not?"* is highly dependent upon future appreciation of the stock price. If the assumptions in Table 6.11 and 6.12 are changed such that the stock price appreciates at an annual rate of more than 14 percent, the early exercise provides a higher terminal value. At rates of appreciation less than 14 percent, the early exercise results in a lower terminal value.

Table 6.12

Purchase U.S. Series EE Savings Bonds in Year 1 Exercise NQSO in Year 6. Sell the Stock in Year 6 Terminal Value of the Investment (Assuming no State Income Tax)

Year⇒	1	2	3	4	5	6
Purchase bonds[1]	($100)					
Redeem bonds[1]						129
Tax on interest income						$(10)^2$
Exercise NQSO						(100)
Sell stock						193
Social security and Medicare tax						$(1)^3$
Tax on NQSO exercise						$(32)^4$
Net cash flow	($100)					$179

[1] U.S. Series EE savings bonds
[2] tax on savings bonds interest income = 35% x ($129 - 100) = $10; payable not later than April 15, Year 7 with IRS Form 1040
[3] Assumes taxpayer has exceed the social security tax ceiling for the calendar year; Medicare tax = 1.45% x ($193 – 100) = $1
[4] 35% x ($193 - 100) = $32; payable not later than April 15, Year 7 with IRS Form 1040

The alternatives illustrated in Tables 6.11 and 6.12 resulted in the *same* terminal values at the end of five years ($179). The early exercise, however, involved substantially more risk. Consequently, its *risk-adjusted* return is lower than the wait-to-exercise alternative.

As discussed earlier, it is theoretically possible to determine the minimum rate of appreciation in the stock price that must occur after the date of option exercise, in order for the exercise early alternative to *appear* attractive. The following section shows that such appearances can be misleading...and *costly*. It illustrates that an outright purchase of the stock, while continuing to hold the option, is preferable to early exercise of the option.

RETAINING THE NQSO AND BUYING THE STOCK OUTRIGHT

If the expectation is that the stock price will appreciate substantially, it naturally follows that *retaining* the nonqualified stock option, and buying the stock outright, is usually preferable to buying the stock by exercising the option. This strategy allows the optionee to retain the advantages of holding the option while reaping any benefits than stem from owning the stock.

See Table 6.13. The example in Table 6.13 assumes (1) that the optionee's federal marginal income tax rate is 35 percent, (2) an option exercise price of $80 per share, which was the stock price on option grant date, *and* (3) a current stock price of $100 per share.

Alternative A is to purchase one share of stock at $100 and *retain* the NQSO to purchase one share at $80. Alternative A requires a total investment of $100.

Alternative B is to *exercise* the NQSO by paying $80 to purchase one share of stock that has a fair market value of $100. The $20 excess of the fair market value of the stock on the date of exercise over the exercise price is taxed as ordinary compensation income, at a marginal income tax rate of 35 percent. The income tax liability on that $20 gain is $7. Alternative B requires a total investment of $87.

Clearly, Alternative A is preferable to B. When he selects Alternative A, the optionee effectively pays $13 (see Table 6.13 "Alt A-B") to retain an option that has an *intrinsic value* of $20 (the $100 fair market value of the stock minus the $80 exercise price of the option) and a *fair market value* that may be worth substantially more than $20, depending upon a number of factors, including the amount of time remaining until the option's expiration date. The more time remaining, the more valuable is the option.

Table 6.14 clearly illustrates that when the optionee exercises early he literally discards his option. He throws it into the waste receptacle.

In Table 6.14, the optionee holds an option to purchase one share of stock at an exercise price of $100. The fair market value of the stock is $100.

If he pays $100 to buy the stock outright (and retains the option), he holds one share of stock *and* an option to buy one share of stock at $100. This scenario is identified in Table 6.14 as Alternative A.

Table 6.13

Retaining the NQSO and Buying the Stock (Alternative A) versus Exercising the NQSO (Alternative B)

Alt A	Buy 1 share @ $100 per share	$100
	Retain option to purchase 1 share @ $80	0
	Total investment Alternative A	$100
Alt B	Exercise:buy 1 share @ $80 per share	80
	Income tax @ 35% on $20 gain	7
	Total investment Alternative B	$ 87
Alt A-B	*Difference in amount of investment*	$ 13

Instead, if he exercises the option, he pays the $100 exercise price and he holds one share of stock. *But* his option is gone. This scenario is identified in Table 6.14 as Alternative B.

Clearly, Alternative A is preferable to B. See "Alt A-B" in Table 6.14 which illustrates that the optionee effectively pays *nothing* to retain the option when he chooses Alternative A.

Table 6.14

Retaining the NQSO and Buying the Stock (Alternative A) versus Exercising the NQSO (Alternative B)

Alt A	Buy 1 share @ $100 per share	$100
	Retain option to purchase 1 share @ $100	0
	Total investment Alternative A	$100
Alt B	Exercise:buy 1 share @ $100 per share	100
	Income tax @ 35% on $0 gain	0
	Total investment Alternative B	$100
Alt A-B	*Difference in amount of investment*	$ 0

Stated another way, when he exercises the option early, he sacrifices the option. The option that he sacrifices has value, a value which could be substantial depending upon a number of factors including the volatility of the stock and the amount of time remaining until the option's expiration date.

IIB. EARLY EXERCISE - UNVESTED NQSOS

The previous section addressed the early exercise of a *vested* nonqualified stock option (NQSO). The same analysis applies to the exercise of an *unvested* NQSO when such exercise is followed by a valid IRC Section 83(b) election.

If the optionee exercises an *unvested* nonqualified stock option and on the date of option exercise the stock acquired by such exercise is *both* subject to a substantial risk of forfeiture *and* not transferable, the recognition of income is delayed. If the optionee files a timely IRC Section 83(b) election, he accelerates the recognition of ordinary compensation income to the date of option exercise.

In the situation described above, the IRC Section 83(b) election effectively makes the exercise of an *unvested* NQSO equivalent to the exercise of a *vested* NQSO for purposes of federal income tax. Consequently, the analysis in *"Early Exercise - Vested NQSOs"* applies to the early exercise of *unvested* NQSOs *if* the optionee makes the Section 83(b) election.

7

ISO Tax Traps

This chapter shows why companies that grant incentive stock options would do employees a service if they would issue a warning with such grants – much like cigarette manufacturers warn smokers of the dangers from smoking. A warning might include language like this:

> Exercising an incentive stock option and continuing to hold the ISO-stock beyond December 31 of the year of ISO exercise could result in federal alternative minimum tax consequences so severe that proceeds from your eventual sale of the ISO-stock may be insufficient to pay any AMT liability that would be due with your federal income tax return on April 15 of the year following ISO exercise.

This chapter discusses some common ISO traps in the following sections:

- *Large Bargain Element Followed by Collapse of Stock Price*
- *$3,000 Annual Limitation on AMT Capital Losses*
- *No Limit on Compensation Income*
- *Sale of ISO-Stock is Prohibited*
- *Charitable Donation of ISO-Stock*

LARGE BARGAIN ELEMENT FOLLOWED BY COLLAPSE OF STOCK PRICE

The optionee should be alert to the possibility that he could fall victim to an ISO trap if he holds ISO-stock beyond December 31 of the year of ISO exercise, and all of the following statements are true:

- There was a large bargain element on ISO exercise date.

- The bargain element triggered AMT.

- Proceeds from his eventual sale of ISO-stock are substantially less than what the fair market value was on ISO exercise date.

The next example shows that even though Beverly has no gain on her sale of ISO-stock, the Internal Revenue Service ends up with her money and she ends up with a non-interest-bearing tax credit – the AMT credit – that she can use to reduce her future regular income tax liability, but only to the extent her regular income tax liability exceeds her tentative minimum tax. It also illustrates the income tax consequences, and federal income tax reporting, under two different scenarios:

- *Scenario #1:* The optionee sells her ISO-stock, in a *disqualifying* disposition, in the year of ISO exercise (that is, she sells in Year 1).

- *Scenario #2:* The optionee sells her ISO-stock, in a *qualifying* disposition, in the year after ISO exercise (that is, she sells in Year 2).

Example: *Optionee exercises an ISO, the bargain element is large, and proceeds from the eventual sale of such ISO-stock equal her ISO exercise price (that is, she has no economic gain):* On January 5, Year 1, Beverly exercises ISOs to buy 1,000 shares of ABC Corporation stock at $50 per share. She does not make a same-day sale of the ISO-stock. At the time of exercise, she expects that she will sell the stock on January 15, Year 2, a date that is more than 12 months after her date of option exercise *and* more than two years after the option grant date – so that the sale of stock would result in 100 percent of any gain being taxed as long-term capital gain.

The FMV of the stock on the January 5, Year 1 date of option exercise is $100 per share. The "bargain element" – the fair market value of the stock on the date of option exercise minus the option exercise price – is $50 per share ($50,000 bargain element on 1,000 shares). On December 31, Year 1, the fair market value of her ISO-stock is only $50 per share, the same price she paid to exercise the options on January 5, Year 1.

Under Scenario #1 below, Beverly sells the stock for $50 per share on December 31, Year 1, in a disqualifying disposition. Under that scenario, the IRS holds none of her money. Under Scenario #2 below she sells the stock for $50 per share on January 15, Year 2, in a qualifying disposition. Under that scenario, the IRS holds $14,000 of her money and gives her a $14,000 AMT credit. Note that Beverly has *no economic gain or loss* under either scenario.

SCENARIO #1: SELL ISO-STOCK IN YEAR 1

Under this scenario, Beverly makes a disqualifying disposition by selling the stock in Year 1 for $50 per share (total proceeds equal $50,000), which is the same price she paid to exercise the ISO. ABC Corporation reports no compensation income on her IRS Form W-2 for Year 1 because compensation income equals the *lesser* of her gain, if any, *or* the $50,000 bargain element that existed on ISO exercise date. Further, Beverly does not report the $50,000 "bargain element" that existed on the date of option exercise as income for purposes of AMT.

Beverly escapes without paying *any* income tax on her exercise of ISOs and subsequent sale of ISO-stock. She has zero capital gain, zero capital loss, and zero compensation income. After all, this is equitable, given that she has no economic gain; she bought the stock for $50,000 on ISO exercise date, and she sold it for $50,000.

SCENARIO #1: YEAR 1 FEDERAL INCOME TAX RETURN

Beverly reports $50,000 of gross proceeds from the sale of ABC stock and the $50,000 basis on IRS Form 1040, Schedule D, for the year ended December 31, Year 1. Her capital gain is zero. She reports nothing with respect to such transactions on her income tax return for the year ended December 31, Year 2.

SCENARIO #2: SELL ISO-STOCK IN YEAR 2

Under this scenario, Beverly holds the ISO-stock beyond December 31, Year 1, which triggers the recognition of taxable income in Year 1 for purposes of AMT only. She sells the stock for $50 per share (total proceeds equal $50,000) on January 15, Year 2, in a qualifying disposition. Beverly has no other capital gains or losses in Year 2.

SCENARIO #2: YEAR 1 FEDERAL INCOME TAX RETURN

Beverly reports $50,000 of taxable income, the amount of the bargain element that existed on the ISO exercise date, for purposes of AMT on her Year 1 income tax return (on IRS Form 6251). This $50,000 of income triggers $14,000 of federal AMT (28% x $50,000 = $14,000) that is payable on April 15, Year 2.

In exchange for the $14,000 AMT that she pays on April 15, Year 2, Beverly receives a $14,000 AMT credit that she may use to reduce her *regular* tax on her Year 2 income tax return, but only to the extent that her regular tax *exceeds* her tentative minimum tax, the tax computed under the AMT rules. If she is not able to use the entire $14,000 credit on her Year 2 income tax return, she carries the unused amount to Year 3, and so on, until the AMT credit is fully utilized.

SCENARIO #2: YEAR 2 FEDERAL INCOME TAX RETURN

This section explains that Beverly reports her sale of ISO-stock in two different ways on her Year 2 income tax return – one way for purposes of regular tax, and another way for purposes of AMT.

That is because her ISO-stock has a "dual" basis. The basis for regular tax purposes equals her $50,000 ISO exercise price. The basis for AMT purposes is the $100,000 fair market value on the date of ISO exercise.

Tax reporting for purposes of regular tax: Beverly reports the sale of stock on IRS Form 1040, Schedule D, and has no capital gain or loss for purposes of regular tax because the $50,000 of proceeds from the sale equals the $50,000 basis.

Tax reporting for purposes of AMT: She reports $50,000 of proceeds from the sale and $100,000 of basis for purposes of AMT, which results in a $50,000 capital loss. But IRC Section 1211(b), discussed below, limits her AMT capital loss to $3,000 per year. The $47,000 unused portion of the $50,000 AMT capital loss carries forward to Year 3.

COMPARISON: SCENARIO #1 VERSUS SCENARIO #2

In Scenario #1 Beverly realizes no capital gain or loss and, as one would expect, pays no income tax. In Scenario #2 Beverly doesn't realize any capital gain or loss, either, but she pays $14,000 of AMT in Year 1 and receives a $14,000 AMT credit. In effect, she loans $14,000 to the U.S. Treasury at a zero interest rate, and does not know for sure when she will get the money back, because she is able to use the AMT credit only to the extent that regular tax exceeds tentative minimum tax.

LARGE LOSS ON YEAR 2 SALE OF ISO-STOCK

Under Scenario #2 above, Beverly pays $50,000 to exercise ISOs in Year 1 and sells the stock in Year 2 for $50,000. She does not suffer a capital loss but she does suffer from the AMT trap, where the U.S. Treasury is holding $14,000 of her cash (because she paid $14,000 of AMT). She also holds a $14,000 AMT credit that may take years to utilize.

Beverly's situation is not ideal. But, fortunately, the $50,000 proceeds from her sale of stock on a date after December 31, Year 1, and before April 15, Year 2, exceed the $14,000 of alternative minimum tax that is due on April 15, Year 2, with her income tax return for Year 1.

The next example illustrates that Janet is not so fortunate because the price of her ISO-stock crashes. She too exercises ISOs in Year 1 and sells the stock after December 31, Year 1, but before April 15, Year 2, in order to pay her Year 1 income tax liability. Proceeds from her sale, however, are dwarfed by the Year 1 income tax liability that she must pay on or before April 15, Year 2.

Janet's example is based on true stories. Following the general collapse of stock prices that began in 2000, many optionees were forced to sell cars and homes to raise cash sufficient to pay the AMT that was triggered by the exercise of ISOs. Some withdrew money from retirement plans and these withdrawals triggered even more taxes and sometimes penalties for early withdrawal. Many could not raise enough cash and filed bankruptcy.

Example: *The stock price collapses and proceeds from the sale of ISO-stock in Year 2 are dwarfed by the Year 1 AMT liability:* Janet exercises incentive stock options on January 15, Year 1, and does not sell such ISO-stock on or before December 31, Year 1. On the date of ISO exercise the fair market value of the stock is $1,001,000 and Janet's exercise price is $1,000, a difference of $1,000,000 (the bargain element). Janet reports $1,000,000 of income, for purposes of AMT only, on IRS Form 6251 for the year ended December 31, Year 1. That $1,000,000 triggers $280,000 of alternative minimum tax that is due with IRS Form 1040 on April 15, Year 2. The stock price collapses and Janet's proceeds from the sale of her ISO-stock in April Year 2 are only $100,000, which is $180,000 less than the $280,000 of AMT that is due with her Year 1 income tax return on April 15, Year 2.

$3,000 ANNUAL LIMITATION ON AMT CAPITAL LOSSES

Internal Revenue Code Section 1211(b) places a $3,000 annual limitation on the amount of capital losses that an individual may apply against other taxable income such as wages, and interest income.

Does the $3,000 annual limitation apply for purposes of AMT? The answer is clear. The *General Explanation of the Tax Reform Act of 1986*, prepared by the staff of the joint committee on taxation, states that the $3,000 annual limitation applies for purposes of alternative minimum tax.

THE AMT CAPITAL LOSS LIMITATION IS SIGNIFICANT

The AMT capital loss limitation is significant for those whose exercise of ISOs triggers alternative minimum tax. The reason is that the AMT credit that arises can only be used to the extent that regular tax in years after the year of ISO exercise exceeds tentative minimum tax.

In short, the optionee can only use his AMT credit – in a taxable year after the taxable year of ISO exercise – to the extent of the "gap" (discussed below). But, the $3,000 AMT capital loss limitation often reduces the size of the gap that would exist, if such limitation did not exist. The reduction in the size of the gap often adversely impacts the optionee's ability to use the AMT credit.

More specifically, the $3,000 AMT capital loss limitation often results in a higher income tax liability, in taxable years after the taxable year of ISO exercise, than would otherwise result if such limitation did not exist.

TAXABLE GAIN ADJUSTMENT

If the optionee sells ISO-stock after December 31 of the year of ISO exercise, such ISO-stock almost certainly has a dual basis, because basis for purposes of regular tax is the option exercise price, and basis for purposes of AMT is the fair market value on the date of ISO exercise.

Naturally, if the basis is different for purposes of regular tax and AMT, the taxable capital gain or loss from the sale of such stock is different. Table 7.1 shows how to compute the difference in taxable gain or loss for purposes of regular tax versus AMT.

Table 7.1
Sale of ISO-Stock: How to Compute the Taxable Gain Adjustment That Arises Due to the $3,000 AMT Capital Loss Limitation

Example:

	AMT	Reg Tax
Proceeds from sale of ISO-stock	50,000	50,000
Basis (1)	100,000	10,000
Gain (loss) on sale of ISO-stock	(50,000)	40,000

This example assumes there are no other capital gains or losses for the year.

Computation of the negative $43,000 taxable gain adjustment:

	(A) AMT	(B) Reg Tax	(A) - (B) Adjustment
Other capital gains (losses)	0	0	
Gain (loss) on sale of ISO-stock (detail above)	(50,000)	40,000	
Net capital gain (loss) for the year	(50,000)	40,000	
Taxable capital gain (loss) for the year (2)	(3,000)	40,000	**(43,000)**

(1) AMT basis = FMV on date of ISO exercise; Regular Tax basis = option exercise price

(2) IRC Section 1211(b) places a $3,000 annual limitation on net capital losses

Note in Table 7.1 that for purposes of AMT, the optionee's total capital losses from the sale of stocks are $50,000 (all from the sale of his ISO-stock, because this example assumes he has no other capital gains or losses) but only $3,000 is deductible in the current year; the remaining $47,000 carries forward to the next year.

This $3,000 deductible capital *loss* is $43,000 less than the $40,000 net capital *gain* for purposes of regular tax. The $43,000 difference between the two amounts, as explained below, is an important number because tentative AMT is higher than it would be if the $3,000 AMT capital loss limitation did not exist.

THE "GAP"

The "gap" is an informal term that refers to the excess, if any, of the optionee's income tax liability computed under the regular income tax over his liability computed under the rules for computing AMT. In tax jargon, the gap is the excess of his regular income tax liability over his tentative minimum tax.

> The gap is an important number because it effectively *limits* the amount of AMT credit that the optionee may use to reduce his regular income tax liability. As this section explains, the $3,000 annual AMT capital loss limitation can reduce the gap and therefore make it more difficult to use the AMT credit.

The next example is labeled Scenario #2A because it is based on the facts from Scenario #2 earlier in this chapter, in which Beverly triggers $14,000 of AMT. Scenario #2A illustrates how the $3,000 AMT capital loss limitation reduces the gap, making it more difficult for Beverly to use the AMT credit and resulting in a tax liability in Year 2 that is $13,000 higher than it would be if such capital loss limitation did not exist.

Table 7.2 summarizes Scenario #2A and shows:

- The tax consequences that *would* occur *if* there was not a $3,000 AMT capital loss limitation

- The tax consequences under current law under which there *is* a $3,000 AMT capital loss limitation

- The difference between the two, which shows the $13,000 tax increase (summarized in Table 7.2, column G) that the $3,000 AMT capital loss limitation has on Beverly's Year 2 tax liability

Example: Scenario 2A: *Beverly can only deduct $3,000 of her $50,000 capital loss for purposes of AMT. That causes her to pay $13,000 more tax in Year 2 than she would pay if the $3,000 AMT capital loss limitation did not exist:* In scenario #2 above, Beverly does not sell her ISO-stock in Year 1 and she pays $14,000 of alternative minimum tax in Year 1. She receives a $14,000 AMT credit that she may use to reduce regular income tax in taxable years after Year 1. In Year 2 she sells the stock for $50,000 and reports no capital gain or loss for purposes of regular tax. She suffers a $50,000 capital loss for purposes of AMT. But she can deduct only $3,000 for purposes of AMT, due to the AMT capital loss limitation.

If she would have been able to deduct the entire $50,000 AMT capital loss, her tentative minimum tax would have been $88,000. Instead it is $101,000. Her regular income tax liability is $100,000. Since regular tax exceeds tentative minimum tax there is no gap. Her Year 2 income tax liability is therefore $101,000, the greater of $101,000 tax computed under the regular income tax, or $100,000 tax computed under AMT rules. In short, the $3,000 AMT capital loss limitation prevents Beverly's AMT liability from falling below her regular tax liability. The result (please see Table 7.2, column G) is that she pays $13,000 more tax in Year 2 than should would have to pay if the $3,000 AMT capital loss limitation did not exist. She carries the entire $14,000 credit forward, hoping to use some or all of it in Year 3.

Table 7.2

How the $3,000 AMT Capital Loss Limitation Limits Use of the $14,000 AMT Credit

	Text Scenario 2A: Gap = $0	
	If loss limitation did not apply (1)	With $3,000 loss limitation (2)
(A) Year 2 Regular Tax (before AMT Credit)	$100,000	$100,000
(B) Year 2 Tentative Minimum Tax	$88,000	$101,000
(C) Year 2 Gap = (A) minus (B) but not less than zero	$12,000	$0
(D) Year 2 AMT Credit (lesser of $14,000 or (C) but not less than zero	$12,000	$0
(E) Carryover of AMT Credit to Year 3 = $14,000 minus (D)	$2,000	$14,000
(F) Year 2 Regular Tax (after AMT Credit) = (A) minus (D)	$88,000	$100,000
(G) Year 2 Tax Liability (greater of B or F)	$88,000	$101,000
Difference		**$13,000**

Tax impact: $13,000 tax increase in Year 2 (see column G) and a $14,000 (instead of $2,000) AMT credit carryover to Year 3 (see column E)

(1) These are the income tax consequences that would result if the $3,000 loss limitation did not apply for purposes of AMT

(2) These are the income tax consequences under current law where the $3,000 loss limitation does apply for purposes of AMT

NO LIMIT ON COMPENSATION INCOME

IRC Section 422 places a (favorable) limitation on compensation income.

Section 422(c)(2) states that if the optionee makes a disqualifying disposition, he recognizes *ordinary compensation income* on the date of such disposition to the extent of the *lesser* of:

(a) the excess of the fair market value of the stock on the date of ISO exercise over the option exercise price (that is, the bargain element),

   or,

(b) the excess, if any, of the amount received in the disposition over the option exercise price (that is, the actual gain - if any)

   if "such disposition is a sale or exchange with respect to which a loss (if sustained) would be recognized to such individual."

In practice, this (more favorable) income tax treatment applies most of the time, because in most cases *if* there would be a loss on the sale of ISO-stock such loss *would* be deductible on the optionee's income tax return. For example, the optionee sells the stock through a brokerage firm to an unrelated person and does not buy substantially identical stock (including the same stock that he sold) or securities within 30 calendar days of the disqualifying disposition of ISO-stock; within 30 calendar days covers the 61-day period that starts 30 days before the disqualifying disposition and continues for 30 days after the disqualifying disposition.

The following is a discussion of the trap that can cause the optionee to recognize a large amount of compensation income – whether he has an actual gain, or a loss, on the disposition. In fact, if the stock price declines substantially after the option exercise date, the income tax liability on such compensation income may exceed the proceeds from his sale of stock.

Regulation 1.422-1(b)(2)(ii) states that the favorable limitation on compensation income (that is, compensation income is limited to the *lesser* of (a) or (b) above) does *not* apply when the disqualifying disposition is one of three kinds of transactions:

- sale described in IRC Section 1091 (relating to wash sales),

- gift,

  or,

- sale described in IRC Section 267 (sales between related persons)

That is because, *if* the optionee *would* suffer a loss in any of these three types of transactions, the loss would not be recognized (that is, the optionee would not be able to deduct such loss on his income tax return).

The key words are "*if*" and "*would.*" It doesn't matter that the optionee might have a *gain* on the sale of his ISO-stock. He still gets tripped up by this trap because *if* the gain *would* have been a loss, such loss would *not* be recognized – it would *not* be deductible.

Regulation 1.422-1(b)(2)(ii) provides that if the limitation on compensation income does not apply, the optionee recognizes compensation income in the amount of the *bargain element* (that is, the fair market value of the stock on the date of option exercise over the option exercise price) that existed on the date of ISO exercise. The next three sections illustrate the three types of transactions mentioned above, showing that the optionee falls into a trap whereby he recognizes compensation income in the amount of the bargain element that existed on ISO exercise date even if his disqualifying disposition does not provide him with sufficient proceeds to pay the tax liability that is triggered by such compensation income.

SALE DESCRIBED IN IRC SECTION 1091 – WASH SALES

The first kind of transaction described above occurs when the optionee sells ISO-stock and within a period beginning 30 days before the date of sale or disposition and ending 30 days after such date (a total of 61 calendar days), the taxpayer has acquired, or has entered into a contract or option to acquire, substantially identical stock or securities. IRC Section 1091 states that the term "stock or securities" shall, except as provided in regulations, include contracts or options to acquire or sell stock or securities.

Table 7.3 presents a summary of the next example.

Example: Optionee sells ISO-stock and repurchases the same stock within 30 calendar days: Amy exercises incentive stock options on January 15, Year 1, and pays $1,000 to buy 1,000 shares of ABC stock. The fair market value of the stock on ISO exercise date is $1,001,000. Therefore, the bargain element is $1,000,000. The stock price on December 20, Year 1, is $100,000 and Amy sells her ISO-stock at that price in a disqualifying disposition. She purposely sells the stock before January 1, Year 2 – in order to avoid the recognition of $1,000,000 (the bargain element) of taxable income in Year 1 for purposes of AMT – because holding the stock beyond December 31, Year 1, would have triggered $280,000 of AMT ($1,000,000 taxable income x 28 percent = $280,000), which is substantially more than the $100,000 fair market value of the stock.

But, on December 21, Year 1, Amy makes a costly mistake by repurchasing 1,000 shares of ABC stock. The December 21 purchase falls within the 61-day period that runs from 30 days before her December 20, Year 1 sale of ISO-stock until 30 days after her December 20, Year 1 sale of ISO-stock. Therefore, the December 20 sale of ISO-stock is a "sale described in IRC Section 1091." Consequently, Regulation 1.422-1(b)(2)(ii) provides that Amy must recognize ordinary *compensation* income in Year 1 in the amount of the $1,000,000 bargain element that existed on the date of ISO exercise.

Basis of ISO-stock sold on December 20, Year 1: Amy's basis in the ISO-stock that she sells on December 20, Year 1, is $1,001,000. It consists of the $1,000 option exercise price plus the $1,000,000 of compensation income that she recognizes.

Computation of gain or loss on December 20, Year 1 sale of ISO-stock: Amy realizes a $901,000 loss on the ISO-stock that she sells on December 20, Year 1. That $901,000 loss equals $100,000 of proceeds from the sale minus her $1,001,000 basis in the stock.

IRC Section 1091 provides that *none* of the $901,000 loss is deductible on her Year 1 income tax return; instead, as described below, the $901,000 disallowed loss is added to Amy's basis in ABC stock that she purchases on December 21, Year 1.

Basis of ABC stock purchased on December 21, Year 1: Amy pays $100,000 to buy 1,000 shares of ABC stock on December 21, Year 1. Her *basis* in the 1,000 shares is $1,001,000, which consists of the $100,000 purchase price plus the $901,000 disallowed loss from the December 20, Year 1 sale of ISO-stock.

Holding period for ABC stock purchased on December 21, Year 1: IRC Section 1223 provides that Amy's *holding period* for the 1,000 shares that she buys on December 21, Year 1, begins on January 15, Year 1, the date she exercised her ISOs to buy the ISO-stock.

Summary of income tax trap that Amy falls into: Amy pays income tax on $1,000,000 of compensation income. Her $100,000 of proceeds from the sale of ISO-stock falls well short of the tax liability on that $1,000,000. On December 21, Year 1, she holds "new" shares of ABC stock that have a $1,001,000 basis and a $100,000 fair market value; it means that Amy has the potential to sell the new shares and report a $901,000 capital loss. The problem is that IRC Section 1211(b) places a $3,000 annual limitation on the deductibility of net capital losses. If she sells the new stock for $100,000, she realizes a $901,000 capital loss that she may use to absorb other capital gains – if she has any. If Amy's capital losses exceed her capital gains, she may apply such excess – up to a maximum of $3,000 per year – against ordinary income (for example, wages and interest). If her net capital loss exceeds $3,000, she carries such excess forward to her Year 2 income tax return.

CAUTION: "SALE DESCRIBED IN SECTION 1091"

The "wash sale" described in the example above is clear-cut. The question then arises, *"Are there other possible traps related to IRC Section 1091"?* The answer is "Yes."

The IRS might successfully argue that if the optionee receives a stock option *grant* within the 61-day period that runs from 30 days before the date of his disqualifying disposition of ISO-stock until

30 days after such date, his disposition of ISO-stock is a "sale described in IRC Section 1091." That would trigger compensation income in the amount of the bargain element that existed on the ISO exercise date.

Example: Employee receives a stock grant within 30 days of making a disqualifying disposition of ISO-stock: On December 2 Irene receives a stock option grant for 1,000 shares of ABC stock. On December 9 she makes a disqualifying disposition of 1,000 shares of ABC ISO-stock. The IRS may successfully argue that the December 9 sale of stock is a "sale described in IRC Section 1091" because the December 2 grant date is within 30 days of the December 9 sale. If so, Irene recognizes compensation income in the amount of the bargain element that existed on the date of ISO exercise.

Another potential trap could be that the optionee's purchase of employer stock through an employee stock purchase plan (ESPP) within the 61-day period that runs from 30 days before the date of a disqualifying disposition of ISO-stock until 30 days after such date would make the disqualifying disposition of ISO-stock a "sale described in IRC Section 1091." If so, that too would trigger compensation income in the amount of the bargain element that existed on ISO exercise date.

GIFTS

The second kind of transaction described earlier occurs when the optionee gifts ISO-stock (including gifts to non-spouse individuals and charitable organizations) that he has not held for the required holding periods (that is, more than two years after grant date, and more than 12 months after option exercise date). This second kind of transaction also triggers compensation income in the amount of the bargain element that existed on the date of ISO exercise.

Example: Gift of immature ISO-stock to charity triggers compensation income in the amount of the bargain element that existed on ISO exercise date: In an earlier example, Amy sells the ISO-stock on December 20, Year 1, in a disqualifying disposition and buys back the same stock within 30 days (that is, she triggers the wash sale rule). She recognizes $1,000,000 of compensation income. If, instead, she *donates* the immature ISO-stock on December 20, Year 1, to a charitable organization, she also would recognize $1,000,000 of compensation income in Year 1 in accordance with Regulation 1.422-1(b)(2)(ii). That $1,000,000 is the amount of the bargain element that existed on the date of ISO exercise. Amy would report $100,000 – the fair market value of the stock on the date of donation – as a *charitable deduction* on IRS Form 1040, Schedule A.

Example: Gift of ISO-stock to spouse does not trigger the recognition of compensation income: IRC Section 424(c)(4) provides that a transfer of ISO-stock between spouses is *not* a disposition. Therefore, if Amy gives her ISO-stock to her spouse, such gift does *not* trigger the recognition of income – even if the transfer occurs before Amy has satisfied the holding period requirements.

SALE DESCRIBED IN IRC SECTION 267 – RELATED PERSONS

The third kind of transaction described earlier occurs when the optionee sells ISO-stock, which he has not held for the required holding periods, to a related party. Such disqualifying disposition of ISO-stock that is a "sale described in IRC Section 267" also triggers compensation income in the amount of the bargain element that existed on the ISO exercise date.

A "sale described in IRC Section 267" is a sale to a related party (for example, a family member). But, the definition of "related party" under Section 267 extends beyond family members. It includes trusts, corporations, and other business entities that are related to the optionee or to a member of his family.

Example: The sale of ISO-stock to optionee's son is a "sale described in IRC Section 267": The following is based on Regulation 1.422-1(b)(2)(ii). Amy exercises an ISO and pays the $100 exercise price. The fair market value of the stock on the date of option exercise is $200. She sells the ISO-stock to her son for $150 in a disqualifying disposition (that is, she doesn't satisfy the holding period requirements). In fact, Amy sells the stock to her son at a gain (that is, the $150 proceeds exceed her $100 purchase price by $50). *If,* however, she *would* have sold the stock to her son for $99, she *would* have realized a loss. Under IRC Section 267, such loss would not be deductible because Amy's son is a related person. Since her loss (if she had sustained one) would not be deductible, Amy's sale of ISO-stock to her son triggers the recognition of compensation income in the amount of $100, the bargain element that existed on the date of option exercise.

Basis of ISO-stock sold by Amy: Amy's *basis* in the ISO-stock that she sells to her son is $200. That $200 is comprised of her $100 ISO exercise price, plus $100 of compensation income (that is, the bargain element that existed on ISO exercise date) that she recognizes because she sells the stock to a related person.

Computation of gain or loss on Amy's sale of ISO-stock: Amy's sale of stock to her son results in a $50 loss. That loss equals the $150 proceeds from the sale minus her $200 basis. Amy's $50 loss is *not* deductible on her income tax return because IRC Section 267 disallows losses from sales to related persons.

Example: *Amy sells her ISO-stock to the Amy Wilson Irrevocable Trust before satisfying the holding period requirements:* Before satisfying the holding period requirements, Amy sells her ISO-stock to the Amy Wilson *Irrevocable* Trust. Amy's sale is a disposition that triggers compensation income in the amount of the bargain element that existed on the date of ISO exercise.

Example: *Amy transfers her ISO-stock to the Amy Wilson Revocable Trust before satisfying the holding period requirements:* Amy establishes the Amy Wilson *Revocable* Trust and places her ISO-stock in the trust. As described in Chapter 4, the IRS wrote in PLR 9309027 that transfers to a qualifying grantor trust would not be a disposition *if* certain requirements are satisfied.

SALE OF ISO-STOCK IS PROHIBITED

A "lock-up" period typically follows an initial public offering (IPO) of stock. Under a lock-up agreement, which begins on the date of IPO and often lasts about six months, certain shareholders agree not to sell, otherwise dispose of, or hedge any common shares, options, warrants, or convertible securities of the issuing corporation.

If the optionee exercises an ISO, he places himself in a potential ISO trap if:

- an ISO exercise would trigger a substantial amount of taxable income on the ISO exercise date, for purposes of AMT

  and,

- he cannot sell such ISO-stock on or before December 31 of the year of ISO exercise.

The reason he places himself in a potential trap is that if the stock price collapses after ISO exercise date and has not recovered by the end of December, the lock-up agreement prohibits him from selling the ISO-stock on or before December 31 of the year of ISO exercise in order to avoid the recognition of a substantial amount of AMT taxable income. If such AMT taxable income would trigger a large amount of AMT in the year of ISO exercise, the optionee's proceeds from his sale of the ISO-stock after the calendar year of ISO exercise may be less than the AMT liability that would be due on April 15 of the year following ISO exercise.

For example, if the optionee exercises a vested ISO during the lock-up period, such ISO-stock is non-transferable on the date of ISO exercise. But, as discussed in Chapter 3, the lock-up period does *not* constitute a "substantial risk of forfeiture"; it means that the lock-up does not delay the recognition of income. Therefore, the optionee recognizes taxable income on the date of ISO exercise – for purposes of AMT only – in the amount of the excess of the fair market value of the stock on ISO exercise date over the option exercise price. This was the situation addressed in IRS Private Letter Ruling 200338010.

Example: The optionee exercises a vested ISO during the lock-up period. The bargain element is substantial and triggers a substantial amount of AMT. The stock price collapses before January 1 of the next year but the optionee cannot sell her stock on or before December 31 of the year of ISO exercise: On July 5, Year 1, ABC Corporation sells shares in an IPO. On August 5,

Year 1, Rene exercises an ISO and on that date the fair market value of the stock is $110. Her exercise price is $10. Therefore, the bargain element is $100. On December 31, Year 1, the stock price is only $10. Generally – under conditions of a substantial bargain element that would trigger AMT *and* a stock price at the end of December that is substantially below its price on ISO exercise date – an optionee would sell the ISO-stock on or before December 31, Year 1, to avoid the recognition of AMT taxable income in Year 1 in the amount of the bargain element. But, the investment banking firm's underwriting agreement states that from July 5, Year 1, until January 5, Year 2, Rene is covered by a lock-up agreement whereby she cannot sell the ISO-stock until after January 5, Year 2. Rene finds herself paying $28 (28 percent x $100 bargain element = $28) of AMT in Year 1 and on December 31, Year 1, her ISO-stock is worth only $10.

BLACKOUT PERIODS

The optionee's employer likely imposes blackout periods during which the optionee is prohibited from selling the company's stock. The optionee needs to know when the blackout dates will apply in order to take a proactive approach to managing his wealth. In short, it does him no good to be free from the lock-up agreement trap, described above, if he would get tripped up by a blackout period.

Example: Assume the same facts as the example above, except that the lock-up agreement ends on December 27, Year 1. But a blackout period is in place on December 27, 28, 29, 30, and 31 that prevents Rene from selling her ISO-stock.

In short, the optionee should know – *before* he exercises the ISO – that he can sell the ISO-stock on or before December 31 of the year of ISO exercise. Otherwise, he faces the possibility of being caught in a costly ISO trap.

RULE 144 STOCK

As discussed in Chapter 3, SEC Rule 144 does not prohibit the sale of stock in a *private* transaction. If the optionee wants to sell Rule 144 stock on or before December 31 of the year of ISO exercise, he might find a buyer. If he does, the buyer will likely demand a discount from the fair market value of freely-traded stock because of the Rule 144 restriction that accompanies the stock.

CHARITABLE DONATION OF ISO-STOCK

Taxpayers sometimes donate to charity appreciated stock that has a holding period of more than one year. The fair market value of the stock on the date of the donation is deductible as a charitable contribution on IRS Form 1040, Schedule A.

The taxpayer needs to be aware that his ISO-stock may have a special value that other stock in his portfolio does not have – dual basis. Sale of the dual basis stock might allow him to use more AMT credits to reduce his tax liability. Therefore, if he donates ISO-stock that – if sold – would allow him to use more of his AMT credit, he falls into the trap of increasing his cost of AMT (please see Chapter 8 "The Cost of AMT").

In the next example, Lara holds mature ISO-stock that had a large bargain element at the time of ISO exercise. Therefore, the stock has a low basis for purposes of regular tax, and a high basis for purposes of AMT. Consequently, she does not donate her ISO-stock; instead, she sells it and donates other highly-appreciated stock that she has held for more than one year.

Example: *Taxpayer wisely decides to sell mature ISO-stock instead of donating it to charity:* In Year 3, Lara decides to donate $100,000 of stock to charity, and sell $100,000 of stock to raise cash. She owns stock in just two companies – ABC Corporation and DEF Corporation. Each has a $100,000 fair market value and Lara's holding period for each is more than 12 months. Her basis in ABC stock is $1,000, for both regular tax purposes and AMT purposes. Her DEF stock is mature ISO-stock that she bought in Year 1 by exercising ISOs. Her basis is $1,000 for purposes of regular tax and $90,000 for purposes of AMT.

Therefore, if she would sell the ISO-stock for its $100,000 current value, she would report a $99,000 capital gain for purposes of regular tax ($100,000 - $1,000 = $99,000), but only a $10,000 capital gain for purposes of AMT ($100,000 - $90,000 = $10,000). The larger tax on capital gain for purposes of regular tax would substantially increase the "gap" between her regular tax liability and her tentative minimum tax. The increased gap would allow her to utilize AMT credits to reduce her Year 3 income tax liability. Consequently, Lara donates $100,000 of ABC stock to charity and sells $100,000 of ISO-stock. If she would do the reverse (that is, donate ISO-stock and sell ABC stock), she would likely place herself in the suboptimal position of paying more income tax in Year 3 in exchange for retaining 100 percent of her AMT credits into Year 4.

Table 7.3
Disqualifying Disposition of ISO-Stock
Repurchase Stock within 30 Days versus No Repurchase

	Repurchase	No Repurchase
(A) Fair Market Value of ISO-stock on Date of ISO Exercise	1,001,000	1,001,000
(B) Option Exercise Price	1,000	1,000
(C) Proceeds from Sale of ISO-stock	100,000	100,000
(D) Actual Gain (loss) on Sale of ISO-stock = (C) minus (B)	99,000	99,000
(E) Compensation Income Due to Sale of ISO-stock (Note 1)	1,000,000	99,000
(F) Income Tax on Compensation @ 40% Tax Rate = 40% x (E)	400,000	39,600
(G) Basis of ISO-stock sold = (B) plus (E)	1,001,000	100,000
(H) Capital Gain (loss) on sale of ISO-stock = (C) minus (G) (Note 2)	(901,000)	0
(I) Basis of "New" Shares Acquired = $100,000 minus (H) (Note 3)	1,001,000	N/A
(J) Capital Gain (loss) if "New" Shares are Sold for $100,000 = $100,000 minus (I)	(901,000)	N/A

Note 1:

If optionee repurchases the stock within 30 days, compensation income = bargain element on exercise date = (A) minus (B).

If optionee does not make a repurchase of the stock within 30 days, compensation income = lesser of bargain element on exercise date or the actual gain on sale of ISO-stock (if any) = lesser of: (A) minus (B), or (D).

Note 2:

The $901,000 loss on the sale of ISO-stock is a "wash sale" under IRC Section 1091. Consequently, such loss is not a deductible loss. The $901,000 becomes part of the basis of the "new" shares. See Note 3.

Note 3:

This example assumes that the optionee pays $100,000 to repurchase the stock. The basis of the "new" shares = purchase price of "new" shares + the loss disallowed under IRC Section 1091 = $100,000 + $901,000 = $1,001,000.

8

The Cost of AMT

Note: This chapter makes a number of important references to the time value of money, a subject explained in Appendix "*Time Value of Money*." In Chapter 9 "*ISO-Stock: The December 31 Decision*", the optionee uses the information from this chapter when trying to decide whether to hold ISO-stock beyond December 31 of the year of ISO exercise.

Alternative minimum tax can be a worrisome problem. In order for the optionee to know whether, and how much, he *should* worry it is important to project the cost of ISO-induced AMT – preferably *before* he *chooses* to trigger AMT (that is, he *chooses* to trigger AMT when he chooses to hold ISO-stock beyond December 31 of the year of ISO exercise, and the bargain element that existed on ISO exercise date triggers AMT). Choosing to pay AMT on an ISO exercise is a complex *investment decision,* and is one that the optionee sometimes makes without even realizing that he has made it (that is, he is sometimes not aware that holding ISO-stock beyond December 31 has income tax consequences associated with it).

Like any investment of a substantial amount of money, choosing to pay AMT should not be a decision made from the gut; and, as explained below, an out-of-the-box, one-size-fits-all answer generally does not exist. That is one reason for this chapter.

While it is unlikely that one can compute the *actual* cost of the AMT at the time it arises, he can *project* it. A well-prepared projection should serve him well (despite the fact that projections are subject to estimation errors) in making an informed decision with respect to the hold-sell decision on his ISO-stock.

Important: This chapter addresses the cost of AMT that is triggered by the exercise of an incentive stock option (that is, ISO-induced AMT). This chapter **does not apply** to AMT that is triggered by *exclusion items* such as state income taxes and miscellaneous itemized deductions, because AMT that is triggered by exclusion items does not generate an AMT credit.

This chapter discusses the following sections:

- *Economics of ISO-induced AMT*

- *Projected Cost of ISO-induced AMT*

ECONOMICS OF ISO-INDUCED AMT

When an optionee exercises an ISO and holds such ISO-stock beyond December 31 of the year of ISO exercise, he reports taxable income on his income tax return – for purposes of alternative minimum tax only – in the amount of the bargain element that existed on ISO exercise date. He receives an AMT credit in the amount of the AMT that is triggered by such AMT taxable income.

Internal Revenue Code Section 53(c) states that the optionee may use the AMT credit to reduce his regular income tax liability in tax years subsequent to the year of ISO exercise, but only to the extent that his regular income tax liability exceeds tentative minimum tax (that is, his tax liability computed under AMT rules).

In essence, then, ISO-induced AMT is not a tax in the truest sense of the word, because it is totally refundable. As explained below, it is more accurately described as partially a tax and partially a refundable tax deposit.

ISO-induced AMT is a tax in the amount of the opportunity losses that stem from the optionee's inability to earn returns on money that he must send to the IRS with his Year 1 income tax return. It is a refundable tax deposit in the amount of the present value of the AMT credit, which might be described as the *real* amount of AMT credit that he expects to recover from his ability to use such credit to reduce his future income tax liability.

Example: *ISO-induced AMT is partially a tax and partially a refundable tax deposit:* Lena exercises an ISO in Year 1, doesn't sell the stock in Year 1, and therefore the option exercise triggers $100,000 of AMT that she pays when she files her federal income tax return for the year ended December 31, Year 1. Consequently, she receives a $100,000 AMT credit. Lena is able to fully use the credit to reduce her tax liability by $100,000 in Year 2. Present value tables (please see Table A.4 for the present value of $1 to be received in the future) indicate that the $100,000 tax reduction in Year 2 had a present value of only $96,000 in Year 1. Economically, the $100,000 of AMT she pays in Year 1 is a refundable tax *deposit* in the amount of $96,000, and a *tax* in the amount of $4,000. Therefore, the cost of AMT is $4,000, the amount of the AMT tax payment that is really a tax.

In theory, the AMT credit should work as described in the example above. That is, the optionee pays AMT with his income tax return for Year 1 and recovers the AMT tax payment in full – via the AMT credit – when he sells the ISO-stock (in theory, his regular tax liability should exceed his tentative minimum tax liability, in the year he sells the ISO-stock, by an amount that is at least as great as the amount of the AMT credit).

For various reasons, the optionee's regular income tax liability in the year he sells the ISO-stock (in a qualifying disposition), often does not exceed his tentative minimum tax by an amount that is sufficient to utilize the full amount of the AMT credit. In fact, it sometimes takes years to use the entire AMT credit and some optionees are never able to use any of it.

PROJECTED COST OF ISO-INDUCED AMT

The question may arise: *"Why is it important to project the cost of ISO-induced AMT?"* The reason is that, as shown below, such information helps the optionee put the relevant issues into perspective and helps him decide whether to hold ISO-stock beyond December 31 of the year of ISO exercise.

COST-BENEFIT RULE

For some, projecting the cost of AMT is a simple task. For others, it is not.

When the numbers are not large enough to justify the effort or expense of projecting the cost of AMT, optionees will not find it wise to proceed with the analysis. In short, the cost of projecting AMT cost should not outweigh the expected benefit of having such information.

Example: *The cost to project AMT cost exceeds the expected benefit:* In Year 1, Teresa exercised an ISO that had a bargain element of $1,000 on the date of option exercise. If she does not sell the stock in Year 1, the $1,000 bargain element would trigger $260 of AMT and Teresa would receive a $260 AMT credit. Teresa isn't likely to spend much time or money, if any, projecting the cost of AMT because the potential payoff from having such information does not justify such efforts.

HOW TO PROJECT THE COST OF ISO-INDUCED AMT

As explained in the Appendix *"Time Value of Money,"* one dollar to be received in the future is worth less than one dollar. It naturally follows that the present value of every $1 of AMT credit is less than $1 because AMT credits can only be used to reduce an optionee's *future* regular tax liability (and only to the extent that his regular tax liability exceeds his tentative minimum tax liability). The optionee needs to value the AMT credit in order to arrive at the projected cost of AMT.

> The projected cost of ISO-induced AMT is computed as the dollar amount of AMT that the optionee would pay if he holds ISO-stock beyond December 31 of the year of ISO exercise, minus the present value of the corresponding AMT credit.

In order to compute the present value of an AMT credit, the optionee must generally make an income tax projection that shows how much AMT credit he will be able to use in each taxable year.

Some optionees will find that their unique tax situation requires a comprehensive analysis such as the one shown in Table 8.1.

Some optionees will find that the projected cost of AMT is relatively high (stated differently, the present value of the AMT credit is relatively low) because they project that it will take a long time to use the AMT credit, interest rates are unusually high, or both. Other things being equal, the higher the projected cost of AMT, the less attractive it is to hold ISO-stock beyond December 31 of the year of ISO exercise.

Others will find the projected cost of AMT relatively low (stated differently, the present value of the AMT credit is relatively high), for example, because they expect they will be able to use 100 percent of the AMT credit to reduce regular tax in the taxable year immediately following the year of ISO exercise, or interest rates are unusually low, or both.

Example: Projected cost of ISO-induced AMT equals AMT minus the present value of the corresponding AMT credit: Teresa buys ABC Corporation stock by exercising an ISO in Year 1. If she continues to hold such ISO-stock past December 31, Year 1, she will trigger $100,000 of AMT and receive a $100,000 AMT credit. Teresa projects the present value of the AMT credit at $80,000. Therefore, her projected cost of AMT is $20,000, which equals the $100,000 of AMT she would pay minus the $80,000 present value of the AMT credit.

DISCOUNT RATE FOR VALUING AN AMT CREDIT

Determining the appropriate discount rate is a weak link when computing the present value of an AMT credit, which is not an exact science.

First, the timing of future cash flows is generally not predictable with accuracy. Second, the amounts of such cash flows are not predictable with accuracy, either. Third, the discount rate one uses to compute such present value is not one that is determined in a competitive and free market; rather, it is a combination of the current yield on a U.S. Treasury security plus a subjectively-determined risk premium. Unfortunately, the alternative – not valuing a large AMT credit – is not a practical one because that value impacts the decision whether to hold or sell ISO-stock.

The starting point for establishing an appropriate discount rate for discounting projected income tax savings – from utilizing the AMT credit – is the yield on a *U.S. Treasury zero-coupon* security (called *U.S. Treasury Strips*) that matures in the same year as the year in which the optionee expects to use such AMT credit. The rate on the relevant U.S. Treasury security addresses the impact that the passage of *time* has on the value of the AMT credit. The starting point (that is, the yield on the U.S. Treasury security) is then adjusted upwards by a risk premium (the risk premium issue is discussed below).

Example: The yield on a U.S. Treasury security is the starting point for establishing an appropriate discount rate to compute the present value of an AMT credit: Amanda projects that if she holds ISO-stock beyond December 31 of the year of ISO exercise she will trigger $10,000 of AMT that would be payable with her income tax return for Year 1. She also projects that she would be able to use the entire $10,000 AMT to reduce her income tax liability one year later (that is, in Year 2). To establish a starting point for developing an appropriate discount rate, Amanda finds the yield on a U.S. Treasury Strip that matures after one year (that is, one that matures in Year 2).

If the optionee expects to use some of the AMT credit in one year and some in another year (a common scenario), he will need to find the yields on U.S. Treasury Strips with different amounts of time remaining to maturity date. Yields on U.S. Treasury Strips are posted daily in *The Wall Street Journal* under the section entitled *Treasury Bonds, Notes and Bills.*

Example: Different U.S. Treasury yields are applicable when the optionee expects to use some of an AMT credit in one year and some in another year: Esther projects that if she holds ISO-stock beyond the year of ISO exercise, she will trigger $10,000 of AMT in Year 1. She also projects that she would be able to use $3,000 of the corresponding $10,000 AMT credit to reduce her regular tax liability in Year 2 and $7,000 of the AMT credit to reduce her regular tax liability in Year 3. To establish a starting point for valuing the $10,000 AMT credit, she finds the yield on a U.S.

Treasury Strip that matures in Year 2 and the yield on a U.S. Treasury Strip that matures in Year 3.

RISKS OF HOLDING AN AMT CREDIT

With respect to risk, the optionee is not worried that the U.S. Treasury will default on the AMT credit, although there is a possibility that a change in tax law would affect the value of his AMT credit. He *is* worried, or should be, about *when* he will be able to use the credit, however, because money has a time value.

He is also worried about other characteristics of the AMT credit that adversely impact its value. For example, the owner of a U.S. Treasury security perceives that there is zero risk he will not receive *timely* interest and principal payments on the bond because such payments are guaranteed by the federal government. In contrast, the optionee does not know when, if ever, he will be able to use the AMT credit to reduce his future regular income tax liability.

The AMT credit is also inferior to a Treasury security in that the AMT credit is nontransferable (the optionee cannot sell it). He cannot pledge it as collateral, either. Further, the credit has no maturity date.

The AMT credit comes with two more risks – interest rate risk and inflation risk. But the optionee does not increase his subjectively-determined risk premium as compensation for such risks because owners of U.S. Treasury obligations are subject to interest-rate risk and inflation risk, too. Consequently, the current yield on the U.S. Treasury security that serves as the starting point for establishing an appropriate discount rate already "prices in" such risks.

Interest-rate risk is the risk that the *actual* opportunity cost of AMT will be higher than projected, due to a subsequent increase in interest rates. *Inflation-risk* is the risk that the purchasing power of the future tax savings that he reaps from using the AMT credit will be less than expected, because actual rates of future price inflation end up being higher than participants in fixed-income markets had expected at the time the optionee projected the cost of AMT.

RISK PREMIUM FOR VALUING AN AMT CREDIT

After he determines the current yield on the appropriate U.S. Treasury security, the optionee adds a subjectively-determined risk premium to such yield. That is because investors demand compensation, in the form of higher yields, for holding more risky assets.

In the next example, Martha subjectively assigns a two percent risk premium to the current yield on the relevant U.S. Treasury Strip to arrive at a pre-tax discount rate. Another optionee might assign a different risk premium (a higher one, if he would prefer to take the risk of (mistakenly) selling the stock in the calendar year of option exercise, rather than take the risk of (mistakenly) holding the stock beyond December 31).

Example: *See Table 8.1. How to compute the projected cost of ISO-induced AMT:* Martha projects that if she exercises an ISO in Year 1 and holds such ISO-stock beyond December 31, Year 1, she would trigger $100,000 of AMT. She projects that she would reduce her regular tax liability, from using the $100,000 of corresponding AMT credits, by $20,000 in each of Years 2 through 6.

Martha adjusts the yields on U.S. Treasury Strips by a subjectively-determined 2 percent risk premium to arrive at pre-tax discount rates as follows:

U.S.Treasury Maturity Date	U.S.Treasury Current Yield	+ Risk Prem	=	Pre-tax Discount Rate
Year 2	2.62%	2.00%		4.62%
Year 3	4.15	2.00		6.15
Year 4	5.69	2.00		7.69
Year 5	7.23	2.00		9.23
Year 6	8.77	2.00		10.77

Note in this example that the current yields on U.S. Treasuries are higher than actual yields were in early 2005. Higher yields result in a higher discount rate, which results in a lower present value of the AMT credit and, therefore, a higher projected cost of AMT.

Martha's marginal income tax rate is 35 percent. She converts the above pre-tax discount rates into after-tax discount rates as follows:

	Pre-tax Discount Rate	x (1-35% Tax rate)	= After-tax Discount Rate
Year 2	4.62%	.65	3.00%
Year 3	6.15	.65	4.00
Year 4	7.69	.65	5.00
Year 5	9.23	.65	6.00
Year 6	10.77	.65	7.00

In Year 1, Martha computes the present value of the $100,000 AMT credit as follows:

Year 2 $20,000 x (1 divided by 1.03^1)=$20,000 x .97 = $19,400
Year 3 $20,000 x (1 divided by 1.04^2)=$20,000 x .92 = 18,400
Year 4 $20,000 x (1 divided by 1.05^3)=$20,000 x .86 = 17,200
Year 5 $20,000 x (1 divided by 1.06^4)=$20,000 x .79 = 15,800
Year 6 $20,000 x (1 divided by 1.07^5)=$20,000 x .71 = 14,200

Present value of $100,000 AMT credit in Year 1 $85,000

Martha concludes that her projected after-tax cost of AMT is $15,000, which she computes as the $100,000 AMT credit minus the $85,000 present value of such credit. Later in this chapter (and continuing this example into Chapter 9), she takes this $15,000 projected cost into consideration when making a decision whether to sell such ISO-stock in Year 1.

TABLE 8.1: A COMPREHENSIVE EXAMPLE

A comprehensive example is perhaps the best way to explain how one projects the cost of ISO-induced AMT.

Example: Reference Table 8.1. Projected cost of AMT: Martha exercises an ISO on February 1, Year 1. If she holds such ISO-stock beyond December 31, Year 1, she must report the bargain element that existed on February 1, Year 1 as taxable income for purposes of AMT. Martha projects that such taxable income would trigger $100,000 of AMT and she would correspondingly receive a $100,000 AMT credit that would be available to reduce her regular income tax liability (to the extent it exceeds her tentative minimum tax liability) in tax years after Year 1. In Table 8.1 Martha prepares an analysis that shows a projection of when she would be able to use the AMT credits and a projection of the cost of AMT.

LINE BY LINE EXPLANATION OF TABLE 8.1

Lines 1 and 2: Martha prepares an income tax projection for Year 2. She makes a projection for the following year, and subsequent years, if necessary, until such projections show that the entire $100,000 AMT credit will be used.

Line 3: The excess, if any, of her projected regular tax liability over projected tentative minimum tax.

Line 4: The amount ($100,000) of AMT that the ISO exercise would trigger in Year 1 if Martha does not sell such ISO-stock in Year 1.

Line 5: The amount of AMT credit that has not been consumed in previous years and therefore is available for use.

Line 6: The amount of AMT credit that can be used to reduce her tax liability. It equals the excess, if any, of regular tax over tentative minimum tax as shown on Line 3.

Line 7: The present value factor that is used to compute the present value of the dollar amount of AMT credit she projects that she will use this year.

Line 8: The present value of the dollar amount of the AMT credit that the optionee projects she will use this year.

Line 9, col G: The $15,000 projected cost of AMT equals the $100,000 of AMT that would be triggered if she holds the ISO-stock beyond December 31, Year 1, minus the $85,000 present value of the AMT credit.

Lines 10-15: Development of an appropriate after-tax discount rate for valuing the AMT credit.

If Martha holds the stock beyond December 31, Year 1, she pays $100,000 of ISO-induced AMT (Table 8.1, line 4, column A) in Year 1 and receives a $100,000 AMT credit (line 5, column B).

Martha's projected after-tax cost of AMT is $15,000 (Table 8.1, line 9, column G). It consists of the $100,000 (line 4, column A) of AMT that she would pay if she does not sell the ISO-stock on or before December 31, Year 1, minus the $85,000 (line 8, column G) projected present value of the AMT credit.

Martha prepares an income tax projection for Year 2 because tax law says that Year 2 is the first year in which she may use the AMT credit. The projection shows a $20,000 (line 3, column B) excess of regular tax over tentative minimum tax (her tax computed using AMT rules). Therefore, she projects that she will use $20,000 (line 6, column B) of the $100,000 credit to reduce her regular income tax liability by $20,000 in Year 2 and will carry forward to Year 3 the remaining $80,000 AMT credit (line 5, column C).

Since the Year 2 projection shows an AMT credit carryover to Year 3, Martha prepares an income tax projection for Year 3. The Year 3 projection shows that regular tax exceeds tentative minimum tax (line 3, column C) by $20,000. Therefore, she would be able to use $20,000 of AMT credit to reduce her regular income tax liability by $20,000 in Year 3 (line 6, column C).

Martha continues the process until the point where line 6, column G, shows a total AMT recovery in the amount of $100,000 (that is, she projects that she will have used the entire AMT credit).

Martha enters the present value factors on line 7, columns B through F, for the various years based upon the after-tax discount rates on line 15, columns B through F.

She multiplies the present value factors on line 7, columns B through F by the amount of the AMT credit shown on line 6, columns B through F. The results appear on line 8, columns B through F as, "*Present value of AMT credit projected to be used this year.*"

The $85,000 present value of the AMT credit appears on line 8, column G.

The $15,000 projected after-tax cost of AMT appears on line 9, column G, and is computed as the excess of the $100,000 of AMT she would pay if she holds such ISO-stock beyond December 31, Year 1, over the $85,000 present value of the $100,000 AMT credit.

RISK

Projections are subject to estimation errors. Consequently, the *actual* cost of AMT is likely to differ from the *projected* cost. Other reasons, discussed in the section "*Discount Rate,*" include inflation risk and interest-rate risk.

If the actual cost of AMT is greater than the projected cost of AMT, the possibility exists that the optionee incorrectly decides to hold the ISO-stock into Year 2, instead of selling on December 31, Year 1. If the actual cost of AMT is less than the projected cost of AMT, then the possibility exists that he incorrectly decides to sell the stock in Year 1, instead of holding the stock beyond December 31, Year 1.

STOCK PRICE DECLINE MAY INCREASE ACTUAL COST OF AMT

In the previous example, Martha projects the after-tax cost of AMT at $15,000 under various assumptions, one of which is that she will sell the ISO-stock in a *qualifying* disposition (instead of a disqualifying disposition) and receive gross proceeds from such sale that are *equal* to the December 31, Year 1 fair market value (that is, assuming a constant stock price). But future stock prices are subject to a great deal of uncertainty.

If she holds the stock beyond December 31, Year 1 and proceeds from the eventual sale are less than the December 31, Year 1 fair market value, Martha may find it more difficult to use the $100,000 AMT credit than she had projected on December 31, Year 1. This could result in a higher cost of AMT.

One reason it could be more difficult to use the AMT credit is the $3,000 AMT capital loss limitation (please see Chapter 7 "ISO Tax Traps"). In short, Martha could be whipsawed by *two* unfavorable and costly consequences:

- Substantially lower gross proceeds from the sale,

   and,

- A higher cost of AMT

PUTTING THE COST OF AMT INTO PERSPECTIVE

After he computes the projected after-tax cost of AMT, the optionee is one step closer to getting his arms around the relevant issues that drive the December 31 decision.

Example: Putting the projected cost of ISO-induced AMT into perspective: Martha exercises an ISO on February 1, Year 1 and pays $140,000 to buy ABC Corporation stock, which is highly volatile. The fair market value of ABC stock on the date of ISO exercise is $500,000. The fair market value is $300,000 on December 31, Year 1 (a decline of 40 percent since ISO exercise date). She projects that, if she is able to sell the ISO-stock for $300,000 in a qualifying disposition in Year 2 (instead of selling for $300,000 in a disqualifying disposition on December 31, Year 1), she will have converted $160,000 of what would have been ordinary compensation income in Year 1, into $160,000 of long-term capital gain in Year 2. She projects that the conversion would save $32,000 in federal income tax (plus some amount of payroll tax). She evaluates the projected $32,000 tax savings ($160,000 x (35 percent tax rate on compensation income minus 15 percent tax rate on long-term capital gain) = $32,000) in light of the fact that in order to make a qualifying disposition she must continue holding $300,000 of highly volatile stock until February 2, Year 2, and that the projected after-tax cost of AMT is $15,000. Clearly, two optionees will often make *different* choices when faced with *identical* sets of information – because they have unique needs and circumstances, and differing degrees of aversion to risk.

Martha's example above is expanded in Chapter 9 *"ISO-Stock: The December 31 Decision"*.

USE THE AMT CREDIT WISELY

As explained in Chapter 4 under the section entitled *"AMT Planning is Different,"* the optionee sometimes finds it wise to accelerate the recognition of income into a year when he is otherwise subject to AMT *when exclusion items trigger AMT*. That section also explains that tax planning is different when an ISO exercise triggers AMT – because of the AMT credit – and he does not necessarily accelerate income in order to avoid AMT.

Example: *Optionee does not necessarily accelerate the recognition of income simply to use her AMT credit:* Helen has a $100,000 AMT credit. She also has unrealized appreciation in nonqualified stock options (NQSOs). If Helen decides to exercise such NQSOs, it is because an analysis supports such a decision. She would not, however, exercise them simply to accelerate use of the AMT credit.

AMTrecov

Table 8.1
Projected Cost of ISO-induced Alternative Minimum Tax

	(A) Tax Year 1	(B) Tax Year 2	(C) Tax Year 3	(D) Tax Year 4	(E) Tax Year 5	(F) Tax Year 6	(G) Total AMT Credit
Income tax projections:							
1 Projected regular income tax liability		$100,000	110,000	120,000	130,000	140,000	
2 Minus: Projected tentative minimum tax		80,000	90,000	100,000	110,000	120,000	
3 **Excess (if any) of regular income tax over tentative minimum tax**		20,000	20,000	20,000	20,000	20,000	
		=======	=======	=======	=======	=======	
Projected cost of AMT:							
4 Holding ISO-stock beyond December 31, Year 1 triggers this much AMT	100,000						
5 Amount of AMT credit available to reduce regular tax this year		100,000	80,000	60,000	40,000	20,000	100,000
6 AMT credit used this year (greater of zero or line 3 but not more than line 5)		20,000	20,000	20,000	20,000	20,000	
7 Present value factor from line 15		0.97	0.92	0.86	0.79	0.71	
8 Present value of AMT credit projected to be used this year (line 6 x line 7)		19,400	18,400	17,200	15,800	14,200	85,000
							-------
9 **Projected cost of AMT (line 6 - line 8)**							15,000
							=======
Development of discount rate for computing present value of AMT credit:							
10 Pre-tax yield-to-maturity on U.S. Treasury Strip maturing this year		2.62%	4.15%	5.69%	7.23%	8.77%	
11 Subjectively-determined risk premium for holding an AMT credit		2.00%	2.00%	2.00%	2.00%	2.00%	
12 Pre-tax discount rate appropriate for valuing AMT credits to be used this year		4.62%	6.15%	7.69%	9.23%	10.77%	
		======	======	======	======	======	
13 After-tax discount rate (line 12 x (1 - marginal income tax rate on line 14))		3.00%	4.00%	5.00%	6.00%	7.00%	
14 Taxpayer's marginal income tax rate		35.00%	35.00%	35.00%	35.00%	35.00%	
15 **Present value factor corresponding to the discount rate on line 13 *** (see Appendix, Table A-4)		0.97	0.92	0.86	0.79	0.71	

* In Year 1, the PV factor for $1 to be received after 1 year (that is, in Year 2) is .9709
In Year 1, the PV factor for $1 to be received after 2 years (that is, in Year 3) is .9246
In Year 1, the PV factor for $1 to be received after 3 years (that is, in Year 4) is .8638
In Year 1, the PV factor for $1 to be received after 4 years (that is, in Year 5) is .7921
In Year 1, the PV factor for $1 to be received after 5 years (that is, in Year 6) is .7130

9

ISO-Stock: The December 31 Decision

This chapter is directed to an individual who exercised an incentive stock option and still holds such ISO-stock as the end of the calendar year of ISO exercise approaches.

For one reason or another, the optionee decided to hold the ISO-stock at the time of option exercise (instead of making a same-day sale) because *at that time* the risk/reward tradeoff and his unique needs, circumstances, and appetite for risk favored such a decision. But stock prices are continually in a state of flux, and a stock price that led to the exercise-and-hold strategy on date of option exercise may have changed – perhaps drastically. Generally, a substantial decline in stock price after the date of option exercise is a warning sign that the optionee might find it wise to sell at least some of the ISO-stock that he bought earlier in the year.

The optionee faces a decision so important it could lead to a phenomenal after-tax annualized rate of return on his ISO-stock, or bankruptcy, or something in between.

Should he sell the stock on or before December 31, Year 1, or is the potential for income tax savings from a sale in a qualifying disposition (as opposed to a sale on December 31, which would be a disqualifying disposition) so great in relation to the risk that he should continue holding the stock?

The answer depends on several factors:

- The amount of projected income tax savings he would realize if he would continue to hold such ISO-stock just long enough to satisfy the special holding period requirements for long-term capital gain treatment (other things being equal, the greater the projected income tax savings, the more likely he will find it wise to hold the stock beyond December 31)

- How many days beyond December 31 he must continue holding such ISO-stock in order to satisfy the special holding period requirements for long-term capital gain treatment (other things being equal, the fewer the number of days he must hold the stock beyond December 31, the more likely he will find it wise to hold such stock beyond December 31)

- The projected after-tax cost of the AMT, if any, that would be triggered by holding such ISO-stock beyond December 31 (other things being equal, the lower the projected cost of AMT, the more likely he will find it wise to hold the stock beyond December 31)

- Volatility of the stock (other things being equal, the lower the volatility, the more likely he will find it wise to hold the stock beyond December 31)

- The optionee's unique needs and circumstances, and appetite for risk

This chapter demonstrates how an optionee approaches the often difficult decision in order to increase the likelihood of making the choice that is right for him, given his unique circumstances, because the December 31 question generally does not have a "one size fits all" answer. In fact, different optionees will often make different decisions when each owns the *same* ISO-stock, which had been purchased on the *same* option exercise date for the *same* option exercise price.

This chapter consists of the following sections:

- *Projected Payoff from Holding ISO-Stock*
- *Risk of Holding ISO-Stock*

The section covering the projected payoff from holding ISO-stock discusses topics that include:

- Projected income tax savings

- Projected after-tax cost of AMT

- Projected net benefit, which equals the projected income tax savings minus the projected after-tax cost of AMT

- Annualized projected after-tax "return"

The section covering the risk of holding ISO-stock just long enough to satisfy the special holding period requirements discusses topics that include:

- Income tax risk and investment risk

- The "break-even" stock price

- Probability that the stock price will decline below the "break-even" stock price during the period that the optionee waits to satisfy the special holding period requirements

After reading this chapter, the optionee should be able to put his arms around the extremely important issue of whether to hold ISO-stock beyond December 31.

More specifically, he should be able to establish perspective by having the following information:

- Projected income tax savings from holding ISO-stock just long enough to satisfy the special holding period requirements

- The annualized projected net benefit "return" from holding ISO-stock just long enough to satisfy the special holding period requirements

- The estimated "break-even" stock price at which the optionee would be more or less indifferent between a sale of ISO-stock on December 31, Year 1, or a sale on the first day that such sale would be treated as a qualifying disposition

- The estimated probability that holding ISO-stock beyond December 31, Year 1, will yield after-tax net proceeds (from a sale of such stock on the first day that such sale would satisfy the special holding period requirements) that equal or exceed the "break-even" stock price

- How to avoid a "nightmare" scenario if he chooses to hold ISO-stock beyond December 31 of the year of ISO exercise

PROJECTED PAYOFF FROM HOLDING ISO-STOCK

When the optionee holds ISO-stock beyond December 31 with the intention of satisfying the special holding period requirements for long-term capital gain, he makes a trade. He recognizes taxable income, for purposes of AMT only, in the year of ISO exercise, in exchange for the possibility of reaping an income tax savings by selling such stock after satisfying the special holding period requirements. But, as discussed below, holding ISO-stock beyond December 31 is often accompanied by substantial risk.

A rational, informed investor who exercised an ISO and still owns such ISO-stock at the end of December of the year of option exercise generally holds the stock into the next calendar year only when *all* of the following statements are true:

- The projected income tax savings from holding such stock until a date that is more than 12 months after the option exercise date substantially exceeds the projected cost of AMT (in other words, continuing to hold the stock has a substantial *projected net benefit*)

- The risk of holding such stock – from December 31, Year 1, until the first day that is more than 12 months after the option exercise date – is reasonable, relative to the projected net benefit

- He has the ability to bear any adverse financial consequences that would result if proceeds from his eventual sale of stock would be substantially below the current fair market value.

PROJECTED INCOME TAX SAVINGS

Generally, the potential for income tax savings is the carrot that entices the optionee to hold the stock after option exercise. If tax law did not offer the possibility of long-term capital gain treatment on 100 percent of the gain on ISO-stock, it is likely that far fewer would exercise ISOs and continue to hold the stock. Instead, they would likely make a same-day sale.

The *projected* income tax savings from holding ISO-stock into the next calendar year is equal to the excess (if any) of the amount of income tax that *would* result if the stock is sold at the end of the calendar year of option exercise (at its current price) over the amount of income tax that *would* result if the stock is sold (at its current price) on the date that is 12 months and one day after the option exercise date.

Example: *Optionee converts what would otherwise be ordinary compensation income into long-term capital gain by holding ISO-stock for 12 months and one day:* In the previous chapter, Martha exercises an ISO on February 1, Year 1 and the fair market value of the stock is $500,000. Her option exercise price is $140,000. The fair market value on December 31, Year 1, is $300,000 – a decline of 40 percent from ISO exercise date. If she sells her ISO-stock on December 31, Year 1, for $300,000, Martha would trigger $160,000 of ordinary compensation income in Year 1 that would be subject to income tax (and some amount of payroll tax) at her marginal tax rate. In contrast, if she sells the stock for $300,000 on the day she satisfies the holding period requirements, her sale of stock would be treated as a $160,000 long-term capital gain. Martha would effectively convert that $160,000 of (would-be) ordinary compensation income in Year 1 into $160,000 of more-favorable taxed long-term capital gain in Year 2. She projects that such conversion would result in a $32,000 income tax savings (and some amount of payroll tax).

TAX RATE SPREAD

Naturally, the excess (if any) of the projected income tax savings over the projected cost of AMT is greater when the *spread* between the optionee's marginal rate of income tax on ordinary income and his rate of tax on long-term capital gain is larger. Consequently, the optionee who is subject to a higher marginal rate has the potential to reap more income tax savings from converting ordinary income into long-term capital gain.

Example: Other things being equal, the larger the spread between the marginal income tax rate on ordinary compensation income and the tax rate on long-term capital gain, the more attractive it is to hold ISO-stock beyond December 31: Martha's marginal income tax rate is 35 percent and her rate of tax on long-term capital gain is 15 percent. The spread between the two rates of tax is 20 percent. If she converts $160,000 of what would otherwise be ordinary compensation income into long-term capital gain, she reduces her income tax liability by $32,000 (20 percent x $160,000 = $32,000). If, instead, the tax rate spread is only 15 percent, converting $160,000 into long-term capital gain would reduce her income tax liability by only $24,000.

PROJECTED NET BENEFIT

In Table 8.1, Martha projected her cost of AMT at $15,000. In the previous example (continuing the same fact pattern), she also projects a $32,000 income tax savings if she sells the stock for $300,000 (its current price) in a qualifying disposition, instead of for $300,000 on December 31, Year 1, in what would be a disqualifying disposition. Her after-tax projected net benefit from holding the ISO-stock is $17,000, which equals the $32,000 projected income tax savings minus the $15,000 projected cost of AMT.

If the projected net benefit would be minimal or nonexistent, it is generally wise to sell the ISO-stock on or before December 31. But in Martha's case, the projected net benefit of $17,000 is large enough for her to make further inquiry. Next, she evaluates how much risk she would have to take in order to reap the projected net benefit.

ANNUALIZED PROJECTED AFTER-TAX NET BENEFIT

In the previous example, Martha projects a $17,000 after-tax net benefit from holding $300,000 of stock just long enough to satisfy the holding period requirements. The annualized after-tax projected net benefit "return" (using the $17,000 projected after-tax benefit as the "return" in the numerator) depends on how long after December 31, Year 1, she must hold the stock in order to reap such projected net benefit.

Example: Annualized projected after-tax net benefit "return": Martha will satisfy the holding period requirement on February 2, Year 2. If on that date she sells the stock for $300,000 (its fair market value on December 31, Year 1), she projects that she will have earned 5.67 percent ($17,000/$300,000 = 5.67 percent) by holding such stock for approximately 1 month (from December 31, Year 1, until February 2, Year 2). Her annualized projected after-tax net benefit, after taking into account her $15,000 projected cost of AMT, is 68 percent, ignoring monthly compounding (5.67 percent per month x 12 months = 68 percent). Martha may find this projected "return" enticing enough to make further inquiry into how much risk she would have to endure.

It is important to note that the annualized projected after-tax net benefit "return" drops substantially as the number of days required to hold the ISO-stock after December 31 (in order to satisfy the holding period requirements) increases. For example, using data from the previous example, the annualized projected after-tax net benefit "return" falls to approximately 23 percent (5.67 percent per quarter x 4 quarters = 23 percent) if Martha would have to hold such stock for approximately 3 more months (that is, from December 31, Year 1 until April 2, Year 2). A large number of optionees would wisely conclude that the 23 percent figure is not sufficient for them to hold a stock with 70 percent volatility until April 2, Year 2. Instead, they would sell on or before December 31, Year 1.

RISK OF HOLDING ISO-STOCK

The optionee must be aware of two distinct risks when he continues to hold ISO-stock beyond December 31 of the year of ISO exercise. One, *income tax risk*, is a new risk that emerges on January 1 of the year following the year of ISO exercise if the bargain element that existed on ISO exercise date triggers AMT. Another, *investment risk*, is uncertainty with respect to the future fair market value of the ISO-stock.

The optionee will be subject to income tax risk (that is, there is uncertainty with respect to his cost of AMT) if the taxable income he must recognize in the year of ISO exercise, for purposes of AMT, in fact triggers some amount of AMT. One reason is that the cost of AMT is a function of when he will be able to enjoy the future (uncertain) tax savings from the AMT credit. Obviously, the sooner he can use the credit, the better.

The optionee will be subject to investment risk because the fair market value of his ISO-stock will almost certainly fluctuate during the time he waits to satisfy the special holding period requirement.

Further, the income tax risk described above is not independent from the investment risk. In other words, if the stock price plummets, the cost of AMT could increase substantially because (as described in Chapter 7 "*ISO Tax Traps*", with respect to the $3,000 AMT capital loss limitation) it could impede his ability to use the AMT credit.

In short, a plummeting stock price after December 31 is a double-edged sword that can deliver the optionee a disastrous result (for some, that means bankruptcy). Not only does a plummeting stock price reduce gross proceeds from the sale of stock, but the cost of AMT often increases substantially as a result of such lower gross proceeds because lower gross proceeds generally makes it more difficult to use the AMT credit.

BREAK-EVEN STOCK PRICE

Clearly, the fair market value of appreciated ISO-stock could decline by some amount after December 31, Year 1, and yet the income tax savings from making a qualifying disposition (instead of making a disqualifying disposition on December 31) would outweigh (a) the reduction in gross proceeds from the sale, *plus* (b) the cost of AMT that would result from holding beyond year end.

One relevant question is: *How much more decline in stock price could the optionee tolerate, such that he would be more or less indifferent between a sale of such stock on December 31 or a sale on the day that he satisfies the required holding periods?*

If the stock price at the end of December does not exceed the stock price on exercise date, the following equation may be used to estimate that "break-even" point for a non-dividend-paying stock:

$$F = \frac{A - AC + BC - BD + E}{1 - D}$$

Where,

A= December 31, Year 1, fair market value of ISO-stock that optionee will hold beyond December 31, Year 1

B= Option exercise price

C= Marginal tax rate on ordinary compensation income (including payroll tax)

D= Marginal tax rate on long-term capital gain

E= After-tax projected cost of AMT

F= Fair market value at which optionee is more or less indifferent between a December 31 sale of stock or a sale of stock on the date that he will satisfy the holding period requirements (this is the estimated break-even fair market value)

Note: The above equation assumes an interest rate of zero percent on cash equivalents. The estimated break-even fair market value increases as the interest rate on cash equivalents increases because gross proceeds from the December 31 sale can be reinvested during the period that the optionee (if he holds the stock beyond December 31) waits to satisfy the special holding period requirements.

The above equation also assumes that "E," the after-tax cost of AMT remains constant regardless of changes in the stock price; in fact, because of the $3,000 AMT capital loss limitation, "E" is likely to increase (*perhaps substantially*) if the stock price declines from its December 31 level, and likely to decrease if the stock price increases from its December 31 level.

Example: The following data is from Martha's example above:

A = $300,000
B = $140,000
C = 35 percent
D = 15 percent
E = $15,000

A sale of Martha's ISO-stock on or after February 2, Year 2 (approximately one month after December 31, Year 1) would be a qualifying disposition.

Solving for "F," the break-even fair market value, one arrives at $280,000. In short, Martha would be *more or less* indifferent (from an economic point of view) between a sale of ISO-stock on December 31, Year 1, that generates gross proceeds in the amount of $300,000 (and after-tax proceeds of $244,000) or a sale of ISO-stock on the date that she will satisfy the "more than 12 months" holding period and that generates gross proceeds in the amount of $280,000 (a decline from $300,000 to $280,000 is 6.67 percent) and projected after-tax wealth of $244,000. Please see the reconciliation below.

Stated differently, holding the *entire* $300,000 block of ISO-stock long enough to satisfy the holding period requirements for long-term capital gain has a positive payoff provided that proceeds from the February 2, Year 2 sale of stock are more than 93.33 percent (100 percent minus 6.67 percent equals 93.33 percent) of the $300,000 December 31 fair market value. Conversely, it has a negative payoff if the stock price declines by more than 6.67

percent, in which case proceeds from the sale are less than 93.33 percent of the December 31 fair market value.

Reconciliation:

	SELL DEC. 31, YEAR 1	SELL FEB. 2, YEAR 2
Proceeds	$300,000	$280,000
Exercise price	140,000	140,000
Taxable amount	$160,000	$140,000
Tax liability	56,000 (1)	21,000 (2)
Proj. cost of AMT	N/A	15,000
After-tax amounts	$244,000 (3)	$244,000 (4)

(1) $160,000 compensation income x 35 percent = $56,000

(2) $140,000 long-term capital gain x 15 percent = $21,000

(3) $300,000 – $56,000 = $244,000 = *actual* after-tax *proceeds*

(4) $280,000 – $21,000 – $15,000 = $244,000 = *projected* after-tax *wealth*

Note:

This analysis assumes that the optionee earns no interest income, from December 31, Year 1 until February 2, Year 2, on proceeds from a December 31, Year 1 sale of stock. This assumption is not likely to materially affect the results shown in the proof, however.

Also note that "Sell December 31, Year 1" is more or less *equivalent to* "Sell Feb. 2, Year 2", but not *equal to* because the $244,000 after-tax amount in the former is "actual after-tax proceeds in Year 1" and the $244,000 after-tax amount in the latter is what might be described as *"projected after-tax wealth* measured in Year 1".

PROBABILITY OF A POSITIVE PAYOFF

Martha then considers the probability that she will experience a positive payoff if she holds the ISO-stock beyond December 31, Year 1 and sells it on February 2, Year 2, which is the first day that she would satisfy the special holding period requirements.

Martha consults Table 2.4, which shows an estimated probability of 43 percent that a stock with a volatility of 70 percent will decline by more than 5 percent over a one-month holding period if the annual interest rate is 3 percent, and Table 2.3, which shows an estimated probability of 33 percent that the same stock will decline by more than 10 percent over a one-month holding period.

She uses interpolation to estimate the probability that her ISO-stock will decline by more than 6.67 percent, and therefore result in a negative payoff. She arrives at a probability of 40 percent (43 percent minus 1.67/5.00 x (43 percent minus 33 percent) = 40 percent). Stated differently, the estimated probability of a positive payoff is 60 percent (100 percent minus 40 percent equals 60 percent); that is, the estimated probability is 60 percent that proceeds from the sale of stock one-month later will equal or exceed the $280,000 break-even stock price.

It is important to notice that the above analysis evaluates the decision to hold or not hold the *entire* $300,000 block of ISO-stock beyond December 31, Year 1. As explained later, not every share of ISO-stock has the same value to the optionee, and if Martha determines that it is not wise to hold the entire block of stock beyond December 31, Year 1, it is important for her to refine her analysis to determine how much, if any, ISO-stock she could hold such that the risk/reward tradeoff would suit her unique needs and circumstances and appetite for risk.

IF BREAK-EVEN STOCK PRICE EXCEEDS THE CURRENT STOCK PRICE

In the previous example, "F," the break-even fair market value of $280,000 is less than the $300,000 current fair market value. That indicates there is some amount of income tax motivation for holding ISO-stock beyond December 31 (the next step is to determine if such motivation is sufficient in relation to the amount of risk).

If the break-even fair market value "F" would equal or exceed the $300,000 current fair market value, it means that there is not enough income tax motivation for the optionee to hold the ISO-stock beyond December 31.

If he *does* decide to hold the stock when "F" exceeds the current fair market value, it is generally because the optionee feels that the knowledge he possesses with respect to the value of the stock is superior to the knowledge of the market, and that the stock is currently undervalued. Generally, however, it is unrealistic for optionees to believe that their ability to compute the fair market value their employer's stock is superior to the ability of market participants operating in U.S. securities markets.

BREAK-EVEN SENSITIVITY TO PROJECTED AMT COST

It is important to realize that projecting the break-even stock price is not an exact science. Generally, the weakest link in the break-even stock price equation, shown above, is "E," the projected cost of AMT.

For example, if the income tax projection used to project the cost of AMT contains errors that result in the projected cost of AMT being substantially greater than the actual cost (in short, the optionee is able to use the AMT credit much faster than the income tax projection indicates), he could end up selling the ISO-stock on December 31 when he should be holding. The converse is also true. If he understates the projected cost of AMT, he could end up holding the stock beyond December 31 when he should be selling the stock on that date.

One way to approach the uncertainty with respect to "E" is to prepare a sensitivity analysis – that is, by setting "E" at various amounts ranging from zero dollars (that is to say, that the projected cost of AMT is zero) to the dollar amount of AMT that would be triggered by holding the ISO-stock beyond December 31 (that is to say, that the optionee will never be able to use any of the AMT credit, and therefore, 100 percent of the amount of AMT that would be triggered by holding the ISO-stock beyond December 31 would be the projected cost of AMT).

PERSPECTIVE ON HOLDING ISO-STOCK

In the earlier example, Martha is not tossing a coin into the air when trying to make a decision about whether to hold ISO-stock that has declined by 40 percent since ISO exercise date. Her decision to hold or sell the entire $300,000 block of ISO-stock beyond December 31, Year 1 is influenced by the following:

- Projected income tax savings = $32,000, if proceeds from her eventual sale of stock in a qualifying disposition equal the $300,000 fair market value on December 31, Year 1

- Annualized projected after-tax net benefit "return" = 68 percent, if proceeds from her eventual sale of stock on February 2, Year 2 (in what would be a qualifying disposition) equal the $300,000 fair market value on December 31, Year 1

- Approximate break-even stock price = $280,000, a price that is 6.67 percent less than the $300,000 fair market value on December 31, Year 1

- Estimated probability = 60 percent that proceeds from a February 2, Year 2 sale of stock will equal or exceed the $280,000 break-even stock price (as explained in Chapter 2, the estimated probability is derived from the Black-Scholes model, which contains some assumptions that likely are not valid; consequently, by extension, estimated probability derived from such model is certainly a "rough" number)

STOCK PRICE VOLATILITY AND TIME

As shown in the previous example, time is a critical factor in assessing risk. The more days after December 31 that the optionee must hold the ISO-stock in order to satisfy the "more than 12 months" holding period, the more risky it is to hold such stock beyond December 31 – other things being equal.

> While the optionee is powerless over the amount of risk attributable to stock price volatility, he controls the amount of time that his money is subject to such volatility. He is in control of this portion of the risk because he chooses the date of ISO exercise.

Example: *Exercising an ISO at the beginning of January minimizes exposure to the amount of stock price risk one must endure after December 31 of the year of ISO exercise:* Irina exercises an ISO on January 2, Year 1. She will satisfy the "more than 12 months" holding period requirement on January 3, Year 2. Therefore, if she holds her ISO-stock beyond December 31, Year 1, she must endure stock price risk for only two calendar days in Year 2.

ISO-SHARES OFTEN HAVE DIFFERENT VALUES

In the discussion presented earlier, Martha determines that, on December 31, Year 1, her $300,000 block of ISO-stock presented a projected income tax savings of $32,000 and a projected net benefit of $17,000 ($32,000 minus $15,000 projected after-tax cost of AMT = $17,000) and that the projected annualized after-tax net benefit "return" was 68 percent – if she could sell the stock for its current $300,000 fair market value on the first day (February 2, Year 2) that she would satisfy the holding period requirements.

Martha senses that not every one of her 1,000 shares of ISO-stock has the same value (to her) on December 31. She confirms her suspicion using the same equation presented earlier, incorporating information that she uncovered from her Year 1 income tax projection:

$$F = \frac{A - AC + BC - BD + E}{1 - D}$$

More specifically, in the next example, Martha discovers that "F," the break-even stock price, is 13 percent lower than the December 31, Year 1 stock price – if she holds only $150,000 of ISO-stock beyond December 31, Year 1.

That 13 percent tolerance for decline in stock price compares favorably with a break-even stock price that is only 6.67 percent lower than the December 31, Year 1 stock price if she holds the entire $300,000 block of ISO-stock beyond December 31, Year 1. Therefore, Martha concludes that not every ISO-share has the same value (to her) – because of income tax considerations.

The logical extension of this is that, since the projected weighted average after-tax "return" for the entire $300,000 block of stock described above is 68 percent, some shares have a projected after-tax "return" of more than 68 percent (perhaps far more) and some have a projected after-tax "return" of less than 68 percent (perhaps far less).

Example: *If she holds only $150,000 (instead of $300,000) of ISO-stock beyond December 31, Year 1, she could tolerate a 13 percent (instead of a 6.67 percent) decline in stock price:* Martha's income tax projection for Year 1 shows that if she continues to hold only $150,000 (therefore, A = $150,000, and B = $70,000, in the equation above) of ISO-stock into Year 2 and sells the other $150,000 of ISO-stock on December 31, Year 1, she would not trigger any AMT in Year 1 (that is, "E" equals zero in the above equation). That result *could* be due to the fact that the disqualifying disposition of $150,000 of ISO-stock in Year 1 triggers the recognition of ordinary compensation income and increases the gap between regular tax and tentative minimum tax, which allows her to trigger more AMT taxable income without triggering AMT. In short, E, the after-tax cost of AMT, would equal zero – if she would hold only $150,000 (instead of $300,000) of ISO-stock beyond December 31, Year 1. Solving for F, she arrives at a break-even stock price of $131,176, which is almost 13 percent less than the $150,000 current stock price. That means she would be more or less indifferent between sales proceeds of $131,176 on the date that she will satisfy the holding period requirements or sales proceeds of $150,000 on December 31, Year 1.

WHY IDENTICAL ISO-SHARES MAY HAVE DIFFERENT VALUES

It may seem odd that *identical* shares of ISO-stock could have *different* values to the optionee. The reason is AMT. Other things being equal, the more costly is AMT, the less attractive it is for the optionee to hold the stock beyond December 31. In short, the cost of AMT impacts the "options" he has with respect to such stock and, therefore, the stock's value (to him).

The optionee should be aware that he is holding ISO-shares of different value when either of the following conditions exists:

- *Condition #1:* If he holds one share of ISO-stock beyond December 31, Year 1, he would not trigger AMT in Year 1, but if he holds more than one share of ISO-stock beyond December 31, Year 1, he would trigger AMT in Year 1 (therefore, one share has zero AMT cost, and one or more shares do have an AMT cost associated with them if held beyond December 31, Year 1)

- *Condition #2:* If he holds one share of ISO-stock beyond December 31, Year 1, he would trigger $X of AMT in Year 1 but would recover the entire $X in Year 2 by using the AMT credit to reduce his regular tax liability. But, if he holds more than one share of ISO-stock beyond December 31, Year 1, and triggers $X+ of AMT in Year 1, he would *not* be able to recover the entire $X+ of AMT in Year 2 via the AMT credit.

Example: *Reference Condition #2 above:* If Alice holds one share of ISO-stock beyond December 31, Year 1, the ISO-stock triggers $100 of AMT, she receives a $100 AMT credit, and she expects to use the $100 AMT credit to reduce her Year 2 tax liability. Instead, if she holds two shares of ISO-stock beyond December 31, Year 1, she triggers $200 of AMT and receives a $200 AMT credit. But her tax projection shows that she would likely use only $150 of AMT credit in Year 2, and $50 of AMT credit in Year 3. Any AMT credit that can't be used until Year 3 is worth less (that is, has a lower present value) than an AMT credit that can be used in Year 2 – because of the time value of money.

By definition, the lower the present value of the AMT credit, the higher the cost of AMT. In short, Alice is holding two shares of ISO-stock and each has a different value (to her). This information alerts her to the fact that it might not be wise to hold two shares of ISO-stock beyond December 31, Year 1, but it might be wise to hold one share beyond December 31, Year 1.

> When the optionee is alert to the fact that he is holding ISO-shares of different value, he is also alert to the fact that such shares have different economic payoffs, on an after-tax basis. Consequently, if analysis leads him to conclude that it is not wise to hold his *entire* block of ISO-stock beyond December 31 of the year of ISO exercise, he knows that additional analysis might lead him to conclude that he should hold *some* ISO-stock beyond December 31.

THE NIGHTMARE SCENARIO

If the optionee exercises an ISO and holds such ISO-stock beyond December 31, Year 1 (and continues to hold such stock during a protracted decline in the stock price), he faces the possibility that proceeds from the eventual sale could be less than the amount of AMT he must pay when he files his income tax return on April 15, Year 2.

Against the odds, this actually happened to many optionees when stock prices came crashing down during the devastating bear market that began in 2000 and ended in 2002. Some optionees who had exercised ISOs and continued to hold the stock found themselves in bankruptcy court.

Example: *Proceeds from the sale of ISO-stock are insufficient to pay the AMT that is due on April 15, Year 2:* Erica exercises an ISO on April 1, Year 1. She will satisfy the holding period requirements on April 2, Year 2, and intends to sell her ISO-stock on that date. She expects to use some of the proceeds to pay the $100,000 of AMT that will be due when she files her calendar Year 1 income tax return on April 15, Year 2. If the price of her stock comes crashing down such that proceeds from the April 2, Year 2 sale are substantially less than $100,000, Erica may find herself in a liquidity crisis, scrambling for cash to pay the Internal Revenue Service.

AVOIDING THE NIGHTMARE SCENARIO

Table 2.3 shows a 25 percent estimated probability that a stock with 50 percent volatility will decline by more than 10 percent over a one-month holding period – if the risk-free annual interest rate is 3 percent (and, therefore, there is a 75 percent probability that the stock will not decline by more than 10 percent). Stated differently, the estimated probability is 75 percent that the stock price will equal or exceed 90 percent of its current price.

Such probabilities are useful in adding perspective to the decision-making process but they are not infallible. One weakness, from a risk management perspective, is that there is no mention of how large the decline in stock price could be.

Another relevant issue is that an optionee is not likely to have a large number of "opportunities" with respect to ISO-stock. Generally, he will not be presented with the same set of conditions over and over again such that, more or less, 75 times out of 100 he can expect a positive result.

In short, probabilities, expected values, and other wealth-maximizing strategies that rely on present values work well when the investor has the opportunity to repeat the decision several times over the long run. But the majority of optionees will not have numerous opportunities to let probabilities run their course, and holding ISO-stock beyond December 31, Year 1 could result in financial ruin. Optionees can avoid such a scenario by holding sufficient cash reserves, which may mean liquidating at least some or perhaps all their ISO-stock on December 31, Year 1.

Example: *On or near December 31, Year 1, the optionee ensures that he has sufficient cash to pay any balance due on April 15, Year 2, with IRS Form 1040:* Martha determines that she would be unable to meet her financial obligations, if the prices of her ISO-stock and other securities in her non-retirement (taxable) investment account decline substantially during the period after December 31, Year 1, while she waits to satisfy the holding period requirements. To insure against a disastrous result, Martha sells enough securities on or near December 31 such that sales proceeds (after taxes) are sufficient to pay the projected amount of income taxes due on April 15, Year 2.

RAISING CASH ON DECEMBER 31, YEAR 1

In the previous example, Martha's strategy is to sell enough securities on or near December 31, Year 1, so that she has sufficient liquidity on April 15, Year 2. Then she must decide which securities to sell. If she holds only ISO-stock, the answer is simple – she must sell it.

Since the annualized projected after-tax net benefit from holding ISO-stock is high (68 percent), however, she would prefer not to sell ISO-stock on December 31, Year 1. If her unique needs and circumstances are such that she has the ability to bear risk, Martha may be a candidate for a different approach.

For example, she may sell securities, whose expected returns have a high correlation with her employer stock, in an amount sufficient to pay the projected amount of income taxes due on April 15, Year 2 – and hold 100 percent of her ISO-stock beyond December 31, Year 1. Or, she may decide to rebalance her portfolio such that during the period from December 31, Year 1, through the first day that she could sell the ISO-stock in a qualifying disposition, she is holding only ISO-stock and cash equivalents. In fact, there may be a wide range of portfolio-positioning alternatives available to her during the period December 31, Year 1, through the first day that she could sell the ISO-stock in a qualifying disposition.

Example: If the annualized projected net benefit is high, under certain circumstances the optionee might hold 100 percent of her ISO-stock beyond December 31, Year 1, and sell other securities on or near December 31, Year 1: Martha owns ISO-stock of ABC Corporation, a leading software developer and a mature firm. The annualized projected after-tax net benefit from holding the ISO-stock beyond December 31, Year 1, is 68 percent. The value of such ISO-stock, plus the intrinsic value of her employee options to buy such stock, is not large in relation to the fair market value of her overall investment portfolio, nor is it large in relation to her net worth. It means that she has the ability to bear the additional risk that is unique to holding ISO-stock beyond year end. If she decides that she would like to raise cash on or near December 31, Year 1, she sells stocks for whose expected returns are highly correlated with those of ABC Corporation. Consequently, to the extent possible, she sells shares in *other* mature software development companies, and those of other companies in *related* fields, because the share prices of such companies are likely to move in tandem with the price of her ISO-stock.

Example: *The optionee attempts to realize capital losses, or to trigger a minimal amount of capital gains:* In the previous example, Martha decides to liquidate securities other than ISO-stock on or near December 31, Year 1, such that she has sufficient cash to pay her projected income tax liability on April 15, Year 2. Generally, when she selects securities for liquidation she makes an effort to sell those that would trigger large capital losses, or those that would trigger minimal capital gains. She would try to avoid the sale of securities that would trigger large capital gains.

10

ISO-Stock Protection Strategies

This chapter is best described as a defensive one, not an offensive one, because it contains material that illustrates why certain ISO-stock protection strategies generally don't work. Its primary objective is to protect the optionee from an unexpected and unpleasant surprise.

When he exercises an ISO and intends to hold the stock for 12 months and one day in order to receive more favorable income tax treatment, the optionee assumes the risk that the stock price will decline. An interesting question arises:

> *Is there a way to protect the value of appreciated and immature ISO-stock <u>and</u> still receive preferential income tax treatment from the eventual sale of such stock by selling it more than 12 months after ISO exercise date and more than two years after ISO grant date?*

This chapter discusses the following hedging strategies for immature ISO-stock, that address the question presented above:

- *Short Sale Against the Box*

- *Put Option on Identical Stock*

- *Collaring the Stock*

- *Put Option on a Broad-Based Index*

These discussions explain that:

- A short sale against the box is not a viable protection strategy because the IRS treats the short sale as a disposition of the ISO-stock.

- Buying a put option on identical stock, assuming that the purchase of such option is not treated as a disqualifying disposition of the ISO-stock (the IRS has not ruled on this), is not a viable protection strategy because the put option and the stock are considered to be a *straddle* that adversely impacts the holding period of the ISO-stock.

- Assuming that the establishment of a collar is not treated as a disqualifying disposition of the ISO-stock (the IRS has not ruled on this), collaring the stock is not a viable protection strategy because the collar is considered to be a straddle that adversely impacts the holding period of the ISO-stock.

- Buying a put option on a broad-based index is a viable protection strategy, but carries the risk that the value of the broad-based index will not move in tandem with the value of the ISO-stock.

Hedging stock is a specialized area and the tax and regulatory rules, which are not always clear, are sometimes subject to varying interpretations. For these and other reasons, it is important to engage the services of experts that have extensive experience in this area, before entering into any hedging transaction.

SHORT SALE AGAINST THE BOX

An optionee might ask whether he can borrow identical stock from his broker and make a short sale of such stock in order to freeze (protect) the value of his ISO-stock. A short sale of identical stock is called a *short sale against the box*. The next example illustrates the economics of a short sale against the box.

Example: Economics of a short sale against the box: Irina's total portfolio consists of 100 shares of ABC stock (known as a "long" position), which has a current value of $100 per share (total value = $10,000 = 100 shares x $100 per share). If she sells short 100 shares of ABC at $100 per share (known as a "short" position), she freezes the value of her portfolio at $10,000. That is because every subsequent $1 increase in the value of her long position in ABC stock is exactly offset by a $1 decrease in the value of her short position in ABC stock.

SHORT SALE IS A DISPOSITION OF ISO-STOCK

Under tax law, the *qualified* stock option preceded the incentive stock option. Like stock acquired by exercise of an ISO, stock acquired by exercise of a qualified stock option had special holding period requirements in order to receive preferential income tax treatment.

In Revenue Ruling 73-92, the Internal Revenue Service ruled that a short-sale of identical stock, which was made before satisfying the special holding period requirement with respect to the stock he bought by exercising a qualified stock option, constituted a *disposition* of the stock that he bought by exercising such qualified stock option.

In short, a short sale of identical stock is treated as a disposition of the ISO-stock.

Example: Short sale against the box is a disposition of ISO-Stock: On January 2, Year 1, Martha exercises an ISO to buy 100 shares of ABC Corporation stock. On July 1, Year 1, while still holding the ISO-stock that she bought on January 2, she sells short 100 shares of ABC stock. The July 1 short sale is a disposition of 100 shares of ISO-stock. Since the disposition occurs before satisfying the special holding period requirement, it is a *disqualifying* disposition of ISO-stock. Therefore, Martha cannot use a short sale against the box to achieve the dual objectives of protecting the value of her ISO-stock and receiving preferential tax treatment from later satisfying the special holding period requirements.

PUT OPTION ON IDENTICAL STOCK

The buyer (the holder) of a *put* option pays what is called a "premium" (that is, he pays money) for the right, but not the obligation, to *sell* 100 shares of the underlying security at a specific (strike) price until a specific date. Generally, the holder may sell the put option at any time before expiration date, exercise the option, or allow it to expire.

Example: *A put option places a "floor," equal to the put option strike price, under the value of Company A stock:* Linda owns 100 shares of Company A stock and she wishes to protect against a decline in its value. The current price is $100 per share; therefore, the total value of her 100 shares is $10,000. Linda buys a put option on Company A stock for $5 (she pays $500 for the option because one put option gives her the right to sell 100 shares of Company A stock). The put option gives her the right, but not the obligation, to sell 100 shares of Company A stock at $100 per share (that is, she would receive proceeds of $10,000 from the sale of 100 shares at $100 per share) until the option expiration date. In short, the put option protects Linda from a decline in the price of Company A stock below $100 per share during the term of the option, because she can sell it for $100 per share at any time up to option expiration date – even if the price of Company A stock falls to zero.

The purchase of a put option on identical stock might be treated by the IRS as a disqualifying disposition of the ISO-stock. The purchase of a put option is not a viable solution for the specific question at hand – even if the put option is not treated as a disqualifying disposition – because the put option plus the ISO-stock is considered a straddle, which stops the holding period on the stock.

PUT OPTION PLUS STOCK IS A STRADDLE

This section explains that if the optionee holds ISO-stock for not more than 12 months at the time he buys a put option (and such purchase is not treated as a sale or disposition of his stock under any section of tax law) on identical stock, the regulations under IRC Section 1092 provide that the holding period stops on his ISO-stock and starts again (from zero) when he no longer holds the put option. In summary, he gets tripped up by the *straddle* rules under IRC Section 1092 if:

- He buys a put option on Company A stock

  and,

- On the date of such purchase, he has not held the ISO-stock of Company A for more than 12 months.

Under U.S. Treasury Temporary Regulation 1.1092(b)-2T(a)(1), the put option and the ISO-stock constitute a straddle, which is defined by IRC Section 1092(c) to mean offsetting positions with respect to personal property.

Under Temporary Regulation 1.1092(b)-2T(a)(1), the holding period of stock, which has not been held more than one year at the time such straddle was entered into, "...shall not begin earlier than the date the taxpayer no longer holds directly or indirectly (through a related person or flowthrough entity) an offsetting position with respect to that position."

This means that:

- The optionee *loses* all of the holding period on the ISO-stock that had accrued at the time he bought the put option,

  and,

- The holding period on his ISO-stock starts to run (from zero) only after he no longer owns such put or any other position that is "offsetting" to his ISO-stock.

Example: *The put option and the ISO-stock constitute a straddle and the optionee loses all of the holding period that had* *accrued at the time she bought such put option:* On January 2, Year 1, Martha exercises an ISO to buy 100 shares of ABC Corporation stock. On July 2, Year 1, the price of ABC stock is $100 per share and she buys a put option that gives her the right to sell 100 shares of ABC stock at $100 per share. The put option and the ISO-stock constitute a straddle. Martha's purchase of the put option causes her to lose the six months' holding period on her ISO-stock that had accrued from January 2 until July 2, because on the date she bought the put option she had not held the ISO-stock for more than 12 months. The holding period on the ISO-stock starts running again (from zero) when Martha no longer owns the put option or any other position that is offsetting to her ISO-stock.

COLLARING THE STOCK

A collar is a strategy that establishes a floor and a ceiling on the value of the optionee's stock. A collar consists of three positions:

1. The optionee owns shares of Company A stock.

2. He buys a put option that gives him the right, but not the obligation, to sell shares of Company A stock at a price that is *below* the current price (i.e., he is "long" a put option).

3. He sells (that is, he is the writer or grantor) a call option on Company A stock that gives the holder of such option the right, but not the obligation, to buy Company A stock at a price that is *above* the current price (i.e., he is "short" a call option).

The put option and the call option have the same expiration date.

Example: A collar places a floor and a ceiling on the value of the stock: Lynne owns 100 shares of Company A stock. The current stock price is $100. She buys one put option on Company A stock that has a strike price of $90. She sells one call option on Company A stock that has a strike price of $105. Lynne has collared her Company A stock. The put option places a $90 floor on the value of Company A stock because Lynne can sell the stock for $90 even if the market price fall substantially below $90. The call option places a $105 ceiling on the value of her Company A stock because the owner of the call option can buy the stock at $105 even if the market price rises substantially above $105.

The establishment of a collar might be treated by the IRS as a disqualifying disposition of the ISO-stock. The establishment of a collar is not a viable solution for the specific question at hand – even if the collar is not treated as a disqualifying disposition – because the collar plus the ISO-stock is considered a straddle, which stops the holding period on the stock.

COLLAR PLUS STOCK IS A STRADDLE

In Revenue Ruling 2002-66, the Internal Revenue Service ruled that the stock and a collar on such stock is a straddle.

Under Temporary Regulation 1.1092(b)-2T(a)(1), the holding period of stock, which has not been held more than one year at the time such straddle was entered into, is lost if the optionee collars the stock. In summary, the collar protects the value of the ISO-stock but it does not allow the ISO-stock to mature.

Example: The put option, the call option, and the ISO-stock constitute a straddle and the optionee loses all of the holding period on the stock that had accrued at the time she collared such stock: On January 2, Year 1, Martha exercises an ISO to buy 100 shares of ABC Corporation stock. On July 2, Year 1, she collars the stock (that is, she buys a put option and sells a call option on ABC stock). The stock plus the collar is a straddle under Revenue Ruling 2002-66. Therefore, Temporary Regulation 1.1092(b)-2T(a)(1) provides that Martha loses the six-month holding period that had accrued from January 2 until July 2 because, on the date she collared the stock, she had not held it for more than 12 months.

PUT OPTION ON A BROAD-BASED INDEX

The optionee could attempt to protect the value of his ISO-stock by buying a put option on a broad-based index such as the NASDAQ. His purchase of such a put option does not impact his ISO-stock in any way.

The *risk* of this strategy is that the price of his ISO-stock declines and the underlying security or basket of securities does *not* decline or declines by a lesser amount.   If this happens, any gain on the put options will be insufficient to offset the decline in the value of the ISO-stock.

Example: *Optionee exercises an ISO and buys a put option on the NASDAQ 100 index:* Pam exercises an ISO on January 15. On January 16 she buys a put option on the NASDAQ 100 index because her broker advises her that historical returns on her ISO-stock are highly correlated with those of the NASDAQ 100. Pam's purchase of the put option does not affect her ISO-stock.

11

Stock Grants

Companies often grant stock – sometimes in addition to, and sometimes instead of, stock options – in exchange for services. Employees and non-employees are eligible to receive stock grants.

Income taxation of a stock grant differs, depending on whether the stock is *vested*. Stock is vested on grant date if the stock is transferable, *or* is not subject to a "substantial risk of forfeiture" on grant date (please see Chapter 3 for a discussion of the term "substantial risk of forfeiture").

If the stock is vested on the date of grant, Internal Revenue Code Section 83(a) provides that the grantee recognizes *compensation income* on the date of *grant* – in the amount of the excess of the fair market value of the stock on the date of *grant* over the amount the grantee pays for such stock.

If the stock is *not* vested on the date of grant, Section 83(a) provides that the grantee does not recognize compensation on the grant date. He recognizes compensation income on the date the stock vests – in the amount of the excess of the fair market value on the date the stock vests over the amount the grantee pays for such stock.

Since stock grants are generally subject to income tax on *vesting* date, and since optionees are generally not subject to income tax until they *exercise* nonqualified stock options, stock options have an income tax advantage over stock grants. This distinction may be important in that the grantee receiving stock does not enjoy the same opportunity for tax deferral, and the opportunity to control the timing of income recognition, as that afforded to optionees receiving options. It is also significant because the grantee must have cash to pay the associated tax liability that is triggered on vesting date, and may be forced to sell stock that he would prefer to hold.

If the stock is not vested on the date of grant, but the grantee files a Section 83(b) election within 30 calendar days after receiving such stock, he recognizes compensation income on the date of grant – in the amount of the excess of the fair market value of the stock on the date of grant over the amount the grantee pays for such stock – and there are no income tax consequences when the stock eventually vests.

This chapter explains that the grantee should always make what might be described as a "risk-free" Section 83(b) election. A risk-free election is one that does not trigger any compensation income on the grant date. The opportunity for a risk-free election is present when, on the date of grant, the fair market value of the stock equals the grantee's purchase price.

Grantees must be aware, however, that a Section 83(b) election, which is *not* risk-free, is an investment decision – not just a tax decision. In other words, it could result in a lower tax liability, and still be an unwise investment choice. In short, grantees should not assume that the Section 83(b) election is always a wise course of action. Often, it is not.

After examining the alternatives, the grantee will often find that an outright purchase of the grantor corporation's stock – when such alternative is available to the grantee – offers the potential for a greater after-tax return than the potential from a Section 83(b) election on such stock.

A number of companies issue a restricted stock unit ("RSU"), which is generally an unfunded and unsecured promise by the grantor corporation to issue grantor stock to the grantee on vesting date. An RSU is different from a stock grant and is not considered "property" under IRC Section 83. Consequently, the grantee of an RSU cannot make an IRC Section 83(b) election.

This chapter discusses the following sections:

- *Taxation of Stock Grants*
- *Special Tax Rules on Dividend Income*
- *Section 83(b) Election is an Investment Decision*
- *Section 83(b) Election Issues*
- *Taxation of Restricted Stock Units*

TAXATION OF STOCK GRANTS

This section describes the federal income tax and federal payroll tax treatment of stock grants.

As mentioned above, the amount of compensation income that the grantee recognizes – and the date on which such recognition occurs – depends on when the stock *vests*. Therefore, it is important to understand the term "vested stock". The answer is found under Internal Revenue Code Section 83.

VESTED VERSUS NON-VESTED STOCK

Stock is vested on the date of grant if it is *either*:

(a) transferable

or

(b) not subject to a substantial risk of forfeiture

Stated differently, stock is *not* vested on the date of grant if – on grant date – it is *both*:

(a) not transferable

and

(b) subject to a substantial risk of forfeiture

SUBSTANTIAL RISK OF FORFEITURE

As discussed in Chapter 3, a *substantial risk of forfeiture* exists on the date of grant when terms of the transfer give the corporation the right to repurchase the stock at the same price that the stock was sold to the grantee if the grantee ceases to perform services for the corporation before the vesting date.

Example: Stock is not vested on grant date: In Year 1, ABC Corporation sells one share of its common stock at fair market value to Mary, an employee. Under terms of the transfer, Mary forfeits the stock if her employment terminates before January 15, Year 5. Mary's stock is not vested on grant date – even though she is required to pay fair market value to buy such stock – because she cannot sell it and must forfeit the stock if her employment terminates before January 15, Year 5.

STOCK IS VESTED ON GRANT DATE

IRC Section 83(a) provides that if the stock is vested on the date of grant, the grantee recognizes compensation income on the date of grant. The amount of income he recognizes is equal to the excess of the fair market value of the stock on grant date over the price he pays to buy such stock.

Example: Stock is vested on grant date and grantee recognizes compensation income on grant date: On January 15, Year 1, Lucy, an employee of Company A, receives a stock grant from Company A as compensation for services and pays nothing for such stock. The fair market value of the stock on the date of grant is $10,000. Lucy may sell the stock immediately (that is, the stock is transferable). Since she may sell the stock on the grant date, it is vested on grant date. Under IRC Section 83(a), Lucy recognizes $10,000 of ordinary compensation income on the date of grant – the excess of the $10,000 fair market value of the stock on grant date over the amount (zero) she pays for it.

SALE OF STOCK THAT WAS VESTED ON GRANT DATE

The grantee's basis in stock that is vested on grant date is the amount he pays to acquire such stock plus the amount of compensation income that he recognizes on grant date.

Example: Basis equals purchase price plus the amount of compensation income recognized on grant date: In the example above, the stock is vested on grant date. Lucy pays nothing for the stock and recognizes $100 of compensation income. Therefore, her *basis* in the stock is $100, which consists of her purchase price (zero) plus the $100 of compensation income she reports on her individual income tax return.

IRC Section 83(f) provides that the *holding period* of stock begins on the vesting date.

Example: Holding period begins on vesting date: In the previous example, Lucy receives a stock grant on January 15, Year 1 and the stock is vested on grant date. Her holding period for the stock begins on January 15, Year 1, the grant date.

Example: Sale of stock that was vested on grant date: Continuing the example above, Lucy later sells the stock. If proceeds from such sale exceed her $100 basis, she realizes a capital gain. If proceeds are less than $100, she realizes a capital loss. Any gain or loss is long-term capital gain or loss if the sale date is more than 12 months after January 15, Year 1. Any gain or loss is short-term capital gain or loss if the sale date is not more than 12 months after January 15, Year 1.

STOCK IS <u>NOT</u> VESTED ON GRANT DATE AND GRANTEE DOES <u>NOT</u> MAKE SECTION 83(b) ELECTION

IRC Section 83(a) provides that if the stock is not vested on the date of grant, the grantee does *not* recognize compensation income on the date of grant. Consequently, if the stock is not vested on grant date and he does not make a timely Section 83(b) election to recognize compensation income on grant date, the grantee recognizes income on the date the stock vests. The amount of income he recognizes on the date the stock vests equals the excess of the fair market value of the stock *on the date the stock vests* over his purchase price.

Example: *Stock is not vested on grant date and therefore grantee does not recognize compensation income on grant date:* Donna, an employee of Company A, receives a stock grant from Company A and pays nothing for the stock. The fair market value of the stock is $100 on the January 15, Year 1 grant date. Donna's stock is not vested because she forfeits the stock if her employment terminates within 12 months. Donna does not recognize any income on the date of grant because the stock is not vested on the date of grant.

Example: The stock vests and grantee recognizes compensation income on vesting date: Donna continues to work for Company A and satisfies the 12-month employment period. On January 15, Year 2 her stock is vested because it is no longer subject to a substantial risk of forfeiture. The fair market value of the stock on the vesting date is $300. Donna recognizes $300 of ordinary compensation income on the January 15, Year 2 vesting date – the excess of the $300 fair market value on the vesting date over the amount (zero) she pays to acquire the stock.

SALE OF STOCK THAT WAS NOT VESTED ON GRANT DATE AND GRANTEE DID NOT MAKE SECTION 83(b) ELECTION

The grantee's basis in stock that was not vested on grant date is the amount he pays to acquire such stock plus the amount of compensation income that he recognizes on vesting date.

Example: Basis equals purchase price plus amount of compensation income recognized on vesting date: In the previous example, the stock is not vested on grant date. Donna pays nothing for the stock and recognizes $300 of ordinary compensation income on vesting date. Therefore, her basis in the stock is $300, which equals the amount she pays to buy the stock (zero) plus the $300 of compensation income she recognizes on vesting date.

IRC Section 83(f) provides that the *holding period* of stock begins on the vesting date.

Example: Holding period begins on vesting date: In the previous example, Donna receives a stock grant on January 15, Year 1 and the stock is not vested on grant date. Her holding period for the stock begins on January 15, Year 2, the date that the stock vests.

Example: Sale of stock that was not vested on grant date and grantee did not make Section 83(b) election: Continuing the example above, Donna later sells the stock. If proceeds from such sale exceed her $300 basis, she realizes a capital gain. If proceeds are less than $300, she realizes a capital loss. Any gain or loss is long-term capital gain or loss if the sale date is more than 12 months after January 15, Year 2. Any gain or loss is short-term capital gain or loss if the sale date is not more than 12 months after January 15, Year 2.

STOCK IS NOT VESTED ON GRANT DATE BUT GRANTEE MAKES SECTION 83(b) ELECTION

The previous section explains that the grantee does not recognize compensation income on grant date if the stock is not vested on grant date. This section illustrates that the grantee has the power to change the tax consequences for stock that is not vested on grant date by making a Section 83(b) election within 30 days after receipt of such stock.

THE SECTION 83(b) ELECTION

The Section 83(b) election:

- Accelerates the recognition of compensation income (and the associated payroll taxes) from vesting date to grant date

- Changes the amount of compensation income recognized to the excess of the fair market value of the stock on the *grant date* over the grantee's purchase price (instead of the excess of the fair market value of the stock on the *vesting date* over the grantee's purchase price)

- Accelerates the start of the holding period on the stock from vesting date to grant date

IRC Section 83(b) provides that if a grantee performs services and receives non-vested stock in exchange for such services he may *elect* to recognize compensation income, if any, on the *grant date* (if he does not make the election, he will recognize compensation income, if any, on vesting date). If the grantee makes the Section 83(b) election, he recognizes compensation income in the amount of the excess of the fair market value of the stock on *grant date* over the amount he pays to acquire such stock.

The election always changes the *date* (taxation occurs on grant date instead of vesting date) on which the grantee recognizes compensation income. Generally, the election does not change the *total* amount of income that will ultimately be subject to income tax.

And, if the fair market value of the stock on grant date is different from the fair market value on vesting date, the election will have changed the amount of compensation income recognized by the grantee. If the fair market value is higher (lower) on vesting date than on grant date the election will have resulted in less (more) compensation income and a lower (higher) basis in the grantee's stock.

Generally, a grantee makes the Section 83(b) election when he expects (but, he must be aware that expectations may not materialize and the Section 83(b) election is not risk free if it triggers a tax liability) that by doing so he will convert what would have been compensation income, in the absence of a Section 83(b) election, into capital gain. This chapter illustrates these concepts and other relevant issues with respect to a Section 83(b) election.

Example: *Stock is not vested on grant date but grantee makes a Section 83(b) election that triggers the recognition of compensation income on grant date:* Gail, an employee of Company A, receives a stock grant from Company A on January 15, Year 1 and pays nothing for the stock. The fair market value of the stock is $100 on grant date. Gail's stock is not vested because she forfeits the stock if her employment terminates within 12 months. Gail makes a timely Section 83(b) election, which triggers the recognition of ordinary compensation income on grant date. Consequently, Gail recognizes $100 of compensation income – the excess of the fair market value of the stock on grant date over the amount (zero) she pays for such stock – on January 15, Year 1.

RISK-FREE SECTION 83(b) ELECTION

The Section 83(b) election is **risk-free** to the grantee if the fair market value of the stock on the date of grant is *equal* to the grantee's purchase price. That is because the election triggers no compensation income and therefore no income tax and no payroll tax. In short, the grantee invests nothing when he makes the election, yet such election offers him the potential for preferential income tax treatment.

For example, if the stock price is higher on vesting date than it was on grant date, the risk-free election will have resulted in less compensation income. It will also have resulted in a lower basis in his stock. Therefore, if he would sell such stock on vesting date, the election will have converted what would have been ordinary compensation income on vesting date (if he had not made the election) into capital gain on vesting date. Note in this case that the total amount of income subject to tax does not change, but less of the total is characterized as compensation income and more is characterized as capital gain.

Further, a Section 83(b) starts the clock running on the grantee's holding period. This may be an important consideration for grantees that intend to sell the stock as soon as possible, yet reap the benefit of having satisfied the more-than-12 months holding period that is required for the sale of appreciated stock to qualify for long-term capital gain treatment.

In summary, the grantee should *always* make a Section 83(b) election whenever such election would not trigger additional tax. But, as discussed later in this chapter the grantee will often find that a Section 83(b) election, which would trigger additional tax on grant date, is an inferior investment as compared to alternatives of equivalent risk.

No Tax Consequences on Vesting Date

Regulation 1.83-2(a) provides that, if the grantee makes a Section 83(b) election, he does not recognize any taxable income when the stock vests.

Sale of Stock for Which Grantee Had Made a Section 83(b) Election

Regulation 1.83-2(a) provides that the grantee's *basis* in stock that was not vested on grant date but is now vested – *and* for which the grantee had made a Section 83(b) election – is the amount he paid to acquire such stock plus the amount of compensation income that he recognized on grant date.

The previous paragraph describes the basis of stock if the grantee does not forfeit such stock. As explained later in this chapter, if the grantee forfeits the stock (that is, the stock never becomes vested) his basis consists only of the amount he paid to acquire such stock.

Example: *Basis of vested stock equals purchase price plus the amount of compensation income recognized on grant date:* On January 15, Year 1, Tracy, an employee of Company A, receives a stock grant from Company A as compensation for services and pays nothing to acquire such stock. The fair market value of the stock on the date of grant is $10,000. The stock is not vested on grant date. Tracy makes a Section 83(b) election, which triggers $10,000 of ordinary compensation income on grant date. That $10,000 is the excess of the $10,000 fair market value of the stock on grant date over the amount (zero) she pays to acquire it. Tracy's basis in Company A stock will be $10,000 if she does not forfeit such stock (that is, if it eventually vests). That $10,000 basis equals the amount she pays to acquire such stock (zero) plus the $10,000 of ordinary compensation income she recognizes on grant date.

Regulation 1.83-4(a) provides that the *holding period* begins just after the date the stock is transferred to him, if he has made a Section 83(b) election. Accelerating the start of the holding period is an important consideration for grantees who intend to sell the stock as soon as possible (often on vesting date) yet still satisfy the more-than-12-months holding period required for long-term capital gain treatment.

Example: The Section 83(b) election accelerates the start of the holding period to the time of option exercise: In the previous example, Tracy's holding period on the stock that is not vested on grant date begins at the time of option exercise – because she makes a Section 83(b) election. If she had not made the election, her holding period would begin on vesting date.

Example: Sale of stock that was not vested on grant date but for which grantee had made a Section 83(b) election: Continuing the example above, Tracy does not forfeit the stock (that is, it becomes vested) and she sells it. If proceeds from the sale exceed her $10,000 basis, she realizes a capital gain. If proceeds are less than $10,000, she realizes a capital loss. Any gain or loss on the sale is long-term capital gain or loss if the sale date is more than 12 months after the date of option exercise, or short-term capital gain or loss if the holding period is not more than 12 months.

TAX WITHHOLDING FOR EMPLOYEES

Under Regulation 31.3401(a), the term "wages" – for purposes of withholding – includes compensation income that arises when a corporation transfers its own stock (for example, makes a stock grant) to an *employee* as remuneration for services.

Regulation 31.3402(a)-1(c) states that "... employer is required to deduct and withhold the tax notwithstanding the wages are paid in something other than money (for example, wages paid in stocks or bonds)....and to pay over the tax in money. If wages are paid in property other than money, the employer should make necessary arrangements to insure that the amount of the tax required to be withheld is available for payment in money."

Example: Compensation income earned by an employee is subject to withholding: Lillian is an employee of Company A. She recognizes $10,000 of compensation income from a stock grant. Such income is subject to all of the following:

- income tax withholding

- social security tax withholding

- Medicare tax withholding

In practice, the employer generally requires the grantee to write it a check in the amount of the required income tax withholding, social security tax withholding, and Medicare tax withholding on compensation income.

NO TAX WITHHOLDING FOR NON-EMPLOYEES

Generally, withholding on compensation income is not required for an individual who is not an employee.

Example: Generally, compensation income earned by a non-employee is not subject to withholding: Lorie is not an employee of Company A. Like Lillian in the previous example, Lorie receives a stock grant that triggers $10,000 of compensation income. But, unlike Lillian, Lorie's income is generally not subject to income tax withholding, social security tax withholding, or Medicare tax withholding because of her non-employee status. Nevertheless, the $10,000 of compensation income *is* subject to:

- income tax

  and,

- self-employment tax

TAXATION OF STOCK FORFEITURES

If the grantee's stock is not vested on grant date, the possibility exists that he will *forfeit* the stock because, for example, his employment terminates before vesting date.

If he forfeits the stock and must sell it back to the grantor, the grantee's taxable capital gain (or loss) is computed as the difference between his proceeds from such sale and the amount he paid (if any) to acquire the stock.

The next two examples show that in cases where a grantee forfeits the stock, the amount of his taxable capital gain (or loss) is the *same* – whether he had not made a Section 83(b) election (the first example below), or whether he had (the second example below).

The reason that the taxable capital gain (or loss) is the same under both scenarios is that the basis of forfeited stock is the same. That is, basis of forfeited stock equals the grantee's purchase price.

The grantee that makes a Section 83(b) election and later forfeits the stock does not increase his basis by the amount of compensation income he had recognized on grant date. The reason is found under IRC Section 83(b)(1), which provides that if the grantee makes a Section 83(b) election and later forfeits the stock, he receives no deduction for any compensation income that was triggered by such election.

Example: *Grantee does not make a Section 83(b) election and later forfeits the stock:* Jane receives a stock grant from Company A and pays $1,000 for the stock. The fair market value of the stock on the date of grant is $3,000. Terms of the grant provide that Jane forfeits the stock if her employment terminates before November 4, Year 3 (the vesting date) and, if her employment does terminate, she must sell the stock back to Company A for $1,000. Therefore, Jane's stock is not vested on grant date. She does not make a Section 83(b) election. Her employment terminates before vesting date and Company A pays $1,000 to buy her stock. Jane's proceeds from the sale are $1,000 and her basis is $1,000; consequently, she has no taxable capital gain or loss from the sale.

Example: *Grantee makes a Section 83(b) election and later forfeits the stock:* The facts are the same as in the preceding example, except that Jane makes a Section 83(b) election. The election triggers the recognition of $2,000 of compensation income on grant date – the excess of the $3,000 fair market value of the stock on grant date over her $1,000 purchase price. IRC Section 83(b)(1) provides, however, that Jane receives no deduction for the

$2,000 of compensation income she recognized on grant date – if she forfeits the stock. Jane's employment terminates before vesting date and she forfeits the stock. Company A pays $1,000 to repurchase such stock. Jane has incurred an *economic* loss in the amount of tax that was triggered by the $2,000 of compensation income that she recognized on stock grant. But, IRC Section 83(b)(1) limits her basis to $1,000, the amount she paid to buy the stock. As in the previous example, Jane reports on her income tax return $1,000 of proceeds from the sale, and basis in the amount of $1,000; therefore, as in the previous example, her income tax return shows no taxable capital gain or loss from such sale.

Table 11.1
Income Tax Treatment of Stock Grants

Example:

Grantee's purchase price	$ 0
Proceeds from sale of stock to grantor if grantee forfeits non-vested stock	0
Fair market value of stock on grant date	10,000
Fair market value of stock on vesting date	15,000
Proceeds from eventual sale of stock	19,000

Three Different Scenarios	Compensation Income on Grant Date	Compensation Income on Vesting Date	Holding Period Begins	Basis of Stock (1)	Capital Gain (loss) on Eventual Sale of Stock	Capital Gain (loss) if Grantee Forfeits Stock
A Stock is vested on grant date	$10,000 = $10,000 FMV - $0 purchase price (3)	Not applicable; stock is vested on grant date	On grant date	$10,000	$9,000=$19,000 proceeds minus $10,000 basis. Report on IRS Form 1040, Schedule D	Stock is vested on grant date so there is no chance of forfeiture
B Stock is not vested on grant date and grantee does not make Section 83(b) election	None	$15,000 = $15,000 FMV - $0 purchase price (3)	On vesting date	$15,000	$4,000= $19,000 proceeds minus $15,000 basis. Report on Form 1040, Schedule D	Zero (2). Report sale on IRS Form 1040, Schedule D
C Stock is not vested on grant date but grantee makes Section 83(b) election	$10,000 = $10,000 FMV - $0 purchase price (3)	None	On grant date	$10,000	$9,000=$19,000 proceeds minus $10,000 basis. Report on Form 1040, Schedule D	Zero (2). Report sale on IRS Form 1040, Schedule D

(1) Basis equals the amount paid to buy the stock (zero) + the amount of compensation income reported on IRS Form 1040

(2) Capital gain or loss on forfeiture = Proceeds on forfeiture (zero) minus amount paid to buy the stock (zero) = zero

(3) The company includes this amount on IRS Form W-2 for employees. Non-employees receive IRS Form 1099-MISC

Special Tax Rules on Dividend Income

The income tax treatment for dividends received varies, depending on whether or not the stock is vested.

Dividends on Vested Stock

Dividends received by the grantee retain their character as dividend income if the stock is vested.

Example: *Dividends received on the stock are taxable as dividend income, not as compensation income, if the stock is vested on grant date:* ABC Corporation makes a stock grant to Lucy. The stock is vested on grant date. Dividends that she receives on such stock are characterized as dividend income – not as compensation income. ABC Corporation reports such income to the Internal Revenue Service on IRS Form 1099-DIV.

Dividends on Unvested Stock

Whether dividends on unvested stock are characterized as dividend income or as compensation income depends on whether or not the grantee has made a Section 83(b) election for such stock.

Compensation income is subject to income tax, social security tax, and Medicare tax, while dividend income is subject only to income tax. Further, under current law, dividend income receives preferential income tax treatment relative to compensation income.

Regulation 1.83-1(a) provides that the company is the owner of the stock until the stock vests and that any income from such stock that is received by the grantee before vesting date constitutes additional *compensation* income to the grantee. The following example describes the taxation of dividend income if the grantee does not make a Section 83(b) election.

Example: *Dividends received on unvested stock are taxable as compensation income, not as dividend income, if grantee has not made a Section 83(b) election:* Donna receives a stock grant on January 15, Year 1 and the stock does not vest until January 15, Year 2. Donna does not make a timely Section 83(b) election.

Any dividends she receives on such stock during the period the stock remains unvested are characterized as compensation income (not as dividend income) that is reported to her on IRS Form W-2.

TAX TREATMENT OF DIVIDENDS IF GRANTEE MAKES 83(b) ELECTION

Regulation 1.83-2(a) treats the stock as substantially vested and the grantee is considered to be the owner of the stock if the grantee makes a Section 83(b) election. In Revenue Ruling 83-22 the IRS ruled that dividends received by the grantee retain their character as dividend income if the grantee has made a Section 83(b) election.

Example: Dividends received on the stock are taxable as dividend income, not as compensation income, if the grantee has made a Section 83(b) election: Gail receives a stock grant from ABC Corporation. The stock is not vested on grant date. Gail files a Section 83(b) election, which triggers the recognition of compensation income on grant date. In accordance with Revenue Ruling 83-22, dividends that she receives on the stock are characterized as dividend income, not as compensation income.

SECTION 83(b) ELECTION IS AN INVESTMENT DECISION

> The Section 83(b) election for stock grants is sometimes touted as a wise maneuver. Often, it is not.

For example, some grantees have made the election – for stock that was publicly-traded on grant date – on stock received from the grantor at *no cost* because they expected the fair market value of the stock to be substantially higher on vesting date than on grant date. Yet, as shown below, if the grantee expects the fair market value of the stock, which he receives from the grantor at no cost, to be higher on vesting date his financial resources are sometimes better applied by simply buying such stock outright.

Rational, informed investors generally invest only when they expect to be compensated for the risk that such investment entails.

In order to measure the amount of such compensation that a Section 83(b) election might deliver under various scenarios, grantees should always project the annual after-tax return from making an election before investing any money in that election.

Succeeding discussions in this chapter illustrate that making a Section 83(b) election that is not risk-free (that is, when the fair market value of the stock on grant date exceeds his purchase price) generally proves to be a "dream" investment when all of the following statements are true:

- The grantee cannot make an outright purchase of the grantor corporation's stock (that is because an outright purchase of the stock, which appreciates from grant date to vesting date, often yields a higher return than the return from the Section 83(b) election)

- The fair market value of the stock appreciates at a high rate from grant date to vesting date (that is, the election results in substantially less compensation income on grant date than there would have been – in the absence of the election – on vesting date)

- During the period beginning on grant date and continuing through vesting date, the fair market value of the stock appreciates at a rate that substantially exceeds the rate of appreciation on alternative investments (that is, the grantee's "investment" in the Section 83(b) election is not overshadowed by returns he could have earned on alternative investments)

- The grantee's marginal tax rate on compensation income is lower on grant date than on vesting date (that is, he pays tax – on the excess of fair market value on grant date over his purchase price – at a lower tax rate than he would pay in the absence of an election)

- On vesting date, the grantee has satisfied the more-than-12-months holding period, he sells his stock, and his marginal tax rate on long-term capital gain on vesting date is substantially lower than his marginal tax rate on compensation income on vesting date (that is, he converts a large amount of appreciation, which takes place from grant date to vesting date, from what would have been compensation income – in the absence of an election – into long-term capital gain)

IRR ON THE SECTION 83(b) ELECTION

This section explains how to project the after-tax internal rate of return ("IRR") from making a Section 83(b) election. The projection is generally subject to some amount of uncertainty because the timing of relevant cash flows is not 100 percent predictable. More specifically, the full amount of the income tax liability that is triggered on grant date by the Section 83(b) election is not always withheld on grant date.

Six assumptions apply to the discussion that follows:

- The stock does not pay a dividend

- Fair market value of the stock is higher on vesting date than on grant date

- The grantee's marginal rate of tax on compensation income is the same in the taxable year in which the stock is granted as it is in the taxable year in which such stock vests

- In the taxable year in which the stock vests, the grantee's marginal rate of tax on compensation income equals or exceeds his rate of tax on long-term capital gain

- Vesting date is more than 12 months after grant date

- The grantee intends to sell the stock on vesting date

Essentially, the above assumptions imply that the grantee's project "return" from making a Section 83(b) election consists *solely* of the income tax benefit that he hopes to enjoy from converting – into more favorably taxed long-term capital gain – 100 percent of the appreciation in fair market value that occurs from grant date to vesting date. In many cases, this is the platform from which a Section 83(b) election is made.

In short, a grantee generally does not make a Section 83(b) election if he expects little or no appreciation in stock price from grant date to vesting date, or if he expects that his marginal tax rate on compensation income at the time of vesting would not exceed his tax rate on long-term capital gain at the time of vesting.

The choice of whether to make a Section 83(b) election is an investment decision that results in a cash outflow on grant date in exchange for the possibility of tax savings at a future date. The grantee considers the amount of cash outflows he will *certainly* incur (if he makes the election) on grant date, relative to the *projected* cash inflows that are directly attributable to a Section 83(b) election. Such projected cash inflows consist **solely** of the projected tax benefit from converting what would be compensation income on vesting date (if an election would *not* be made, and the fair market value of the stock on vesting date exceeds fair market value on grant date) into capital gain from the sale of such stock on vesting date (if an election *is* made). By taking into account only those cash flows that are attributable solely to the Section 83(b) election, the grantee is able to project the yield that is directly attributable to making the election.

HOW TO PROJECT THE TAX BENEFIT FROM THE ELECTION

Since the expectation of income tax benefits drives the decision to make a Section 83(b) election, the grantee makes a projection of these benefits before making such election.

Based upon the six assumptions presented above, the projected tax benefit, "B," attributable to the conversion of compensation income into long-term capital gain is:

$$B = (P_2 - P_1) \times (R_O - R_C)$$

Where:

P_2 = *projected* fair market value of stock on vesting date

P_1 = *actual* fair market value of stock on grant date

R_O = tax rate on compensation income on vesting date. It is the *projected* amount of income and payroll taxes that would be triggered by the recognition of compensation income on vesting date divided by the amount of such compensation income (expressed as a percentage) – if a Section 83(b) election is *not* made [and where R_O equals or exceeds R_C]

R_C = tax rate on long-term capital gain on vesting date. It is the *projected* amount of capital gain tax that would be triggered by a sale of the stock on vesting date divided by the amount of projected appreciation in fair market value from grant date to vesting date (expressed as a percentage) – if a Section 83(b) election *is* made [and where R_C is less than or equal to R_O]

Example: *Projected tax savings is $3.75, which equals the $15 projected increase in stock price multiplied by the projected 25 percentage point spread - on vesting date - between the marginal tax rate on ordinary compensation income, R_O, and the tax rate on long-term capital gain, R_C:* P_2, the projected fair market value at vesting date is $30. P_1, fair market value on grant date is $15. Therefore, if a Section 83(b) election is *not* made, the projected amount of compensation income that the grantee will recognize on vesting date is $30. Projections show that $30 of compensation income would trigger a total of $12 in income tax and payroll tax on vesting date. Therefore, R_O is 40 percent, the ratio of $12 to $30. The projected tax rate on long-term capital gain, R_C, is 15 percent on vesting date. Therefore, the projected tax benefit from a Section 83(b) election is $3.75, which equals: $(P_2 - P_1) \times (R_O - R_C)$ = $15 x 25 percent.

PROJECTED AFTER-TAX IRR FROM SECTION 83(b) ELECTION

Continuing the previous example, where B = $3.75, the grantee projects the IRR from making a Section 83(b) election, using the following equation and solving for i, the annual internal rate of return:

$$CF_O \times (1+i)^N = CF_O + B$$

Therefore,

$$(1 + i)^N = \frac{CF_O + B}{CF_O}$$

Where:

B   = projected tax savings from Section 83(b) election

CF_O = amount of income tax and payroll tax triggered – on grant date – by the Section 83(b) election

N   = amount of time (in years) from grant date to vesting date

Example: *Section 83(b) election triggers a $6 tax liability on grant date, and the projected tax benefit from such election is $3.75 at the end of a 3-year holding period:* Wanda receives a stock grant that will vest at the end of three years if her employment does not terminate before that time. Therefore, *N*, from the equation above equals 3. The fair market value of the stock is $15 on grant date. Wanda calculates that a Section 83(b) election would trigger a total of $6 of income taxes and payroll taxes on grant date (that is, her marginal tax rate is 40 percent in the taxable year of grant). Therefore, CF_O in the equation above equals $6 (in practice, however, the amount of tax withholding would be less than $6 on grant date and the grantee would pay the remaining balance due when he files his income tax return). She projects that the fair market value of the stock will be $30 at the end of 3 years. She also projects that – if the stock price *is* $30 at the end of 3 years and she does *not* make a Section 83(b) election – the projected income tax and payroll tax on $30 of compensation income that she would have to recognize is $12, which equals 40 percent multiplied by $30. She expects that – if the stock price *is* $30 at the end of three years and she *does* make a Section 83(b) election – a sale of stock on vesting date would trigger capital gain at the rate of 15 percent. Therefore, Wanda projects, B, the tax benefit from a Section 83(b) election, to equal $3.75, computed as the increase in fair market value (from $15 at grant date to $30 at vesting date) multiplied by the excess of the 40 percent marginal rate on compensation income over the 15 percent rate on capital gain. Therefore, the projected cash inflow (**that is attributable solely to making the election**) at the end of 3 years is $9.75, which represents a return of the $6 cash outflow that occurred on grant date (CF$_O$) *plus* the $3.75 projected tax benefit (B).

$$(1 + i)^3 = \frac{CF_O + B}{CF_O} = \frac{\$6 + \$3.75}{\$6} = 1.625$$

After-tax IRR = i = 17.5 percent

Example: *Setting an after-tax return from making a Section 83(b) election, and solving for the required fair market value on vesting date:* In the previous example, Wanda projects a fair market value of $30 on vesting date, which results in an after-tax projected IRR of 17.5 percent from making a Section 83(b) election. In this example, Wanda rephrases the question. She asks herself *"How much would the fair market value have to be on vesting date in order for the Section 83(b) election to yield a 10 percent after-tax return?"* She finds the answer, $22.96, by working through the equation above as follows:

$$(1+.10)^3 = \frac{\$6 + B}{\$6} = 1.331$$

Solving for B, she arrives at $1.986. In short, the projected tax benefit would have to be approximately $1.99 on vesting date in order for the projected after-tax IRR from a Section 83(b) election to equal 10 percent. At this point, she knows the amounts for P_1, R_O and R_C and is able to compute P_2 using the equation above:

$$B = \text{Projected Tax Benefit} = (P_2 - P_1) \times (R_o - R_c)$$

$$1.99 = (P2 - \$15) \times (40 \text{ percent} - 15 \text{ percent})$$

$$P2 = \$22.96 = \text{Projected fair market value on vesting date}$$

In short, if the fair market value of the stock is $22.96 on vesting date and the tax rate differential on vesting date is 25 percent (40 percent – 15 percent = 25 percent), the projected tax benefit on vesting date is $1.99, which is a 10 percent after-tax rate of return compounded annually.

Stated differently, the Section 83(b) election yields an annual after-tax return of 10 percent if Wanda's proceeds from the sale of stock on vesting date equal $22.96. *This 10 percent yield is attributable solely to the income tax benefits that result from the election.*

PROJECTED AFTER-TAX IRR FROM BUYING THE STOCK OUTRIGHT

In the previous section, Wanda receives a grant of stock that has a $15 fair market value on grant date. She projects a doubling of the stock price (to $30 at the end of her 3-year vesting period) which results in a projected 17.5 percent annual after-tax return from making a Section 83(b) election. In the next example, Wanda does not make a Section 83(b) election. Instead, she buys the stock outright and finds that buying the stock outright yields a 22.8 percent annual after-tax return under the same underlying assumptions.

Example: *Wanda buys the stock instead of making the Section 83(b) election:* Same facts as the previous example, except Wanda does not make the Section 83(b) election. Instead, she buys the stock. In the previous example, the $30 projected fair market value on vesting date is two times the $15 fair market value on grant date. In short, she projects that every $1 she invests on grant date will be worth $2 (pre-tax) on vesting date. That $2 pre-tax amount is equal to $1.85 after-tax because the $1 projected long-term capital gain will trigger 15 cents of income tax (15 percent x $1 = 15 cents) if the tax rate is 15 percent on long-term capital gain. As shown below, Wanda's projected annual after-tax return is 22.8 percent on a purchase of stock at $15 and sale of such stock at $30. That 22.8 percent return exceeds the 17.5 percent annual after-tax return she projects for the Section 83(b) election.

The 22.8 percent projected annual after-tax return is computed as follows:

$$(1 + i)^3 = \frac{\$2 \text{ proceeds minus income tax on } \$1 \text{ capital gain}}{\$1 \text{ investment on grant date}}$$

$$= (1 + i)^3 = \frac{\$2 - (15 \text{ percent x } \$1)}{\$1 \text{ investment}}$$

$$= (1 + i)^3 = 1.85$$

$$\text{After-tax IRR} = i = 22.8 \text{ percent}$$

SECTION 83(b) ELECTION VERSUS BUYING THE STOCK OUTRIGHT

The Section 83(b) election is sometimes a wise tax and investment maneuver. But it is often overrated. The above examples show that one does not necessarily achieve his objective of wealth maximization simply by making wise tax decisions.

In the examples above, the 17.5 percent projected annual after-tax return on the Section 83(b) election fell short of the 22.8 percent projected after-tax return on an outright purchase of stock. That is because the projected return from making a Section 83(b) election is comprised *solely* of projected tax benefits from projected favorable treatment of capital gains on vesting date. In contrast, the return on the outright purchase of stock is comprised of projected appreciation in the stock price *and* projected favorable treatment of capital gains on vesting date.

288 / Chapter 11

The reason that the return from a Section 83(b) election is derived *solely* from tax benefits is that the grantee captures the projected appreciation in fair market value *regardless* of whether he makes a Section 83(b) election. More specifically, his share of projected stock price appreciation comes from remaining an employee for the 3-year period.

PORTFOLIO DIVERSIFICATION

The previous section illustrates that Wanda would reap a higher after-tax return if she would not make a Section 83(b) election and, instead, would buy the stock outright. But, perhaps neither of these two potentially high-yielding alternatives (the 83(b) election and the stock purchase) is wise from a portfolio management perspective, because both are essentially investments in stock of the grantor corporation.

For example, grantees whose net worth is comprised mostly of stock in the grantor corporation, unrealized appreciation (intrinsic value) in options to buy the stock of such corporation, and other securities of such corporation should probably avoid both alternatives – because such grantees already have too many eggs in one basket.

SECTION 83(b) ELECTION ISSUES

Making a Section 83(b) election is simple. But, the implications of the election can be significant. Consequently, it is important to understand the relevant issues with respect to the election.

RELEVANT ISSUES WHEN THE ELECTION TRIGGERS ADDITIONAL TAX

As discussed above, the Section 83(b) election is sometimes risk-free. The election is not risk-free, however, when it would trigger the recognition of compensation income and, therefore, income tax or payroll tax, or both, on grant date. Compensation income is triggered whenever the grantee makes a Section 83(b) election and the fair market value of the stock – on the date of grant – exceeds the grantee's purchase price.

In order to make an informed decision whether to make an election that is not risk-free, it is important to understand the relevant issues with respect to such election. They include the following, which are discussed below:

- *Diversification*

- *Actively-traded versus privately-held stock*

- *Fair market value of the stock on vesting date may be lower than on grant date*

- *Preferential income tax treatment of long-term capital gain*

- *Marginal income tax or payroll tax rates on compensation income, or both, may change*

- *Liquidity*

- *Alternative investment opportunities*

- *Holding period*

- *Section 1211(b) annual limitation of $3,000 on deduction of net capital losses*

- *Grantee may forfeit the stock*

- *Dividend income versus compensation income*

- *Grantee's decision inadvertently sends a message to the grantor corporation*

DIVERSIFICATION

When the grantee makes a Section 83(b) election that triggers a tax liability on grant date, he effectively makes an investment in the stock. Before making such investment, the grantee should take into account how much of his net worth is comprised of such stock and the intrinsic value of options to buy such stock. Other things being equal, the Section 83(b) election is more attractive to a grantee whose net worth is mostly comprised of assets other than securities of the grantor corporation and options to buy the stock of the grantor corporation.

ACTIVELY-TRADED VERSUS PRIVATELY-HELD STOCK

The general rule is that the grantee should not make a Section 83(b) election, which would not be risk-free, if the stock is publicly traded. That is because, generally, the grantee should not expect that the fair market value of publicly traded stock is undervalued and therefore will increase substantially from grant date to vesting date, since U.S. markets tend to price actively traded stock at or near true value. Anticipation of a substantial increase in stock price, from grant date to vesting date, is one of the more important reasons for making a Section 83(b) election.

Further, the grantee may buy stock of the grantor corporation – instead of making a Section 83(b) election – since such stock is publicly traded. In the discussion above, buying the stock outright yields a higher return than an election that is not risk-free – when the stock price on vesting date is higher than on grant date.

FAIR MARKET VALUE OF THE STOCK ON VESTING DATE MAY BE LOWER THAN ON GRANT DATE

As mentioned above, one of the most important reasons for making a Section 83(b) election stems from the grantee's expectation that the fair market value of the stock on vesting date will be higher than on grant date.

The Section 83(b) election may prove costly if the fair market value of the stock on vesting date is lower than on grant date. If the stock price is lower on vesting date than it was on grant date, the Section 83(b) election will have resulted in the recognition of more compensation income and payroll taxes on the grant date – than would have been triggered on vesting date if the grantee had not made a Section 83(b) election.

Further, the grantee will also have paid income tax and payroll tax sooner (on grant date) rather than later (on vesting date) – and this is relevant because money has a time value.

Example: *The Section 83(b) election triggers more income tax and payroll tax and accelerates the payment of such taxes because fair market value of the stock on vesting date is less than fair market value on grant date:* On July 1, Year 1, ABC Corporation grants stock to Ellen. Her purchase price is zero. The stock will vest on July 1, Year 3 if Ellen's employment does not terminate before that date. The fair market value of the stock on grant date is $10,000. Ellen makes a timely Section 83(b) election, which triggers $10,000 of compensation income on grant date. That $10,000 of income triggers a total of $3,000 (30 percent x $10,000 = $3,000) in additional income tax and payroll tax. On vesting date, the fair market value of the stock is only $1,000. If Ellen had not made the election, she would have incurred additional tax of only $300 (30 percent x $10,000 = $300) on vesting date. In short, Ellen paid $3,000 additional tax in Year 1 instead of $300 in Year 3 – a difference of $2,700. If Ellen sells the stock on vesting date, she would recognize a $9,000 long-term capital loss – which equals $1,000 of gross proceeds minus her $10,000 basis; the income tax benefit, if any, from that $9,000 capital loss would help to offset at least some of the $2,700 additional tax that she paid because she made the Section 83(b) election.

PREFERENTIAL INCOME TAX TREATMENT OF LONG-TERM CAPITAL GAIN

One of the most important reasons for making a Section 83(b) election stems from the grantee's expectation that the fair market value of the stock on vesting date will be higher than on grant date, *and* on vesting date the rate of tax on capital gain will be substantially lower than the marginal rate on compensation income.

Under current law, the rate of tax on long-term capital gain *is* substantially less than the rate of tax on compensation income. This favorable treatment of long-term capital gain over ordinary compensation income could remain unchanged on and after vesting date, or it could become even more favorable, or it could disappear by the time vesting date arrives.

Example: Congress could eliminate preferential income tax treatment of long-term capital gains: In 1986 Congress passed the *Tax Reform Act of 1986,* which eliminated the preferential income tax treatment of long-term capital gains. As mentioned above, however, long-term capital gains now receive preferential treatment relative to compensation income.

MARGINAL INCOME TAX OR PAYROLL TAX RATES ON COMPENSATION INCOME, OR BOTH, MAY CHANGE

Other things being equal, the Section 83(b) election appears relatively more attractive when the grantee's marginal tax rate on ordinary compensation income is substantially lower in the year of grant than he projects it will be in the year that the stock will vest.

Example: Other things remain constant, but the marginal tax rate on compensation income is higher on grant date than on vesting date and that condition has an <u>adverse</u> impact on the rate of return from making a Section 83(b) election: Eleanor receives a stock grant on January 1, Year 1. The fair market value of the stock is $15 on grant date. Eleanor's purchase price is zero. The stock will vest on January 1, Year 3 if Eleanor's employment does not terminate before such date. In Year 1, Eleanor's marginal rate of tax on $15 of compensation income is 40 percent and therefore a Section 83(b) election triggers $6 of tax on grant date. Congress passes a new tax law in Year 2 that reduces the marginal rate of tax on compensation income to 10 percent effective January 1, Year 3. The fair market value of the stock is $15 on January 1, Year 3. If Eleanor would not have made a Section 83(b) election, she would pay only $1.50 (10 percent x $15 of compensation income = $1.50) of tax on January 1, Year 3 (instead of paying $6 of tax on January 1, Year 1). The Section 83(b) election proves to be a costly investment solely because Eleanor's marginal rate of tax on compensation income is lower on vesting date than on grant date.

Example: Other things remain constant, but the marginal tax rate on compensation income is lower on grant date than on vesting date and that condition has a <u>favorable</u> impact on the rate of return from making a Section 83(b) election: Same facts as the previous example, except that Eleanor's marginal tax rate on compensation income is 10 percent on grant date and 40 percent on vesting date. The Section 83(b) election triggers $1.50 of tax (10 percent x $15 of compensation income = $1.50) on grant date, versus what would have been $6 (40 percent x $15 of compensation income = $6) on vesting date. In short, Eleanor's $1.50 investment on grant date yields a $4.50 gain ($6 - $1.50 = $4.50), which is a substantial after-tax rate of return measured over the two year period that elapsed between grant date and vesting date. Eleanor reaps the $4.50 tax gain even though the fair market value remains unchanged; it is $15 on both grant date and vesting date.

LIQUIDITY

The grantee pays additional income tax or payroll tax, or both, when he makes a Section 83(b) election and the fair market value of the stock on grant date exceeds his purchase price. The grantee cannot sell the non-vested stock if he needs to raise cash before such stock vests. Generally, he will not be able to borrow money from a brokerage firm using such stock as collateral (that is, a margin loan) because the brokerage firm would not be able to sell his non-vested stock in the event that the fair market value of such stock should decline and such decline would be sufficient to trigger a margin call.

The grantee must also be aware of liquidity issues that may arise on *vesting* date if he does *not* make a Section 83(b) election. More specifically, a payroll tax and income tax liability is triggered on vesting date if he does not make an election, and the fair market value of such stock on vesting date exceeds the grantee's purchase price. The grantee should prepare for the possibility that he may need to sell some amount of stock on vesting date – or liquidate other assets on vesting date – if he otherwise will not have sufficient cash on vesting date to satisfy a payroll tax liability or an income tax liability, or both.

ALTERNATIVE INVESTMENT OPPORTUNITIES

As described above, a Section 83(b) election that is not risk free is one that triggers additional tax. If the grantee triggers additional tax at grant date, he forsakes the ability to invest such tax dollars in other investment alternatives.

Naturally, some grantees will have more attractive investment opportunities than will others. Other things being equal, a grantee that has few, if any, attractive investment alternatives is more likely to find the Section 83(b) election a wise decision than would a grantee that has access to numerous investment choices that have high projected rates of return.

Example: The decision to make a Section 83(b) election is generally more attractive to grantees that have few, if any, attractive investment opportunities: Kendra, the CEO of ABC Corporation, often receives invitations to invest in young pre-IPO companies that have exciting growth potential. Karen, an accountant at ABC, has never received such an invitation. Other things being equal, the Section 83(b) election is likely to be more attractive to Karen than to Kendra.

HOLDING PERIOD

Under IRC Section 83(f), the holding period on stock that is not vested on grant date begins on the date such stock vests – if the grantee does not make a Section 83(b) election. If he makes such election, Regulation 1.83-4(a) provides that the holding period begins just after the date he receives the stock.

In short, the Section 83(b) election starts the clock running on the holding period. This might be an important consideration for a grantee that would like to sell such stock as soon as possible, and have any gain or loss on such sale be treated as long-term capital gain or loss.

Example: Grantee expects to sell the stock on vesting date: ABC Corporation makes a stock grant to Elizabeth on January 15, Year 1. The stock will vest on January 15, Year 3. If Elizabeth makes a Section 83(b) election, her holding period starts at the time of grant, and therefore a sale more than 12 months after

January 15, Year 1 would result in long-term capital gain or loss. If Elizabeth does not make a Section 83(b) election, she must sell the stock on a date that is more than 12 months after the January 15, Year 3 vesting date, in order for any gain or loss to be treated as long-term capital gain or loss.

SECTION 1211(b) $3,000 ANNUAL LIMITATION ON DEDUCTION OF NET CAPITAL LOSSES

The $3,000 annual limitation on the deductibility of net capital losses is potentially more restrictive – and therefore potentially more costly in terms of opportunity losses – when the dollar amounts involved are larger.

In short, the Section 83(b) election has the potential to burden the grantee with large capital loss carryovers, which may take years to utilize, or which may never be utilized at all because, if he dies, a capital loss carryover can be used as an income tax deduction by a surviving spouse but cannot be used by a decedent's estate nor by a decedent's heirs.

Example: Grantee makes a Section 83(b) election and the fair market value of the stock is substantially lower on vesting date than it was on grant date: Erica receives a stock grant and the fair market value of the stock is $100,000 on grant date. Erica pays nothing to acquire such stock. The stock is not vested on grant date and Erica makes a Section 83(b) election, which triggers $100,000 of ordinary compensation income on grant date. Her basis in the stock is, therefore, $100,000. On vesting date the fair market value is only $1,000. If Erica sells the stock for $1,000 on vesting date, she reports a $99,000 capital loss on her income tax return. Depending on her income tax situation, it could take years to utilize the entire $99,000 of capital losses because of the $3,000 annual limitation under IRC Section 1211(b). In short, other things being equal, the larger the excess of fair market value on grant date over the grantee's purchase price, the more relevant the Section 1211(b) limitation is to the decision whether or not to make the Section 83(b) election.

GRANTEE MAY FORFEIT THE STOCK

The grantee may terminate his employment with the grantor before vesting date. If so, he forfeits the stock and generally is required to sell the stock back to the grantor at the same price that he had paid to acquire it. As explained earlier, if he forfeits the stock he is not entitled to an income tax deduction for the amount of compensation income that he had recognized – and on which he paid income tax or payroll tax, or both – on grant date as a result of the Section 83(b) election.

DIVIDEND INCOME VERSUS COMPENSATION INCOME

Under current law, dividend income receives preferential income tax treatment relative to compensation income. Further, compensation income is subject to payroll tax and dividend income is not.

Dividends received on non-vested stock are characterized as compensation income if the grantee has not made a Section 83(b) election for such stock. In contrast, dividends received on stock that was not vested on grant date are characterized as dividend income if the grantee has made a Section 83(b) election.

The issue of dividend income versus compensation income is more relevant for stocks that have high dividend yields, and has little or no relevance for stocks that have low dividend yields or pay no dividends at all.

GRANTEE'S DECISION INADVERTENTLY SENDS A MESSAGE TO THE GRANTOR CORPORATION

IRS regulations require the grantee to deliver a copy of the Section 83(b) election to the grantor of the stock at the time he files such election with the IRS (that is, within 30 days after grant date). The grantee's decision to file or not file the election may inadvertently send a message to the board of directors of the grantor corporation.

Example: The grantee does not make a Section 83(b) election and the board of directors of the grantor wonders why not: ABC Corporation issues a stock grant to Paula. The stock, which Paula cannot buy outright because it is not publicly traded, will vest after one year if Paula's employment does not terminate within one year. The fair market value of the stock is $15 on grant date and Paula's purchase price is zero dollars. Grantees who are excited about the prospects for ABC stock over the next year are likely to perceive that the Section 83(b) election is an attractive investment decision, if diversification is not an overriding issue, because on grant date the rate of tax on compensation income substantially exceeds the rate of tax on long-term capital gain – and this relationship is expected to exist on vesting date.

If Paula does not make the Section 83(b) election, ABC's board of directors may infer – correctly or incorrectly – that Paula expects to terminate employment before the end of the one-year vesting period, or that she is not confident that the fair market value of the stock on vesting date will exceed fair market value on grant date, or both.

TAXATION OF RESTRICTED STOCK UNITS

A number of companies offer restricted stock units ("RSU") as compensation for services. Generally, an RSU is an unfunded and unsecured promise by the grantor corporation to issue grantor stock to the grantee at a later date (that is, on vesting date).

RSU IS NOT "PROPERTY" UNDER SECTION 83

A restricted stock unit is different from a restricted stock grant. As mentioned above, the former is generally an unfunded and unsecured *promise* by the corporation to issue grantor stock to the grantee on vesting date if he is still an employee on such date. In contrast, the latter is an actual issuance of stock on grant date, even though such issued stock may or may not be vested on grant date.

Regulation 1.83-3(e) provides, in part, that the term "property" includes real and personal property other than either money or an unfunded and unsecured promise to pay money or property in the future. Therefore, an RSU is not property for purposes of IRC Section 83 and this is an important distinction, as discussed below, which results in disparate tax treatment relative to a grant of restricted stock.

TAXATION ON VESTING DATE

On grant date, the grantor's promise to issue stock to the grantee on vesting date has no tax consequences to the grantee. The grantee generally recognizes compensation income on the date that the RSU vests. The amount of compensation equals the fair market value of the stock on vesting date over the amount (generally, zero) that the grantee pays for such stock.

BASIS AND HOLDING PERIOD

The grantee's basis in the stock he receives on vesting date is the fair market value of such stock on vesting date.

The holding period for such stock begins on the date it is received. In order for gain or loss on its eventual sale to be characterized as long-term capital gain or loss, the sale date must be more than 12 months after the date such stock was received by the grantee.

SECTION 83(b) ELECTION IS NOT AVAILABLE ON RSUs

As discussed above, the grant of a restricted stock unit is a promise and is not property for purposes of IRC Section 83. Therefore, the grantee may not make a Section 83(b) election at the time the RSU is granted.

IRC SECTION 409A IMPACTS RSUs

Before the *American Jobs Creation Act of 2004*, some companies allowed the grantee of a restricted stock unit to delay receipt of the stock to a date subsequent to vesting date, so that he could defer the recognition of compensation income (but, under IRC Section 3121(v)(2), the grantee was not able to defer social security tax and Medicare tax) to such subsequent date. Grantees were relying on IRS Revenue Ruling 77-25, which provided that payments under a deferred compensation plan were subject to income tax on the date such payments are actually or constructively received. The 2004 tax act changed that.

Under IRC Section 409A, grantees will generally recognize compensation income on vesting date.

12

Employee Stock Purchase Plans (ESPP)

This chapter discusses only *qualified* employee stock purchase plans (ESPP) that satisfy the requirements of IRC Section 423, and allow employees to buy employer stock at a discount of up to 15 percent.

It is important to note that IRC Section 409A, discussed in earlier chapters, is "...not intended to change the tax treatment of...options granted under an employee stock purchase plan meeting the requirements of section 423", according to the committee reports to the *American Jobs Creation Act of 2004*.

Employees often reap high returns from participation in an ESPP because of the discount – with relatively little risk if they sell the stock shortly after purchase. Consequently, even risk-averse individuals generally choose to participate. Employees must be aware, however, that participating in such an ESPP is not completely risk free because stock prices fluctuate and an unexpected delay in selling the stock could result in a loss of capital.

The ESPP participant does not recognize taxable income at the time he buys ESPP-stock. He does recognize taxable income, however, when he disposes of it (generally by selling the stock, but other actions such as gifting such stock to a person who is not a spouse are also dispositions).

This control over the timing of income recognition offers an advantage, for those whose marginal income tax rates differ substantially from year to year, because shareholders can choose to recognize taxable income in a year when they are subject to a lower marginal tax rate. Naturally, however, such a strategy is accompanied by the possibility of a decline in stock price that exceeds any tax advantage from recognizing taxable income at a lower marginal tax rate.

Income tax treatment of a stock disposition differs, depending if the disposition is a:

- Disqualifying disposition (a special holding period requirement is *not* satisfied)

  or,

- Qualifying disposition (a special holding period requirement *is* satisfied).

Generally, the *total* amount of income recognized on the sale of ESPP-stock is the *same*, regardless of whether he makes a disqualifying or qualifying disposition. It is the *character* of the income that generally differs and this is usually the driving force behind holding such stock beyond purchase date.

As compared with a disqualifying disposition, a qualifying disposition generally results in more long-term capital gain and less ordinary compensation income than does a disqualifying disposition. Investors favor long-term capital gain over compensation income because the marginal tax rate on such gain is lower than the marginal tax rate on ordinary compensation income.

This chapter discusses the following sections:

- *Income Taxation of ESPP-Stock*

- *ESPP Investment Strategy*

INCOME TAXATION OF ESPP-STOCK

This section covers the offering period, purchase price, disposition of ESPP-stock, gifting ESPP-stock to a person who is not a spouse, and withholding of income and payroll taxes – when the employer stock purchase plan allows the employee to buy stock at a discount of up to 15 percent.

OFFERING PERIOD

Generally, as the employee directs, the employer withholds a specified percentage of the employee's paycheck, or an exact dollar amount, during what is called the *offering period* (often a period of six months, but the period does not have to be six months).

Such withholding is not tax-deductible, which means that the employee buys ESPP-stock with after-tax money. The employer uses the withholding to buy stock for the employee, in accordance with terms of the plan, at the end of the offering period. The plan may also permit the employee to make a lump-sum contribution to the plan during each offering period.

Generally, the employee can change his contribution rate or discontinue contributions, or even withdraw contributions if a request for withdrawal is made before a set number of days before the end of the offering period.

The offering period is significant for another reason. The change in the stock's fair market value from the beginning of the offering period to the end of the offering period dictates investment strategy.

Other things being equal, shareholders will find little or no income tax advantage to holding ESPP-stock beyond purchase date unless the fair market value of such stock on purchase date (that is, at the end of the offering period) is substantially higher than fair market value at the beginning of the offering period. This important point is discussed in more detail later.

PURCHASE PRICE

Terms under an ESPP are not standardized from employer to employer. It is quite common for a participant in an employer stock purchase plan, however, to buy stock at a price that is equal to 85 percent multiplied by the *lesser* of:

(A) the fair market value of the stock at the *beginning* of the offering period,

or,

(B) the fair market value of the stock at the *end* of the offering period

DISPOSITION OF ESPP-STOCK

Internal Revenue Code Section 421(a) provides that the employee does not recognize any taxable income at the time he buys stock through an employer stock purchase plan. In accordance with IRC Sections 421(b) and 423(c), income tax consequences do arise in the year that the shareholder disposes of such stock.

WHAT *IS* AND *ISN'T* A DISPOSITION OF ESPP-STOCK

IRC Section 424(c) provides that the term "disposition" has the same meaning with respect to stock purchased through an employer stock purchase plan (ESPP-stock) as it has with respect to stock purchased by exercising an incentive stock option (ISO-stock) – except for the discrepancy discussed in the next paragraph.

IRC Section 422(c)(3) provides that certain transfers of ISO-stock by insolvent individuals are not dispositions of such ISO-stock. The tax law does not have a corresponding provision stating that certain transfers of ESPP-stock by insolvent individuals are not dispositions of ESPP-stock.

Consequently, the "*What Is, and Isn't, a Disposition*" section in Chapter 4 applies to ESPP-stock as well – except for the discussion relating to certain transfers by insolvent individuals.

DISQUALIFYING VERSUS QUALIFYING DISPOSITION

The income tax consequences that arise from a disposition of ESPP-stock depend on whether the shareholder has satisfied the special holding period requirement under IRC Section 423(a). A disposition of ESPP-Stock is *either* a:

- *Disqualifying disposition* (that is, the special holding period requirement under IRC Section 423(a) has not been satisfied)

  or,

- *Qualifying disposition* (that is, the special holding period requirement under IRC Section 423(a) has been satisfied)

SPECIAL HOLDING PERIOD REQUIREMENT

The shareholder satisfies the special holding period requirement under IRC Section 423(a), and therefore makes a qualifying disposition of ESPP-stock, if such disposition occurs *after* the *later* of two dates:

(A) 12 months after the stock is transferred to him

   or,

(B) Two years after option grant date (that is, two years after the beginning of the offering period)

Example: Length of offering period is less than one year: The beginning of the six-month offering period is January 1, Year 1. Sheila buys stock through the ESPP at the end of such offering period. Sheila satisfies the special holding period requirement only if she disposes of the stock more than two years after the beginning of the offering period (more than two years after January 1, Year 1) because the date that is two years after the beginning of the offering period is later than the date that is 12 months after the stock is transferred to her.

If a shareholder makes a *qualifying* disposition, any amount characterized as capital gain or loss is long-term capital gain or loss because the sale date in a qualifying disposition is, by definition, more than 12 months after purchase date.

If the shareholder makes a *disqualifying* disposition, any amount characterized as capital gain or loss could be either short-term capital gain or loss, *or* long-term capital gain or loss. It is long-term capital gain or loss if the sale date is more than 12 months after purchase date, and short-term capital gain or loss if the sale date is not more than 12 months after purchase date.

TAXATION OF A DISQUALIFYING DISPOSITION

If the shareholder makes a disqualifying disposition of ESPP-stock, he recognizes compensation income in the amount of the *bargain element* (that is, the excess of the fair market value of the stock on the date of purchase over the shareholder's purchase price). This statement is true regardless of the amount of proceeds from the sale. In short, he recognizes compensation income in the amount of the bargain element even if the stock price collapses after purchase date and he realizes a loss on the sale.

Generally, the shareholder also recognizes some amount of capital gain or loss from the sale as illustrated in the example below.

The shareholder's basis in the stock is comprised of his purchase price plus the amount of compensation income that he recognizes as a result of the disposition.

Under IRC Section 421(b), any increase in income that is attributable to a disqualifying disposition is treated as an increase in income in the taxable year in which such disposition occurs. In other words, taxation is deferred until the taxable year in which the shareholder disposes of the ESPP-stock.

Example: Sale of ESPP-stock triggers compensation income in the amount of the bargain element even though shareholder realizes a loss on the disposition: Sheila chooses to participate in her employer's ESPP. The plan allows employees to buy stock at a price equal to 85 percent multiplied by the lesser of (a) fair market value at the beginning of the offering period, *or* (b) fair market value at the end of the offering period. Fair market value at the beginning of the offering period is $100 and fair market value at the end of the offering period is $120. On June 30, Year 1, Sheila pays $85 per share, which is 85 percent multiplied by $100, the fair market value at the beginning of the offering period. On January 15, Year 2, she sells the stock for $84 in a disqualifying disposition (that is, she realizes a $1 economic loss). IRC Section 421(b) provides that Sheila recognizes $35 of compensation income on January 15, Year 2. That $35 is the amount of the bargain element that existed on purchase date ($120 fair market value on purchase date minus $85 purchase price = $35).

Example: *Basis of ESPP-stock equals purchase price plus the amount of compensation income recognized:* In the previous example, Sheila pays $85 to buy the stock and recognizes $35 of compensation income on the date of sale. Her basis in the stock is $120, which equals $85 plus $35.

Example: *Capital gain or loss on sale of ESPP-stock in a disqualifying disposition:* In the previous two examples, Sheila receives $84 of gross proceeds from the sale of stock that has a $120 basis. In addition to the $35 of compensation income she reports on her income tax return, Sheila also reports a $36 capital loss, which equals gross proceeds in the amount of $84 minus her $120 basis. The $36 loss is a short-term capital loss because the January 15, Year 2 sale date is not more than 12 months after the June 30, Year 1 purchase date.

TAXATION OF A QUALIFYING DISPOSITION

If the shareholder *does* satisfy the special holding period requirement described above, the disposition of ESPP-stock is a *qualifying disposition.*

Under IRC Section 423(c), ordinary compensation income from a qualifying disposition is limited to the *lesser* of:

(A) The amount, if any, by which the fair market value of the stock at the *beginning* of the offering period exceeds the option price computed "as if the option had been exercised at such time"

or,

(B) Actual gain, if any, on the sale of stock (if the disposition is not a sale of stock, then paragraph (B) equals the fair market

value of the stock on the date of disposition minus the
amount paid to buy such stock)

The words "if any" in paragraphs (A) and (B) mean that if the
amount computed under paragraph (A) is less than zero, then (A)
equals zero. Likewise, if the amount computed under paragraph
(B) is less than zero, then (B) equals zero.

The statutory language describing the computation of paragraph
(A) is somewhat cumbersome, but the computation of the amount
under paragraph (A) is quite simple.

(A) equals the percentage discount (for example, the percentage
discount is 15 percent if the employee's purchase price is equal to
85 percent multiplied by the lesser of (a) fair market value at the
beginning of the offering period, or (b) fair market value at the end
of the offering period) multiplied by the fair market value of the
stock at the beginning of the offering period.

In short:

(A) = Percentage discount x Fair market value of stock at
    beginning of offering period

The amount computed under paragraph (B) is simply the
amount of the shareholder's gain, if any, on his sale of stock. That
is, the excess of proceeds from such sale over his purchase price.
As mentioned above, if the shareholder's proceeds from such sale
do not exceed his purchase price (that is, he has realized a loss),
then (B) is zero. In short:

(B) = Actual gain (B = zero, if there is an actual *loss*)

Example: *Amount determined under paragraph (A) above equals the percentage discount multiplied by the fair market value of the stock at the beginning of the offering period:* The fair market value of the stock is $100 at the beginning of the offering period. The ESPP terms state that the employee's purchase price is equal to 85 percent multiplied by the *lesser* of:

(a) Fair market value at the beginning of the offering period

   or,

(b) Fair market value at the end of the offering period.

Therefore, the amount determined under paragraph (A) above is $15, computed as the 15 percent discount multiplied by the $100 beginning fair market value.

Strangely enough, the special computation under paragraph (A) sometimes results in more onerous income taxation from a qualifying disposition than from a disqualifying disposition. That anomaly arises when the fair market value of the stock is lower at the end of the offering period than it was at the beginning of the offering period, *and* proceeds from the sale of stock exceed the fair market value of the stock at the end of the offering period. The following example illustrates this point.

Example: *Qualifying disposition of ESPP-stock:* Sheila participates in her company's ESPP. The fair market value of the stock is $100 at the beginning of the offering period. The fair market value is $80 at the end of the offering period. Sheila pays $68 (85 percent x $80 = $68) to buy the stock. Later, she sells the stock for $100 in a qualifying disposition. Since the sale is a qualifying disposition, IRC Section 423(c) limits the amount of compensation income that the shareholder must recognize to the lesser of the amount computed under paragraph (A) or paragraph (B) described above.

Computation under paragraph (A): The actual bargain element that exists on the date she buys the stock is $12 ($80 fair market value minus $68 purchase price = $12) and this is the amount of compensation that *would* have been triggered had Sheila made a disqualifying disposition. But, Sheila does not make a disqualifying disposition; she makes a qualifying disposition.

Therefore, in order to determine the amount of compensation income she recognizes, she makes two computations – one under paragraph (A) described above and one under paragraph (B) described above. (A) is $15, which is the $100 fair market value at the beginning of the offering period multiplied by 15 percent, the amount of her purchase discount.

Computation under paragraph (B): Sheila pays $68 to buy the stock. She sells the stock for $100. Her gain is $32. Therefore, the amount computed under paragraph (B) above is $32, the actual gain on the sale.

Compensation income is the lesser of (A) or (B): Sheila's compensation income is $15, the lesser of $15 computed under paragraph (A), or $32 computed under paragraph (B). Note that compensation income in the amount of $15 is actually *higher* than the $12 of compensation income that *would* have been triggered if Sheila had made a disqualifying disposition (this anomaly – more onerous taxation from a qualifying disposition than from a disqualifying disposition – is discussed below).

Basis of stock sold equals purchase price plus the amount of compensation income recognized: Sheila's basis of the stock she sells is $83, which equals the $68 she paid to buy such stock plus $15 of compensation income she recognizes upon disposition of such stock.

Capital gain or loss on a qualifying disposition is long-term capital gain or loss: Sheila reports a $17 capital gain on IRS Form 1040, Schedule D. That $17 equals $100 proceeds from the sale minus her $83 basis. The capital gain or loss is long-term capital gain or loss because the sale is a qualifying disposition (in order to be a qualifying disposition the sale date must be more than 12 months after purchase date).

Qualifying Disposition May Trigger More Compensation Income than Would a Disqualifying Disposition

Taxpayers logically expect that a qualifying disposition always results in more favorable income tax treatment than a disqualifying disposition. Unfortunately, tax law does not always seem logical.

The previous example illustrates that under certain circumstances *more* compensation income is triggered by a qualifying disposition of ESPP-stock than would be triggered by a disqualifying disposition.

More compensation from a qualifying disposition occurs when two conditions exist:

- The fair market value of the stock is lower at the end of the offering period than it was at the beginning of the offering period

  and,

- Proceeds from the sale of such stock exceed the fair market value of such stock at the end of the offering period

The amount of *additional* compensation income that is triggered if the shareholder makes a qualifying disposition instead of a disqualifying disposition depends upon the amount of proceeds the shareholder receives from his sale of stock.

When the fair market value of the stock declines during the offering period, there is a ceiling (that is, a maximum) on the amount of *additional* compensation income, however, that could conceivably be triggered by a qualifying disposition instead of a disqualifying disposition.

The shareholder has the information necessary to compute the ceiling on the date that he buys the ESPP-stock. The ceiling, computed as follows, is illustrated in the next example:

Ceiling = Percentage discount x Decline in fair market value
during the offering period

Example: *Fair market value declines during the offering period and the shareholder computes the maximum amount of additional compensation income that could conceivably result from making a qualifying disposition, instead of a disqualifying disposition of ESPP-stock:* In the previous example, Sheila buys ESPP-stock at a 15 percent discount from the *lesser* of:

- Fair market value at the beginning of the offering period

  or,

- Fair market value at the end of the offering period.

The fair market value declined by $20 – from $100 at the beginning of the offering period to $80 at the end of the offering period. At the time she buys the stock (that is, at the end of the offering period), Sheila knows that the maximum amount of additional compensation income that could conceivably result from making a qualifying disposition instead of making a disqualifying disposition is $3. That $3 equals the 15 percent discount multiplied by the $20 decline in fair market value during the offering period.

Example: Additional compensation income increases basis and therefore reduces the amount of capital gain, or increases the amount of capital loss, on sale of ESPP-stock: Same facts as the previous example. Sheila sells the stock for $100 in a qualifying disposition. Her basis in the stock sold is $83, which consists of her $68 purchase price plus $15 of compensation income. If she had sold the stock in a disqualifying disposition, her basis would have been only $80 ($68 purchase price plus $12 of compensation income). The $3 increase in compensation income that results from a qualifying disposition means that Sheila recognizes a $17 capital gain ($100 – $83 = $17) from a qualifying disposition instead of a $20 capital gain ($100 – $80 = $20) from a disqualifying disposition – a difference of $3.

Example: The adverse tax consequences from recognizing additional compensation income described above: In the previous example, Sheila determined that she could potentially recognize up to $3 more ordinary compensation income (and therefore recognize $3 less long-term capital gain) if she satisfies the holding period requirement than if she makes a disqualifying disposition. Her marginal income tax rate on ordinary compensation income is 35 percent (including payroll taxes) and her marginal tax rate on long-term capital gain is 15 percent – a differential of 20 percentage points. She anticipates that her marginal tax rates will not change during the next two years. Sheila projects that the *maximum* tax increase that she would suffer from satisfying the special holding period requirement and therefore recognizing $3 more compensation income is only 60 cents, which equals $3 multiplied by the 20 percentage point differential in tax rate.

Anomaly is a Disincentive to Holding ESPP-Stock

The tax anomaly described above – the potential for more adverse consequences from a qualifying instead of a disqualifying disposition – presents a relatively minor tax disincentive to holding ESPP-stock beyond the date of purchase. Generally, if the shareholder decides to hold the stock, he does so for non-tax reasons.

IF THERE IS GAIN, THERE IS COMPENSATION INCOME

If the shareholder realizes a gain on a qualifying disposition of ESPP-stock that he had purchased at a discount, he recognizes some amount of ordinary compensation income when he disposes of such stock. In short, it is impossible for 100 percent of gain from the sale of stock in a qualifying disposition to be characterized as long-term capital gain.

One arrives at this conclusion after working through the limitation on compensation income provided by IRC Section 423(c).

As discussed earlier, IRC Section 423(c) provides that compensation income equals the *lesser* of:

(A) The percentage discount multiplied by the fair market value of the stock at the beginning of the offering period

   or,

(B) The actual economic gain, if any, from the sale.

Clearly, (A) is a positive number whenever the employee is able to buy ESPP-stock at a discount. (B) is a positive number whenever he sells the stock at a gain. Consequently, if he sells the stock at a gain, both (A) and (B) are positive numbers. That means if there is gain, there is ordinary compensation income.

COMPENSATION INCOME HAS A CEILING AND A FLOOR

At the time he buys ESPP-stock at a discount, the employee knows that if he holds such stock long enough to satisfy the special holding period requirement, there is a maximum amount of ordinary compensation income that he would eventually recognize on the sale of such stock. As shown in the example below, that ceiling is computed as the purchase discount percentage (for example, 15 percent) multiplied by the fair market value of the stock at the beginning of the offering period.

The previous statement is true regardless of the amount of proceeds his receives from an eventual sale. As discussed later in this chapter, when the stock price has appreciated substantially during the offering period, this ceiling on compensation income is a factor that sometimes motivates the shareholder to continue holding the stock long enough to satisfy the special holding period requirement.

Compensation income also has a floor. The floor is zero (that is, it is impossible to have a negative amount of compensation income). That statement is true because, under the limitation on compensation income provided by IRC Section 423(c), the shareholder recognizes no ordinary compensation income from the sale of stock unless he realizes an economic gain.

In summary, if he is able to buy ESPP-stock at a discount, he knows on the purchase date the maximum and minimum amounts of ordinary compensation income that he would recognize if he would sell the stock in a qualifying disposition.

Example: If the shareholder makes a qualifying disposition, there is a ceiling and a floor on the amount of compensation income: ABC Corporation's ESPP allows Sheila to buy stock at a 15 percent discount from the lesser of (a) the fair market value of the stock at the beginning of the offering period, or (b) the fair market value at the end of the offering period. The fair market value of the stock was $100 at the beginning of the offering period. Sheila knows on the date that she buys the stock that if she eventually sells the stock in a qualifying disposition the minimum amount of compensation income she would recognize would be zero and the maximum would be $15. That $15 maximum is computed as her 15 percent purchase discount multiplied by the $100 fair market value at the beginning of the offering period. The actual amount of compensation she recognizes, if any, depends on the amount of proceeds she receives from the sale.

CERTAIN SALES OF ESPP-STOCK ARE NOT DISQUALIFYING DISPOSITIONS

As explained in Chapter 4, the *American Jobs Creation Act of 2004* added IRC Section 421(d), which provides that the required sale of ISO-stock (pursuant to a "certificate of divestiture" as defined in IRC Section 1043) by an "eligible person" (please see Chapter 4 for the definition of that term), in order to comply with federal conflict of interest requirements of the federal government, is not a disqualifying disposition, regardless of how long the stock was actually held. Under Section 421(d), that same treatment applies to ESPP-stock.

Deferral of Gain on Certain Sales of ESPP-Stock

IRC Section 1043(a) provides that the taxpayer may *elect* to defer taxation of the capital gain (that is, to elect nonrecognition treatment) from the sale of ESPP-stock described above, if he buys "permitted property" (please see Chapter 4 for the definition of that term) during the 60-day period beginning on the date of sale.

Gain will only be recognized to the extent the amount realized from the sale exceeds the cost of the permitted property. IRC Section 1043(b)(3) states that permitted property "...means any obligation of the United States or any diversified investment fund approved by regulations issued by the Office of Government Ethics." IRC Section 1043(c) provides that any gain deferred reduces the basis of the permitted property purchased.

GIFT OF ESPP-STOCK TO NON-SPOUSE DONEE

IRC Section 424(c)(4) provides that a gift of ESPP-stock to one's spouse, or a transfer to one's spouse incident to divorce is not a disposition.

Gifts to others, including gifts to charitable organizations, *are* dispositions under IRC Section 424(c)(1). Such dispositions, if made *before* satisfying the special holding period requirement, trigger compensation income to the donor in the amount of the

316 / Chapter 12

bargain element, which equals the fair market value of the ESPP-stock on the date of purchase over the donor's purchase price.

This section describes the income tax rules that apply under two different scenarios where the shareholder makes a gift of ESPP-stock, which constitutes a disposition under IRC Section 424(c)(1), *after* having satisfied the special holding period requirement for such stock:

- *Scenario #1:* The basis of the stock in the hands of the donee is *not* greater than the fair market value of such stock on the date of gift (please see the first example below)

- *Scenario #2:* The basis of the stock in the hands of the donee *is* greater than the fair market value of such stock on the date of gift (please see the second example below)

Regulation 1.423-2(k)(2) Example 4 offers guidance in the situation where the shareholder makes a gift of stock after having satisfied the special holding period requirement. The next example is adapted from that Example 4.

Example: *Scenario #1: Donor's basis of ESPP-stock carries over to the donee because donor's basis does not exceed the stock's fair market value on the date of the gift:* The fair market value of the stock is $100 at the beginning of the offering period and $110 at the end of the offering period. Sheila pays $85 to buy the stock, where the purchase price is computed as 85 percent multiplied by the lesser of (a) fair market value at the beginning of the offering period, or (b) fair market value at the end of the offering period. Later, after satisfying the special holding period requirement, she (the "donor") gives the stock to her daughter, Lynn (the "donee"). The fair market value of the stock on the date of the gift is $150. Sheila recognizes $15 of compensation income on the date of the gift, computed as the lesser of $15, her 15 percent purchase discount multiplied by the $100 fair market value at the beginning of the offering period, or $65, the excess of the $150 fair market value on the date of the gift over her $85 purchase price. Therefore, Sheila's basis in the stock is $100, computed as her $85 purchase price plus the $15 of compensation income she recognizes. At the time of the gift, Sheila's $100 basis becomes

Lynn's basis under IRC Section 1015(a) because Sheila's $100 basis does not exceed the $150 fair market value of the stock on the date of the gift.

The next example is based on Regulation 1.423-2(k)(2) Example 5. Again, the shareholder makes a gift of ESPP-stock after having satisfied the special holding period requirement. It shows how to determine the donee's basis when the donor's basis exceeds the fair market value of the stock on the date of the gift.

Example: Scenario #2: *Donee's basis of ESPP-stock does not carry over to the donee. Instead, donee has one basis for determining gain from the eventual sale of ESPP-stock and a different basis for determining loss:* Same facts as the previous example except that the fair market value of the stock on the date of the gift is $75, not $150. Sheila recognizes no compensation income, computed as the lesser of $15, her 15 percent purchase discount multiplied by the $100 fair market value at the beginning of the offering period, or $0, the excess of the $75 fair market value on the date of the gift over her $85 purchase price. Sheila's basis equals $85, computed as her $85 purchase price plus zero compensation income that she recognizes as a result of the gift. Under IRC Section 1015(a), $85 becomes Lynn's basis, as of the time of the gift, for purposes of determining the amount of *gain* she recognizes from a future sale of the stock. IRC Section 1015(a) provides that Lynn's basis for purposes of determining the amount of *loss* she recognizes from a future sale of the stock is only $75, the fair market value of the stock on the date of the gift. That enigma regarding Lynn's two different basis amounts is described below.

BASIS OF STOCK ACQUIRED BY GIFT

IRC Section 1015(a) provides that the basis of stock acquired by gift is the same as the donor's basis (that is, the donor's basis carries over to the donee), *except* in the case where the fair market value of the stock on the date of the gift is less than the donor's basis.

As shown in the previous example, if the fair market value of the stock on the date of the gift is less than the donor's basis, the donee has one basis for determining gain, and a different basis for determining loss, on his eventual sale of such stock. The rule under IRC Section 1015(a) is as follows:

- The donee's basis for determining *gain* from his eventual sale of stock is the same as the donor's basis (in the previous example, that amount is $85)

- The donee's basis for determining *loss* from his eventual sale of stock is the lower of (a) the donor's basis, or (b) fair market value of such stock at the time of the gift (in the previous example, that amount is $75)

The next three examples apply the facts from the previous example to show how the IRC Section 1015(a) basis rule is applied when Lynn eventually sells the ESPP-stock that she had received as a gift.

Example: Proceeds from sale of stock are less than $75: Lynn's basis for determining loss is $75. If she sells such stock for $70, she recognizes a $5 capital loss ($70 proceeds minus $75 basis = $5 capital loss).

Example: Proceeds from sale of stock equal or exceed $75 but do not exceed $85: If proceeds from her eventual sale of stock equal or exceed $75 but do not exceed $85, Lynn recognizes no capital gain or loss.

Example: Proceeds from sale of stock exceed $85: Lynn's basis for determining gain is $85. If she sells such stock for $90, she recognizes a $5 capital gain ($90 proceeds minus $85 basis = $5 capital gain).

NO WITHHOLDING, NO FICA, AND NO FUTA

Neither the purchase of ESPP-stock nor the disposition of ESPP-stock triggers federal income tax withholding, social security tax withholding, or Medicare tax withholding. The following discussion explains the legal authority for such treatment.

The *American Jobs Creation Act of 2004* ("2004 Tax Act") added language to IRC Section 421(b), which provides that federal income tax withholding is not required on any increase in income attributable to a *disqualifying* disposition of ESPP-stock.

The 2004 Tax Act also added language to IRC Section 423(c), which provides that no federal income tax withholding shall be required with respect to any amount treated as compensation under IRC Section 423(c) – in other words, no withholding on compensation income recognized in connection with an ESPP discount. That means compensation income triggered by a *qualifying* disposition of ESPP-stock (discussed above) is not subject to income tax withholding.

The 2004 Tax Act also added IRC Section 3121(a)(22), which provides that remuneration on account of the transfer of stock to any individual pursuant to an exercise of an option under an employee stock purchase plan, or remuneration on account of any disposition by the individual of such stock – is not considered "wages" for purposes of social security tax and Medicare tax. In short, neither the purchase nor the disposition of such ESPP-stock triggers social security tax or Medicare tax (these two taxes are called FICA taxes).

Further, the 2004 Tax Act added IRC Section 3306(b)(19), which exempts from the definition of FUTA "wages" any remuneration described in the previous paragraph. It means that such remuneration is exempt from federal unemployment tax.

ESTIMATED TAX PAYMENTS

Since, as described above, federal income tax is not withheld on gain from the disposition of ESPP-stock, shareholders may need to make estimated tax payments (with IRS Form 1040ES), or request that employers withhold additional income tax on or before December 31 – in order to avoid the possibility of incurring a penalty for underpayment of estimated tax.

Example: Marilyn sells ESPP-stock in a qualifying disposition. She recognizes $20 of compensation income, and $100 of long-term capital gain. Her marginal tax rate on ordinary income is 35 percent, and her tax rate on long-term capital gain is 15 percent. The sale of ESPP-stock triggers income tax in the amount of $22, which equals $7 (35 percent x $20 of ordinary income) plus $15 (15 percent x $100 of long-term capital gain). If she does not make estimated tax payments, or request that her employer withhold additional income tax, Marilyn may find that she has a balance due to the Internal Revenue Service on April 15 of next year when she files IRS Form 1040.

ESPP INVESTMENT STRATEGY

World-class financial experts at a hedge fund that spiraled downward in the late 1990s thought they had developed a risk-less or nearly risk-less money-making portfolio. Time proved otherwise.

Buying ESPP-stock at a substantial discount from fair market value is not risk-less either (because, for example, an unexpected event could cause the stock price to decline below the shareholder's purchase price before he has had an opportunity to sell). But, buying ESPP-stock at a substantial discount is probably as close to a risk-less investment that most employees will ever get – if they make a same-day sale.

GENERAL RULE: MAKE A SAME-DAY SALE

Shareholders will generally find that a same-day sale of stock is appropriate from a diversification standpoint. Sometimes, however, the diversification issue is overshadowed by other considerations.

For example, there may be a compelling *non-tax* reason for holding the stock (for example, management may frown upon same-day sales). Or, the owner holds ESPP-stock with the intention of selling it on January 2 of the next taxable year because he expects that his income during such year will be subject to a lower marginal tax rate.

More likely, the shareholder does not make a same-day sale, even though such sale might be prudent from a diversification standpoint, because of income tax considerations. For example, by holding the ESPP-stock he may have the *potential* to convert a substantial amount of what would be compensation income if he would make a disqualifying disposition of such stock, into long-term capital gain if, instead, he would make a qualifying disposition.

Finally, continuing to hold such ESPP-stock must be weighed against the possibility that doing so might place a cash constraint on his ability to participate to the maximum in the next offering period under the employer stock purchase plan (that is, if his money is tied up in the stock he may not be able to participate fully in the next offering of ESPP-stock). Continuing to hold the stock must also be considered in light of the possibility that the fair market value of the ESPP-stock could decline substantially.

The discussions that follow with respect to an ESPP investment strategy revolve around the *change* in fair market value that occurs during the offering period. The relationship between the fair market value at the end of the offering period and fair market value at the beginning of the offering period is an important consideration with respect to investment strategy.

POTENTIAL FOR TAX SAVINGS DRIVES INVESTMENT STRATEGY

At the time they buy ESPP-stock, many plan participants (mistakenly) expect that they will *automatically* reap a substantial income tax savings – by converting what "would be" compensation income if they would make a disqualifying disposition of such stock, into long-term capital gain if, instead, they would make a qualifying disposition. Therefore, they sometimes mistakenly hold ESPP-stock with the intention of satisfying the special holding period requirement.

As explained below, there is nothing "automatic" about reaping substantial income tax savings by making a qualifying disposition of ESPP-stock. Therefore, it is important to identify the conditions that offer the *potential* for substantially more favorable tax treatment and weigh this potential against the possibility of a substantial and irreversible decline in stock price.

KEY POINT: FMV_E MINUS FMV_B IS SUBSTANTIAL

As explained below, substantial tax-saving potential exists when FMV_e (fair market value at the *end* of the offering period) *substantially* exceeds FMV_b (fair market value at the *beginning* of the offering period).

The potential for substantially favorable income tax treatment (that is, when FMV_e substantially exceeds FMV_b) turns into *truly* favorable income tax treatment when:

- The shareholder sells such stock in a qualifying disposition

  and,

- Proceeds from the stock sale are substantially higher than the shareholder's purchase price

Example: $FMV_e - FMV_b = \$101$, shareholder sells ESPP-stock in a qualifying disposition, and proceeds from the sale equal fair market value on purchase date: Fair market value at the end of the offering period is $201, and fair market value at the beginning of offering period is $100. ($FMV_e - FMV_b = \$201 - \$100 = \$101$). Tina pays $85, which is 85 percent times the lesser of $100 or $201, to buy the stock. If she sells the stock for $201 in a same-day sale, she recognizes $116 of compensation income, the amount of the bargain element ($201 - $85 = $116) that exists on purchase date. Instead, if she holds the stock and sells it for $201 in a qualifying disposition, she would recognize only $15 of compensation income, the lesser of the $15 bargain element that existed on purchase date or her $116 actual gain on sale ($201 - $85 = $116). That is, she recognizes $101 less compensation income which means that her basis is $101 less and therefore she recognizes $101 more long-term capital gain. In short, the stock price does not change ($201 on purchase date versus $201 on sale date) and Tina reaps a substantial income tax savings from satisfying the special holding period requirement (that is, the qualifying disposition triggers $101 less compensation income and $101 more long-term capital gain, relative to a disqualifying disposition).

But, shareholders are aware that stock prices *do* change and that the risk associated with continuing to hold the stock often far outweighs the hope of reaping an income tax advantage from continuing to hold such stock. In the previous example, Tina continues to hold $201 of employer stock, which could decline substantially in value during the period that she waits to satisfy the special holding period requirement.

The next example is conceptually similar to the one immediately above, and again, proceeds from the sale are equal to fair market value on purchase date. The difference is that FMV_e minus FMV_b is only $1, not $101. Note that, relative to the income tax consequences that would result from a disqualifying disposition on purchase date, the shareholder does *not* reap a substantial income tax benefit from holding the stock and later making a qualifying disposition.

Example: $FMV_e - FMV_b = \$1$, shareholder sells such stock in a qualifying disposition, and proceeds from the sale equal fair market value on purchase date: Fair market value at the end of the offering period is $101, and fair market value at the beginning of the offering period is $100. ($FMV_e - FMV_b = \$101 - \$100 = \$1$). Robin pays $85, which is 85 percent times the lesser of $100 or $101, to buy the stock. If she sells the stock for $101 in a same-day sale, she recognizes $16 of compensation income, the amount of the bargain element that exists on purchase date. Instead, if she holds such stock and sells it for $101 in a qualifying disposition, she would recognize only $15 of compensation income, the lesser of the $15 bargain element that existed on purchase date or her $16 actual gain on sale ($101 - $85 = $16). That is, she recognizes $1 less compensation income which means that her basis is $1 less and therefore she recognizes $1 more long-term capital gain. In short, the stock price does not change ($101 on purchase date versus $101 on sale date) and Robin reaps hardly any income tax savings from satisfying the special holding period requirement (that is, the qualifying disposition triggers $1 less compensation income and $1 more long-term capital gain, relative to a disqualifying disposition).

In the previous example, Robin continues to hold $101 of stock – that could decline substantially in value – while she waits to satisfy the special holding period requirement.

"POTENTIAL" HAS A DARK SIDE

The shareholder must be alert to the fact that the "potential" for income tax savings described above has a dark side.

If there is potential for converting a substantial amount of "would-be" compensation income into long-term capital gain (that is, if FMV_e is substantially greater than FMV_b), the shareholder will suffer *harsh* income tax consequences (that is, he will realize a substantial amount of compensation income that likely triggers a substantial amount of tax, *and* a large capital loss that might not be fully deductible in the year of sale because of the $3,000 annual limitation on deducting net capital losses) if:

- He sells such ESPP-stock before satisfying the special holding period requirement

  and,

- Proceeds from the sale are substantially less than fair market value was at the end of the offering period

In short, the shareholder experiences harsh income tax consequences when he continues to hold the stock after purchase date and later sells it – at a price that is much lower than what the fair market value was on purchase date – in a disqualifying disposition. The next example illustrates this nightmare scenario that shareholders should make every effort to avoid.

Example: $FMVe - FMVb = \$100$, shareholder sells the stock in a <u>disqualifying</u> disposition, and proceeds from the sale are substantially less than fair market value was on purchase date: The fair market value of the stock is $100 at the beginning of the offering period and $200 at the end of the offering period (the date of purchase). Therefore, $FMV_e - FMV_b = \$100$. Sheila's purchase price is $85 (85 percent x the lesser of $100 or $200 = $85). She does not make a same-day sale. The stock price later collapses and Sheila sells it for $50, *before* satisfying the special holding period requirement. Her disqualifying disposition triggers $115 of ordinary compensation income on sale date, which is the bargain element that existed on purchase date ($200 - $85 = $115). Sheila's basis in the stock is $200, which equals her $85 cost plus the $115 of compensation income she recognizes on sale date. She reports a $150 capital loss on IRS Form 1040, Schedule D ($50 sales proceeds minus $200 basis = $150 capital loss). The capital loss is short-term if she held the stock for 12 months or less, and long-term if she held it more than 12 months.

The facts in the next example are the same as the one immediately above, except that Sandra makes a qualifying disposition. Consequently, the income tax consequences are far more favorable than in the above example. It demonstrates that if the shareholder has held the stock through a steep decline in its price, he will often find it wise to bear the risk of a further decline in exchange for the substantially more favorable income tax consequences that he would enjoy from making a qualifying disposition.

Example: *FMVe – FMVb = $100, shareholder sells the stock in a* _qualifying_ *disposition, and proceeds from the sale are substantially less than fair market value was on purchase date:* The fair market value of the stock is $100 at the beginning of the offering period and $200 at the end of the offering period (the date of purchase). Therefore, $FMV_e - FMV_b = \$100$. Sandra's purchase price is $85 (85 percent x the lesser of $100 or $200 = $85). She does not make a same-day sale. The stock price later collapses and Sandra sells it for $50, *after* satisfying the special holding period requirement. Her qualifying disposition triggers zero ordinary compensation income on sale date, which is the lesser of (A) $15 (15 percent x $100 = $15) or (B) $0, the amount of her actual gain, if any. Sandra's basis in the stock is $85, which is her $85 purchase price plus zero compensation income. She reports a $35 long-term capital loss on IRS Form 1040, Schedule D ($50 sales proceeds minus $85 basis = $35 capital loss). The capital loss is a long-term capital loss because the sale date is more than 12 months after purchase date.

PARTICIPATE TO THE MAXIMUM ALLOWED

It is well-established that employees should participate in an employer stock purchase plan that allows participants to buy stock at a substantial discount, and allows participants to make a same-day sale of ESPP-stock.

Generally, employees should be buying the *maximum* amount of ESPP-stock that the plan permits.

Example: Employees need to consider their ability to draw on other assets in order to maximize participation in an ESPP that allows employees to buy stock at a discount and make a same-day sale of ESPP-stock: ABC Corporation's ESPP allows employees to purchase stock at a price which equals 85 percent multiplied by the lesser of fair market value at the beginning of the offering period or fair market value at the end of the offering period. The plan also permits a same-day sale of stock. Monika finds that, if she would buy the maximum amount of stock that the plan allows, her net paycheck from ABC would not be sufficient to pay her monthly living expenses. Monika makes a projection of cash inflows and outflows. She determines that she could contribute the maximum amount to the ESPP and still meet monthly living expenses because she has other assets (for example, a money market account) to draw upon to finance any shortfall that might arise.

STRATEGY IF HOLDING ESPP-STOCK LIMITS PARTICIPATION

Some employees will find that they cannot hold ESPP-stock long enough to satisfy the special holding period requirement without compromising their level of participation in the next offering under the ESPP.

Generally, employees facing such a dilemma should make a same-day sale of stock. The reason is that buying stock at a substantial discount is almost risk-less, and converting the "potential" for tax savings into "actual" tax savings (by making a qualifying disposition instead of making a disqualifying disposition) and a positive rate of return is subject to great uncertainty because stock prices are random and unpredictable.

Example: Substantial potential for tax savings but holding ESPP-stock would make it difficult to participate in the next offering under the plan: Nancy is able to buy ESPP-stock at a substantial discount and make a same-day sale of such stock.

FMV_e substantially exceeds FMV_b, which means there is potential for substantial tax savings if she makes a qualifying disposition. But, Nancy has financial constraints such that if she continues to hold the ESPP-stock long enough to satisfy the special holding period requirement, she will not have enough financial resources to participate in the next offering under the ESPP. Nancy makes a same-day sale.

Worksheet for the Sale of ESPP-Stock
(if the purchase discount does not exceed 15 percent)

FOR DETERMINING THE AMOUNT OF COMPENSATION INCOME, BASIS OF THE STOCK SOLD, AND CAPITAL GAIN OR LOSS FROM THE SALE

1. Fair market value at beginning of offering period _____

2. Fair market value at end of offering period _____

3. Purchase discount *percentage* (not more than 15 percent)*

   ____%

4. Amount employee paid to purchase ESPP-stock _____

5. Proceeds from his sale of ESPP-stock _____

Complete this section if the sale is a *disqualifying* disposition (that is, the special holding period is *not* satisfied)

6. Compensation income (line 2 minus line 4) _____

7. Basis of stock sold (line 4 plus line 6) _____

8. Capital gain or loss (line 5 minus line 7) _____

Complete this section if the sale is a *qualifying* disposition (that is, the special holding period *is* satisfied)

9. Line 1 multiplied by line 3 _____

10. Gain (if any): Line 5 minus line 4 (not less than zero) _____

11. Compensation income (lesser of line 9 or line 10) _____

12. Basis of stock sold (line 4 plus line 11) _____

13. Capital gain or loss (line 5 minus line 12) _____

*For example, enter 15 percent on line 3 if the purchase price equals 85 percent multiplied by the *lesser* of: (A) the fair market value of the stock at the beginning of the offering period, or (B) the fair market value of the stock at the end of the offering period.

13 _____

IRS Form 1040 Reporting

NONQUALIFIED STOCK OPTIONS

GRANT DATE

Generally, the optionee does *not* report to the Internal Revenue Service the fact that a corporation granted him a nonqualified stock option, because in most cases the option does not have an ascertainable fair market value on the grant date.

TAX REPORTING FOR THE YEAR OF EXERCISE

Generally, the exercise of a nonqualified stock option results in the recognition of ordinary compensation income in the amount of the excess, if any, of the fair market value of the stock on the date of exercise over the exercise price.

- The corporation reports the income as *wages* on the optionee's IRS Form W-2 *"Wage and Tax Statement" regardless* if the optionee sells the stock that he acquires by exercising the option. The optionee reports those wages on page 1 of IRS Form 1040.

- If the income is *not* reported to the optionee as wages on IRS Form W-2, the optionee should report the income as *"Wages"* on IRS Form 1040, page 1 accompanied by an explanation that he attaches to his return.

TAX REPORTING FOR THE YEAR OF SALE

Every sale of stock must be reported on IRS Form 1040, Schedule D *"Capital Gains and Losses"*. This statement is true regardless if the sale results in a capital gain, a capital loss, or no capital gain or loss.

In most cases, the optionee recognizes a *capital gain or loss* on the date of sale, even when he sells the stock on the same date that he exercises the option, because stock prices sometimes fluctuate from one minute to the next.

- The optionee reports the sale of stock on IRS Form 1040, Schedule D.

- If the holding period is longer than 12 months, gain or loss is taxed as long-term capital gain or loss. If the holding period is not longer than 12 months, gain or loss is taxed as short-term capital gain or loss.

INCENTIVE STOCK OPTIONS

GRANT DATE

The optionee does *not* report to the Internal Revenue Service the fact that he has been granted an incentive stock option.

TAX REPORTING FOR THE YEAR OF EXERCISE

Generally, an ISO exercise results in taxable income for alternative minimum tax purposes in the amount of the excess of the fair market value of the stock on the date of exercise over the exercise price – *whether or not* the stock is sold during the calendar year of exercise.

- If the stock is *not* sold during the calendar year in which the option is exercised, the optionee reports the income in Part I of IRS Form 6251 *"Alternative Minimum Tax – Individuals"* for the tax year in which the exercise occurs.

- If the stock *is* sold in the calendar year of exercise, the optionee does *not* report the income on IRS Form 6251 – although it *is* subject to alternative minimum tax – because the income is already included in the optionee's computation of regular taxable income. In short, no entry is required on IRS Form 6251 if the optionee exercises the option and sells the stock in the same calendar year.

TAX REPORTING FOR THE YEAR OF SALE

As discussed earlier with respect to nonqualified stock options, *every* sale of stock previously acquired by exercise of an incentive stock option must be reported on IRS Form 1040, Schedule D *"Capital Gains and Losses"* for the tax year in which the stock is sold. For example, the optionee reports a sale of stock that occurs on December 5, Year 2 on his income tax return for the year ended December 31, Year 2.

NON-DISQUALIFYING DISPOSITIONS

- The optionee reports the sale of stock on IRS Form 1040, Schedule D. The difference between the sales proceeds and the exercise price (his basis in the stock) is taxed as *long-term* capital gain or loss.

- The optionee recognizes less income for purposes of AMT than he does for purposes of the regular tax. The optionee must ensure that his tax return reflects a higher AMT basis in the stock sold than his (lower) basis for purposes of regular tax. He must also ensure that his tax return reflects the $3,000 capital loss limitation, when applicable.

DISQUALIFYING DISPOSITIONS

If the optionee sells the stock in the <u>same</u> calendar year that he exercises the ISO:

- *If proceeds from the sale are less than the ISO exercise price:*

   The optionee does not recognize any ordinary compensation income. He reports the sale of stock on IRS Form 1040, Schedule D. The sale results in a *short-term* capital *loss* in the amount of the difference between the sales proceeds and the exercise price (his basis in the stock).

- *If proceeds from the sale are greater than or equal to what the fair market value was on the date of ISO exercise:*

   The employer reports *wages* to the optionee on IRS Form W-2 in the amount of the excess of the fair market value of the stock on the date of exercise over the exercise price. The optionee reports these wages on IRS Form 1040, page 1.

   If the income is *not* reported to the optionee as wages on IRS Form W-2, the optionee should report the excess of the fair market value of the stock on the date of exercise over the exercise price as *"Wages"* on IRS Form 1040, page 1 accompanied by an explanation that he attaches to his return.

   The optionee reports the sale of stock on IRS Form 1040, Schedule D. The excess of the sales proceeds over the fair market value of the stock on the date of exercise (his basis in the stock) is taxed as *short-term* capital gain.

- *If proceeds from the sale are greater than the exercise price but less than what the fair market value was on the date of ISO exercise*:

  The employer reports *wages* to the optionee on IRS Form W-2 in the amount of the excess of the proceeds from the sale over the exercise price. The optionee reports these wages on IRS Form 1040, page 1.

  If the income is *not* reported to the optionee as wages on IRS Form W-2, the optionee should report the excess of the proceeds from the sale over the exercise price as *"Wages"* on IRS Form 1040, page 1 accompanied by an explanation that he attaches to his return.

  The optionee reports the sale of stock as a short-term capital gain or loss on IRS Form 1040, Schedule D. The amount of the gain or loss is equal to the difference between the sales proceeds and the optionee's basis in the stock. His basis in the stock is equal to the sum of the exercise price *plus* the amount of ordinary compensation income (wages) that he recognizes (which is generally reported to him on IRS Form W-2) as a result of the disqualifying disposition.

- The optionee reports nothing on IRS Form 6251 because the income tax consequences for purposes of regular tax are the same as for purposes of alternative minimum tax.

If the optionee sells the stock in the year <u>following</u> the calendar year that he exercises the ISO:

- *If proceeds from the sale are less than the ISO exercise price*:

  The optionee does not recognize any ordinary compensation income. He reports the sale of stock on IRS Form 1040, Schedule D. The sale results in a *capital loss* in the amount of the difference between the sales proceeds and the exercise price (his basis in the stock). If the holding period is not longer than 12 months (which is most often the case in a disqualifying disposition), the loss is taxed as a short-term capital loss. If the holding period is longer than 12 months, the loss is taxed as a long-term capital gain or loss.

The optionee must ensure that his tax return reflects a higher AMT basis in the stock sold than his (lower) basis for purposes of regular tax. He must also ensure that his tax return reflects the $3,000 capital loss limitation, when applicable.

- *If proceeds from the sale are greater than or equal to what the fair market value was on the date of ISO exercise:*

  The employer reports *wages* to the optionee on IRS Form W-2 in the amount of the excess of the fair market value of the stock on the date of exercise over the exercise price. The optionee reports these wages on IRS Form 1040, page 1.

  If the income is *not* reported to the optionee as wages on IRS Form W-2, the optionee should report the excess of the fair market value of the stock on the date of exercise over the exercise price as *"Wages"* on IRS Form 1040, page 1 accompanied by an explanation that he attaches to his return.

  The optionee reports the sale of stock on IRS Form 1040, Schedule D. The excess of the proceeds from the sale over the fair market value of the stock on the date of exercise (his basis in the stock) is taxed as capital gain, short or long-term depending if the holding period is longer than 12 months.

  The optionee must ensure that his tax return reflects a higher AMT basis in the stock sold than his (lower) basis for purposes of regular tax. He must also ensure that his tax return reflects the $3,000 capital loss limitation, when applicable.

- *If proceeds from the sale are greater than the exercise price but less than what the fair market value was on the date of ISO exercise*:

  The employer reports *wages* to the optionee on IRS Form W-2 in the amount of the excess of the proceeds from the sale over the exercise price. The optionee reports these wages on IRS Form 1040, page 1.

  If the income is *not* reported to the optionee as wages on IRS Form W-2, the optionee should report the excess of the proceeds from the sale over the exercise price as *"Wages"* on IRS Form 1040, page 1 accompanied by an explanation that he attaches to his return.

  The optionee reports the sale of stock on IRS Form 1040, Schedule D. The amount of the capital gain or loss is equal to the difference between the sales proceeds and the optionee's basis in the stock. His basis in the stock is equal to the sum of the exercise price *plus* the amount of ordinary compensation income (wages) that he recognizes (which is generally reported to him on IRS Form W-2) as a result of the disqualifying disposition. If the holding period is longer than 12 months, the gain or loss is taxed as long-term capital gain or loss. In most cases, however, the holding period is not longer than 12 months in which case the gain or loss is taxed as short-term capital gain or loss.

  The optionee must ensure that his tax return reflects a higher AMT basis in the stock sold than his (lower) basis for purposes of regular tax. He must also ensure that his tax return reflects the $3,000 capital loss limitation, when applicable.

APPENDIX_____

Time Value of Money

The terms of every well-planned, wealth-maximizing transaction reflect the fact that money has a *time value*. This discussion is important because option values also reflect the time value of money.

The time value of money (otherwise known as "present value"), is a core concept for those striving to maximize their wealth. This chapter sets the foundation for more advanced discussions, found in Chapter 8 *"The Cost of AMT"*, and Chapter 9 *"ISO-Stock: The December 31 Decision"*, which should help optionees decide whether to hold or sell ISO-stock.

This chapter discusses the following sections:

- *Introduction to Present Value*

- *Discount Rate*

- *Present Value of Option Exercise Price*

INTRODUCTION TO PRESENT VALUE

The *present value* of one dollar received today is obviously one dollar. The present value of one dollar to be received one year from today is less than one dollar. One dollar received today is worth more than one dollar to be received in the future because a dollar received today may be invested at some positive rate of return.

Perhaps one of the easier ways to grasp this sometimes confusing topic is by analyzing the promised payments on a bond. That is because the price of a bond is simply the present value of future payments promised by the bond issuer to the bond owner.

BOND PRICE IS SIMPLY ITS PRESENT VALUE

This section uses a 30-year, non-callable coupon bond to illustrate the concept of present value and to show that the price of a bond is simply the present value of promised future cash flows under the bond's indenture.

For example, the principal amount of a bond is generally $1,000 and the issuer of a 30-year bond promises to make the following payments to the owner of such bond:

- Fixed semiannual interest payments for 30 years (a total of 60 interest payments of $X each, depending upon the coupon rate)

  and,

- One $1,000 principal payment at the end of 30 years

The coupon rate is the bond's stated annual interest rate. The issuer promises the owner of an 8 percent, $1,000 principal amount, 30-year coupon bond a total of $80 (8 percent x $1,000 = $80) each year over the life of the bond.

Interest payments are generally made semiannually, which means that the issuer promises $40 ($80 annually divided by 2 = $40 semiannually) at end of every six-month period – totaling 60 interest payments over the 30-year expected life of the bond.

Stated differently, the semiannual interest rate is 4 percent (8 percent divided by 2). See Table A.1 for a snapshot of the promised cash flows on an 8-percent, 30-year bond.

Table A.1						
Promised Cash Flows on an 8-percent, 30-year Bond						
END OF MONTH ⇒	6	12	18	24	30	360
END OF PERIOD ⇒	**1**	**2**	**3**	**4**	**5**	**60**
Cash receipt (in $)	40	40	40	40	40	1,040

Note that the issuer promises to pay $1,040 to the owner at the end of Year 30 (that is, at the end of Period 60 or the End of Month 360 as shown in Table A.1). That $1,040 consists of the final $40 interest payment *plus* the $1,000 return of principal.

The total amount of promised payments is $3,400 over a period of 30 years ($2,400 of interest income and a $1,000 return of principal). But, for the reasons discussed in the next section, not one rational, informed investor would be willing to pay $3,400 for such a promise in an arm's length transaction. In short, that is because money has a time value.

EACH PROMISED PAYMENT HAS A DIFFERENT VALUE

Since the issuer promises to make each of the 60 equal semiannual interest payments on a different *date*, bond market participants place a different *value* on each payment. It is such an important concept that it is worth repeating. *Each and every one of the 60 equal semiannual interest payments has a different value.*

The $40 semiannual interest payment to be received at the end of semiannual period 1 is worth *more than* the $40 interest payment to be received at the end of semiannual period 2. Likewise, the $40 payment to be received at the end of semiannual period 2 is worth *more than* the $40 payment to be received at the end of semiannual period 3, and so on.

PV = Promised Payment x PV Factor

This section explains that the present value of each promised payment equals the amount of such promise multiplied by the applicable present value factor (please see the next section for a discussion of the present value factor).

For example, notice in Table A.2 that the $40 interest payment expected at the end of semiannual period 1 has a present value of only $38.46 if bond market participants price the bond to yield an 8 percent annual pre-tax return. The value is only $38.46, and not $40, because market participants value every $1 promise to be received at the end of semiannual period 1 at just 96.15 cents.

Proof that $1 to be received at the end of semiannual period 1 has a value of 96.15 cents is that 96.15 cents invested at 8 percent for six months results in an end of period value of $1 (96.15 cents x 1.04 = $1).

The $1,000 fair market value of the bond (if the bond is priced to yield exactly 8 percent) equals the sum of the present value of each of the 60 promised cash flows (59 of which equal $40 and one of which equals $1,040). Stated differently, the present value equals the present value of an annuity for 30 years, *plus* the present value of the $1,000 return of principal.

Table A.2

How to Compute the Present Value of Promised Cash Payments on an 8-percent, 30-year Bond

	END OF SEMIANNUAL PERIOD					
	1	2	3	4	5	60
Expected cash receipt(in $)	40	40	40	40	40	1,040
Present value factor	.9615	.9246	.8890	.8548	.8219	.0951
Present value-cash receipt(in $)	38.46	36.98	35.56	34.19	32.88	**98.90**

PRESENT VALUE FACTOR

Notice the term *present value factor* in Table A.3. The present value factor reflects the *time value of money.*

For example, if investors require a 4 percent return semiannually, they pay 96.15 cents for every dollar they expect to receive at the end of semiannual period 1 (that is, at the end of six months). They pay 92.46 cents for every dollar they expect to receive at the end of semiannual period 2. They pay only 9.51 cents for each dollar they expect to receive at the end of semiannual period number 60 (that is, after 30 years). Table A.3 shows how to compute present value factors.

Table A.3

How to Compute the Present Value Factor

END OF SEMIANNUAL PERIOD "N"	COMPUTATION OF PRESENT VALUE FACTOR
1	1 divided by $(1+i)^1$ = .9615
2	1 divided by $(1+i)^2$ = .9246
3	1 divided by $(1+i)^3$ = .8890
4	1 divided by $(1+i)^4$ = .8548
5	1 divided by $(1+i)^5$ = .8219
.	
.	
.	
60	1 divided by $(1+i)^{60}$ = .0951

where i = 4% = .04 (the semiannual interest rate = 8% divided by 2)

Other things being equal (that is, holding "N" constant), the present value factor decreases (increases) as "i", the interest rate, increases (decreases). Other things being equal (that is, holding "i" constant), the present value factor decreases (increases) as "N", the time remaining until the cash receipt, is extended (shortened).

DISCOUNT RATE

As one can see from reading Table A.3, the present value factor decreases as the discount rate, i, increases. The reason is that the denominator in the expression "$(1+i)$" increases as i increases. Likewise, the present value increases as the discount rate decreases. Naturally, then, the discount rate is critical to arriving at the present value of a projected series of cash flows.

In the previous example, bond market participants price the bond to yield exactly 8 percent, which is also the coupon rate on the bond. Since they are willing to accept a yield (8 percent) that is exactly equal to the coupon rate, they by definition price the bond at its $1,000 par value.

If bond market participants had demanded a yield in excess of the coupon rate, they would have priced the bond below $1,000. Likewise, if they had demanded a yield less than the coupon rate, they would have priced the bond above $1,000. Why? It is the time value of money at work.

DISCOUNT RATE UNDER CERTAINTY

It is well established that investors demand compensation, in the form of higher yields, for assuming risk. Since U.S. Treasury securities are deemed to be free from the risk of default, investors accept a lower yield than they would on a security such as a corporate bond that is not free from default risk.

When investors discount a promise of future cash flows using a default-free discount rate (for example, the discount rate used to price a U.S. Treasury security), they have taken into account the impact that *time* has on value. Implicit in that rate, at least to some degree, is the market's perception of future price inflation.

Investors use the interest rate on a U.S. Treasury security plus a *risk premium* (discussed later) to arrive at an appropriate interest rate for discounting a promise of future cash flows when there is a risk of default by the issuer.

RISK OF PRICE INFLATION

Securities markets "price" expected inflation into the yield on conventional U.S. Treasuries (that is, Treasury securities that are not indexed for inflation) but the investor receives no guarantee that the amount of expected price inflation priced into the security at the time of purchase will equal the "actual" rate of future price inflation, as measured, for example, by the Consumer Price Index. In short, uncertainty is present. Even conventional U.S. Treasury Bills are subject to inflation risk.

Example: Conventional short-term U.S. Treasury securities are not free from the risk of price inflation: Investors were especially concerned about price inflation during the 1970s. There were periods when many investors preferred to hold shares in a mutual fund that held U.S. Treasury securities with an average maturity of a few days rather than buy three-month U.S. Treasury Bills at auction.

DISCOUNT RATE UNDER UNCERTAINTY

This topic is relevant to holders of incentive stock options because exercising ISOs, and holding such ISO-stock beyond December 31 of the year of option exercise, triggers taxable income for purposes of AMT. If that income triggers AMT, the optionee receives an AMT credit. In order to make an informed decision as to whether he should hold the stock beyond December 31, he needs to value that credit. And, as described in Chapter 10, there is uncertainty with respect to such credit. Consequently, he needs to develop an appropriate discount rate under conditions of uncertainty.

Bond market participants price fixed-income securities of an issuer other than the U.S. Treasury to reflect the fact that such securities *do* have default risk.

Since investors demand compensation for default risk, they use a higher discount rate to value the promise by such issuer (the higher interest rate results in a lower present value and that is the way investors extract the compensation they require in order for them to buy the security). The excess of such higher discount rate over the discount rate on a U.S. Treasury security that promises identical cash flows is called the *risk premium.*

Market participants also discount *projected* cash flows at a discount rate that reflects uncertainty as to *both* the amount and timing of such cash flows. For example, the future cash flows, if any, on a share of common stock are highly uncertain as to the amount of such cash flows and the date they will be received. In short, there are no promises to holders of common stock – only projections of cash flows. Even the "indicated" dividend on stock is not certain because the board of directors of the company may decide to reduce the amount of such dividend or not pay a dividend at all.

Example: *Corporate bonds contain a risk premium:* The U.S. Treasury and ABC Corporation issue long-term bonds at the same time. The two issues promise identical cash flows. The interest rate on the corporate bond is 7 percent. The interest rate on the U.S. Treasury bond is 6 percent. Therefore, the risk premium is 1 percent. That 1 percent is the amount of pre-tax compensation that investors demand for assuming default risk on the corporate bond, and other inferior attributes such as the fact that interest income on a corporate bond is subject to state and federal income tax while the interest income on a U.S. Treasury security is subject only to federal income tax.

DISCOUNT RATE USING UTILITY FUNCTIONS

Some investors choose to address the uncertainty issue separately – using utility functions – instead of adding a risk premium to the default-free discount rate. A discussion of utility functions, however, is beyond the scope of this book.

THE "APPROPRIATE" DISCOUNT RATE UNDER UNCERTAINTY

The selection of an appropriate discount rate under conditions of uncertainty is crucial since the present value computation, and ultimately accept-reject and buy-sell decisions, depend on it. If the discount rate used to discount projected cash flows is higher (lower) than it "should be", the present value of such cash flows is lower (higher) than it "should be".

Fortunately, a default-free discount rate – which forms the base from which an appropriate discount rate is determined – is available daily in competitive U.S. securities markets. As discussed above, the default-free rate is simply the interest rate the investor could earn by purchasing a U.S. Treasury security that would generate cash flows that would more or less replicate those that he expects to receive on the investment under evaluation. That default-free rate adjusts the value of future cash flows to reflect the impact that *time* has on value. It also adjusts the value of future cash flows to reflect *expected* price inflation.

When future cash flows are uncertain (for example, those from owning stock) or there is not a comparable, actively-traded security to offer guidance on how much the risk premium "should be", such risk premium is, by default, subjectively determined.

Here lies potential for error. This is exactly the problem optionees that hold incentive stock options face, for example, when they attempt to compute the present value of an AMT credit, an asset that has value but is not publicly-traded.

Further, since different investors have different appetites for risk, they would likely assign different risk premiums to the same set of promised future cash flows. Nonetheless, despite the challenge of assigning value to an AMT credit, the alternative of pretending that an AMT credit is worth 100 percent of face value (when it certainly is not) is not a sensible substitute for making an effort to value an AMT credit before incurring ISO-induced AMT.

Example: *Valuing an AMT credit:* Lonnie exercises an incentive stock option in Year 1. If she does not sell such ISO-stock on or before December 31, Year 1, she will incur $100,000 of AMT and, in exchange for such $100,000, receive a $100,000 AMT credit. The AMT credit has value but the question is, "how much?" Lonnie must make a reasonable attempt to value such credit – using the time value of money – in order to make an informed decision on whether to hold the ISO-stock beyond December 31, Year 1 (Please see Chapter 8 *"The Cost of AMT"* for a discussion of how to value an AMT credit, and Chapter 9 *"ISO-Stock: The December 31 Decision"*).

PRESENT VALUE OF OPTION EXERCISE PRICE

Table A.4 shows the present value of one dollar that is expected to be received in one lump sum *in the future*, under various discount rates. The numbers in the table are computed using annual compounding.

The next example show how one projects the *minimum* value of an employee stock option, which gives the employee the right to buy a non-dividend-paying stock that is assumed to have zero volatility. In short, an option should have some amount of value simply because the optionee has the right to pay the exercise price in the future.

Example: *Present value of option exercise price on a non-dividend-paying stock:* Katherine receives a 10-year nontransferable option to buy employer stock at $100. The stock does not pay a dividend. The fair market value of the stock on the date of grant is $100. The present value of $100 to be paid at the end of 10 years is $74.41 ($100 x .7441 PV Factor from Table A.4 = $74.41) if the after-tax default-free discount rate is 3 percent. In other words, if Katherine places $74.41 in an investment account that yields 3 percent after-tax, the after-tax value of the account will grow to $100 at the end of Year 10. That $100 is the amount she would need to pay the $100 option exercise price at the end of Year 10. In effect, then, her option has a value of at least $25.59 on the date of grant ($100 current stock price - $74.41 present value of option exercise price = $25.59) notwithstanding the fact that the fair value of such option is decreased by the nontransferable provision, and increased by the fact that the volatility of the stock price almost certainly exceeds zero.

Table A.4
Present Value of $1.00
(assuming annual compounding)

DISCOUNT RATE > $1 RECEIVED END OF YEAR	1%	2%	3%	4%	5%	6%	7%	8%	9%	10%
1	0.9901	0.9804	0.9709	0.9615	0.9524	0.9434	0.9346	0.9259	0.9174	0.9091
2	0.9803	0.9612	0.9426	0.9246	0.9070	0.8900	0.8734	0.8573	0.8417	0.8264
3	0.9706	0.9423	0.9151	0.8890	0.8638	0.8396	0.8163	0.7938	0.7722	0.7513
4	0.9610	0.9238	0.8885	0.8548	0.8227	0.7921	0.7629	0.7350	0.7084	0.6830
5	0.9515	0.9057	0.8626	0.8219	0.7835	0.7473	0.7130	0.6806	0.6499	0.6209
6	0.9420	0.8880	0.8375	0.7903	0.7462	0.7050	0.6663	0.6302	0.5963	0.5645
7	0.9327	0.8706	0.8131	0.7599	0.7107	0.6651	0.6227	0.5835	0.5470	0.5132
8	0.9235	0.8535	0.7894	0.7307	0.6768	0.6274	0.5820	0.5403	0.5019	0.4665
9	0.9143	0.8368	0.7664	0.7026	0.6446	0.5919	0.5439	0.5002	0.4604	0.4241
10	0.9053	0.8203	0.7441	0.6756	0.6139	0.5584	0.5083	0.4632	0.4224	0.3855